WITH THE COMPLIMENTS
OF
THE INTERNATIONAL CULTURAL SOCIETY OF KOREA
C.P.O. BOX 2147 SEOUL, KOREA

POSTWAR KOREAN SHORT STORIES

An Anthology

■

Translated and Edited with an Introduction
by
Chong-un Kim

Second Edition

■

SEOUL NATIONAL UNIVERSITY PRESS
AND
THE CENTER FOR KOREAN STUDIES
UNIVERSITY OF HAWAII

Distributed Outside Korea by
The University Press of Hawaii, Honolulu

ISBN 0-8248-0833-9

CONTENTS

PREFACE

During the past twenty years or so I have translated a number of Korean short stories and other literary works into English. While a few pieces were solicited by the editors of journals, the bulk of them were singled out by me for translation because I liked them.

Coincidentally, most of the stories I chose for the present volume were written since the Korean War. Hence, the title: *Postwar Korean Short Stories: An Anthology.* However, this volume is not an anthology in the proper sense of the word in that I made no conscious efforts to have it representative. The names of a few rather notable writers—writers whose works one would normally expect to find in an anthology of this nature—are missing, whereas the stories of some relatively lesser-known writers have found their way into this book. In other words, the criterion for selection was a rather ephemeral one, namely, my own personal taste. Inclusion or exclusion from this volume should in no way be cause for glee or despair on the part of our writers.

Despite my apologia, the reader will find a wide variety of stories in the book: there are, of course, examples of war realism along with social realism; there are what I like to call stories of atmosphere, whose main strength is the general drift of the narrative rather than the plot; at least one tale draws heavily on fantasy; some may properly be called stories of ideas, in which intellectual themes are tapped and developed as their plots unfold; and there are even some stories that can be described as black humor. Moreover, the style, the shade and tone, and the structure of the stories are diverse. In short, these stories display a variety of perspectives and situations as well as many storytelling techniques.

The Western reader, to whom this collection is mainly addressed, might find some of the stories quite different from what he or she is accustomed to and therefore difficult to comprehend. This is only natural: literary conventions differ, as do the whole pattern and texture of the cultures involved. The difficulty, however, is not insurmountable. I am certain that a sympathetic reader will have no trouble finding enough elements which are common to all literatures. The only misgivings I have in this regard relate to the quality of my translation—whether or not I have adequately bridged the two cultures. I know I am not a Chapman, but I have done my best to avoid any unnecessary injustices to our writers.

I would like to say a few words of acknowledgment. All but one or two of these stories originally appeared in *Korea Journal,* a publication in English issued by the Korean Commission of UNESCO in Seoul. Mr. Paik Syeunggil, the editor-in-chief of the journal, should receive at least half the credit for this book, for it was he who prodded me to translate all these stories. A number of other persons helped—obtaining hard-to-find material and performing the arduous work of copyreading and proofreading. Among them were Robert Snyder, a Peace Corps Volunteer assigned to Seoul National University, and Kang Jinbaik, my assistant at the university. To these and others I am deeply grateful for devotion and assistance. I goes without saying that the final responsibility for translation rests with me.

Chong-un Kim

INTRODUCTION

An introduction to works of fiction produced during the postwar decades in Korea is, in some sense, obliged to present an overview of some prominent and significant historical and sociopolitical facts. Literature deals with the quality of life, and life is willy-nilly affected by society and history. Moreover, it is even necessary for us to have recourse to such knowledge when the literature is primarily addressed to those with different experiences, as is the case with this collection of stories. This introduction, then, is intended to familiarize the reader with an entire literary period not simply the works in this collection.

I. The Landscape

The first and most epic event is the Liberation of 1945. Though brought about gratis as an outcome of the termination of World War II, it was nevertheless a major historical change without equal in the long history of the country. It opened the floodgates, as it were, of history. It freed the country from the fetters of Japanese colonial rule and promised the long-sought national independence. These in themselves were important enough, and the jubilation and excitement that took hold of the country—our version of *Sturm und Drang*—is understandable. What gives ultimate importance to the Liberation as a historical event, however, lies in what it has brought in its wake to the Korean people: the tragic territorial division. Surely, the path of nation-building would not have been easy to tread without the division of the country, but this fatal division made the path even thornier and more perilous, throwing the country into a welter of unnatural tension, turmoil, and, at one point, bloodshed. The division was the price, as it were, of the Liberation. In this sense, the Liberation was not gratuitous, after all.

The celebrated battle between the "pure literature" camp and the "tendentious literature" camp that took place in the immediate postliberation years paralleled the larger battle that was being waged between the two opposing ideological camps. A people with practically no ideological knowledge, except perhaps the ideal of Wilsonian national self-determination, was suddenly thrown into the vortex of a chaotic war of ideas. Thus the establishment of separate governments in the North and the South, with its attendant sociopolitical developments, was in a sense a preparation for the larger, more deathly, clash—a lull before a tempestuous storm.

In spite of this manifest rivalry, the South was hopelessly unprepared against Northern aggression. The bloody fratricidal war that broke out in 1950 was soon augmented by the armies of other countries. The swift and sweeping pendulumlike shifts of frontline battles ravaged the cities and the countryside alike and laid waste the entire land. A sense of doom reigned, and survival became the paramount concern. The uneasy truce that ended the three years of bitter and devastating strife did not alter this in any essential way. Nothing was achieved except universal destruction and uprooting, physical and spiritual. The physical scar of the war would heal with time, but the spiritual trauma was less likely to follow suit. Thus the war left indelible marks on the consciousness of the people. The horrors and nightmares of the war were replaced by dire postwar economic conditions and moral confusion.

An ineffectual and corrupt government characterized the rest of the 1950s. In spite of the large amount of U.S. aid, economic recovery was slow. The cleavage widened between the few who were fattened by sponging off foreign aid and the masses. This together with the accumulated dissatisfaction directed against the autocratic regime culminated in the April 19 uprising of 1960.

Indeed, the early 1960s was a period of unprecedented political turmoil. In the April uprising, students forced the late strongman Syngman Rhee to step down. A new government was formed by election, but it was toppled by the May 16 military revolution in 1961. The Third Republic was born in 1963, after two years of military government. All these events came at a dizzy speed, heightening the level of political consciousness and sharpening the novelist's or poet's critical awareness of sociopolitical reality.

In the face of the colossal political events, one is apt to overlook the subtler changes in intellectual temper that took place toward the end of the 1950s and into the early 1960s. This new trend was essentially cultural and concerned itself with self-reflection and criticism directed against the indiscreet acceptance of foreign ideas and cultures that more or less inundated the national life after the Liberation. It was an endeavor to reassert cultural identity, our version of the search for a usable past. This entailed a heightened interest in historical consciousness. The more recent, as well as the remote, history of the country was subjected to intense scrutiny in an effort to see the present in a clearer light. Thus a flood of fiction based on actual history appeared.

Of the years after May 16, one can say that two problems stand out as the paramount issues of concern: modernization and national security. The latter is not a new problem. It is a semipermanent condition that dates back to the cease-fire of 1953 or earlier. The ever-present threat of aggression in the face of the uneasy North-South confrontation has become part of Korean consciousness, and it is to this condition that some of the political measures that curb democratic ideals are attributed.

Modernization, however, is another thing. As it turned out, it was construed as synonymous with industrialization. The introduction of a planned economy, together with massive international loans, launched the nation into an orbit of unprecedented economic development. The gross national product soared. Even taking the population increase into account, the figures are impressive: during the same period per capita GNP rose from $76 to $513. It goes without saying that the bulk of the growth resulted from the increase in export-oriented industrial production, and the emergence of industrial tycoons and financial combines has become an established fact.

This kind of rapid economic growth poses a host of social problems: neglect of distribution of wealth in favor of a high rate of development; corrupt and unethical behavior on the part of the economic elite, as displayed by their mode of accumulating wealth and conspicuous consumption; the unnatural growth of cities; the ever-widening gap between the urban and agrarian modes of life. Indeed, the social problems would have been acute enough without the negative aspects of rapid economic growth. During the postwar decades the population of the Republic more than doubled. This in itself is a difficult enough problem, but it is heightened by the shift of population, the migration of farmers to larger cities. Seoul has grown by roughly seven times during this period. The influx of population is usually accommodated by what may be called outer-urban cores (as distinct from sub-urbia) that cancerously grow in clusters around the peripheries of large cities, almost overnight sometimes, places for "second-class" city dwellers without the decent features of cities by any standard. In 1945, the Korean lifestyle was more or less homogeneous; after thirty years, it appears that the population has been divided into three neat groups: the urban, the outer-urban, and the rural.

These are some of the noteworthy features of the postwar land-scape that have fashioned the life and temper of the Korean people in the past three decades. But what of the patterns in postwar literature itself? Ihab Hassan wrote in connection with the rela-tionship between literature and age:

> It is the privilege of every age to consider its predicament unique, and it is its hope that the predicament may prove the most gravid history has known.
> Such illusions are not always idle; for they are the stuff of which men make the record of the speeding days, heightening their moment with some articulate show of pride, wonder, or despair.[1]

I believe that this statement in its entirety is applicable to our situation. Looking back on the postwar period as a whole, writers of fiction have responded rather fairly to what they perceived to be the predicament of their times. Overwhelmed, occasionally, by the enormity of the sudden and inimical turn history takes, they nevertheless manage to record and fashion images of man that honestly grapples with their age in an attempt to mediate the contradictions of culture and even to create some new consciousness.

To discuss the manner and mode of their literary efforts is more elusive than to do the same for history or society. From among many images of man portrayed by writers I have chosen three as dominant and have given them the rubrics of the Walking Wounded, the Inspired Rebel, and the Victimized Aesthete. Their order is roughly chronological but frequent overlapping cannot be avoided. I might add that these are only what I believe to be dominant; many brooks and tributaries that convey equally important, and refreshing literary currents are reluctantly left aside.

II. The Walking Wounded

What is more appropriate with which to start an account of postwar literature than the fiction dealing with the war itself? In this case, however, it is almost embarrassing to note the curious absence of the usual kind of war fiction. I do not mean it literally, of course, but, relatively speaking, the Korean War produced no great, not even fair, war novels commensurate with the import of the tragic event itself. Even those sparse exceptions that managed to come into being strangely shunned the frontline activities and looked away from the scene of senseless and efficient violence and unspeakable ravages. No portrayals of heroism or military valor adorned the fiction of the war-torn country.

Why? Was the abruptness and immediacy of impact and the proximity and involvement of milieu too great to give Korean writers necessary perspective and detachment? Perhaps so. But this surmise holds true only to a certain extent. The real reason must be sought perhaps in the tragic nature of the war itself: it was a civil war in which no real or worldly gain or glory was at stake except that elusive thing called ideology. An instinctive abhorrence of portraying tragic fratricidal battles probably lay at the root of this.

This summary dismissal of war material does not mean that the war had little effect on the fiction of the period. On the contrary, the war was the central and omnipresent core of the situation, the shadow as well as the substance, the protagonist as well as the antagonist, of virtually all the novels and stories produced during the first decade of the period. Only what may be called the legacy of the war—the vast dehumanizing aspects of the war, alienation from self, society, and nature—rather than the war efforts and activities themselves loomed large in fiction. The huddled and uprooted figure dumbfounded by the sense of universal and irrevocable loss; the small people wandering among the ravaged ruins wondering half-seriously where the next meal would come from; the man perplexed by the sudden shift and cleavage in moral ground; the intellectual figure groping for an adequate answer with regard to the condition of man in the face of metaphysical anguish and despair brought about by the war— these are the images of man that populate the fictional works of the period. They are the people maimed by the legacy of the war, and Korean literature finally catches up with the general mode of the postwar fiction of the world. They are the wounded people, physically or spiritually, or both, and the general tone is largely despairing and apocalyptic.

The sense of painful loss is perhaps best caught in the first story of this anthology. Written in the early stage of the period by an older writer, Kim Tongni, "Father and Son" (1951) deals with an ill and decrepit father at the end of a long and arduous journey to visit his son, who has not written home since his enlistment. As a peasant, the father's most important concern has been farming, but now the urge to see his son precludes all else, though the information concerning his son's military address is only half-certain. The journey will cost money, which he does not have. Besides, it is "one of the busiest and most important periods in farming," and thus "setting out on a long journey might seriously damage his fall crop" for the year. "Well, so what? What's a little debt when a body is withered from coughing, worrying, and has had no sleep and is longing for a glance of his son's face? He felt he would be able to cope with anything after the visit."[2] So he borrows heavily and sets out.

The father finally meets his son after a long and hard journey, but neither really has anything to say to the other, and they part after a brief and inarticulate meeting, the son going back to his post, the father going on the long trudge home. The sense of acute pain and loss is wonderfully captured without lapsing into easy sentimentality. Perhaps this is a good place to introduce the judgment of a recent American reviewer:

What is pleasing to the westerner is the insight into Korean rural life and character, and the complete lack of artifice in the presentation of the story. I think of this piece as representatively Korean because of its virtual lack of plot and the starkness of its presentation. More is left unsaid than stated; and in today's mass communication world with its floods of words the restraint is most attractive and the story becomes, curiously, not only traditional but very modern. If a picture is worth a thousand words, the unstated may at times be worth a thousand pictures.[3]

The withered old woman in "A Sketch" (1957) by Yi Hoch'ŏl offers another example. At the outset of the sketch, the old woman, living alone on a hillside far from the village, is dismayed, while feeding her pigs, by the ominous cawing of a crow coming from among the branches of the huge pine tree that is the altar for the village's shamanistic rites. The rest of the story describes her fervent, almost maddened, and inarticulate prayers in front of the sacred pine tree and reports a few incidents related to the arrival of a curt letter from the lonely dwelling place, and the mysterious felling of the pine tree. Nothing is stated explicitly, but piecing together this information tells us that the letter was an official letter from the army notifying her of the death in battle of her only grandson and that the tree was felled by the old woman, who blamed the tree for not answering her prayers. The hillside becomes completely deserted. What survives the general decaying and perishing is the ominous cawing of the crow—the messenger of doom.

That the image of man as the Walking Wounded is not limited to the aged is exemplified in "Shorty Kim" (1957) by Song Pyŏngsu. By placing a boy in his early teens as the protagonist of the story, Song succeeds in depicting the distorting effect of war on the very young and the mode in which the dehumanizing war violates the innocent world of childhood.

Shorty Kim is a war orphan who works in an American army camp near the front line as a pimp. He fled the city of Seoul to go there, for the war-torn city only meant to him either the bullying of the boss of the child-beggar syndicate or the tyranny of the orphange owner who abused the orphans to draw more war-relief material. Here in the camp town life is not all that easy, though he finds solace in the sisterly love extended to him by Darling, a prostitute for whom he works.

He has become immune to the insensitive and animallike behavior of the American soldiers, and in a way he realizes instinctively that it is the very source of his and Darling's livelihood. What baffles him most is the behavior of some of his fellow Koreans who come into daily contact with him in his line of work.

Take the houseboy for the company commander, for instance.
The boy was, in fact, a protégé of Shorty Kim when they fled
the orphanage in Seoul, but now the boy lords over him because
he is a pet of the captain while Shorty Kim is only a pimp for
a sickly prostitute who waits on soldiers in an abandoned air-
raid bunker. Then there is the middle-aged Clubfoot, a fake
disabled veteran who works in the mess hall. All the Korean
workers know that Clubfoot is always behind large or small thefts
that plague the camp. And recently Clubfoot has wanted to
"borrow" American dollars from Darling despite her repeated
refusals.

One day the houseboy brings an American soldier to the
bunker. When the soldier leaves, the houseboy demands Darling's service for himself. Enraged, Darling and Shorty Kim drive
him out of the bunker. Later that day, the bunker is raided by
the military police and Darling is taken away in a jeep. She bids
Shorty to join her in a day or two in front of the PX in Seoul
and not to forget about the eight hundred dollars hidden in the
bunker. Later, Shorty Kim seeks out the houseboy, believing that
it was he who had informed on Darling. While they are bickering, they find out who the true informer was; they find Clubfoot
leaving the bunker in haste with the money. In the ensuing fight
with Clubfoot, Shorty Kim is easily overpowered and faces imminent death, but at the critical moment Clubfoot is stabbed with
a pearl-handled knife by the houseboy. Together they flee for
Seoul, leaving behind the precarious security of the camp town.
While running, Shorty Kim says to himself:

> No more camp town. It's fearful. Yankees are fearful, too. Come to think
> of it. The Bulldog (the bullying soldier) is even more fearful than the boss
> in Seoul, and MPs are more hateful animals than traffic cops. I must get
> out of here as soon as possible and seek out Sister Darling in Seoul. If
> only I could run into tenderhearted Sister Darling in Seoul—then nothing,
> not even the bundle of dollar bills and all the rest would be of any
> consequence...
> If only I could throw myself into her embrace and cry to my heart's
> content...[4]

The landscape is grim. There is no parcel of peaceful land
for Shorty Kim to dwell in, except perhaps in the fragile arms
of Sister Darling.

The pattern of disintegration of moral order is another recurring theme of postwar fiction. The despair and the hollow sense, another legacy of the war, breeds, in characteristic self-abandonment, new kinds of love ethics and moral codes that challenge the established norms of behavior. Thus the young heroine in Son Sohŭi's "The Glen in the Sun" (1957) asserts that her only concern is how to get the maximum pleasure and fun out of her youth. In Han Malsuk's "The Precipice of a Myth" (1957), a college coed goes to bed with just about any man in return for a semester's tuition fee, a plain meal, or overnight accommodation. Let us now examine in some detail one or two stories that deal more or less directly with the lost sense of moral bearings.

A story included in this volume, Son Ch'angsŏp's "Walking in the Snow" (1956) is a good example. Mr. Ko, a meek and good-hearted former teacher of art, is a middle-aged artist who makes a living by drawing magazine illustrations. His sedate life is suddenly jostled by the appearance of a former student, Kwansik, whom he has not seen in fifteen years. Kwansik tells Mr. Ko that he has no place to turn to now that he has lost his job in an unauthorized clinic, where he had acted as an assistant doctor on the strength of his army experience as a corpsman. The good-hearted teacher, shy, proper, and emotionally incapable of saying no, a true Korean-style schlimalz, is imposed upon by Kwansik, and he moves into Mr. Ko's single room. "Just for a week, no more," says the former student, but that week stretches into months. That is not all. There is no end to the youth's audacity; he wears Mr. Ko's socks, underwear, and even the best suit he saves for special occasions. In time, he brings his girlfriend to the place, and she soon becomes a semipermanent house guest, too. Thus Mr. Ko finds himself involved in an impossible situation.

The girl is a sharp-witted aspiring playwright. Although Kwansik openly confesses that he wants to marry the girl, everyone, including the bridegroom-hopeful himself, knows that he is no match for her. She is pert and proud sometimes, but she has a certain freshness and sweetness to which the older gentleman is attracted. When he asks her why she wants to be a playwright of all things, she asks, "Why, is not life itself a play?"

"Do you think so? Is life really but a play? I should think life has its sincere aspects, too."

"That's only a façade. You pretend to yourself that others are sincere but it takes a real actor to make others believe he is sincere. Of course, that is the ultimate goal of dramatic acting itself."[5]

For this kind of fresh insight and others, Mr. Ko finds himself involved in an exceedingly complex emotional situation. It gets further complicated when Kwansik volunteers to be a matchmaker between the teacher and a rich widow. When the youth persists in spite of repeated firm refusals, Mr. Ko says to the young man: "What are you saying? Seems to me it's more like being hired out as a stallion. I don't want that kind of marriage." To this, the youth, a strangely distorted kind of Machiavellian, counters:

You are incorrigible! What are any of us but merchandise? As long as we are to be sold, we should make sure we are sold into wealth. Besides, I have a stake in this marriage. I can cook up something really big with that woman's money as bait.[6]

This is all beyond Mr. Ko, but what is really above and beyond him is the youth's suggestion that he announce, falsely, his inter vivos engagement to the widow to be able to claim the inheritance when it is made known that the widow was slain by an unknown murderer the night before. When the outraged school teacher refuses, Kwansik runs out of the house to the funeral to see what can be done. Infuriated, Mr. Ko leaves the house to walk aimlessly in the snow.

A writer included here who more or less dealt with the same problem is Sŏ Kiwon. His story, "The Uncharted Map" (1956), is a notable example. However, whereas Sŏn's story concentrates on revealing the emerging pattern and on presenting the perplexity and ambivalence that grip the older generation, Sŏ's story not only delimits the new pattern but also suggests, though faintly, some possibilities of the new pattern as a viable norm of existence in the changed landscape.

Two war veterans, Sangdŏk and Hyŏngnam, who have lost in the war the dreams of their college days and must now live in sloth in search of impulsive pleasures, and Yunju, a simple

girl who wanders aimlessly through the postwar void, are the three
main characters of the story. Introspective Hyŏngnam runs into
Sangdŏk, a former comrade-in-arms, when he finds himself down-
at-the-heels in Seoul. He is invited to live with the latter, but
he finds that Sangdŏk is living with Yunju, whom the latter met
one day in a characteristically haphazard fashion in front of a
movie house.

Soon, Hyŏngnam, a former art student, emerges as the sole
breadwinner for this motely family, drawing tawdry signboards
and posters for movie houses. With this, however, the subtle
psychological tension among the three mounts, and finally
Sangdŏk offers Hyŏngnam joint ownership of Yunju. After a
series of intricate and barbed psychological exchanges, the suggested joint ownership becomes a fact.

But they run into a crisis when Yunju announces her pregnan-
cy. Taken aback, the two men suggest abortion, but Yunju laughs
in their faces and leaves the house for good, almost cheerfully,
declaring that the baby will be hers and hers alone.

The story divides itself into two phases. The first is the desolate
and aberrant condition of the postwar spiritual scene in which
individuals are willy-nilly made to face life in frustration and the
resultant perverted value system. It is that grey land inhabited
by the Walking Wounded. Hyŏngnam, the central intelligence,
so to speak, of the story, muses at one point:

> ...What happened to his ambition as an art student in the College of Fine
> Arts, and his desire to create, and all those intoxicatingly beautiful im-
> ages! What filled his mind now were the shrill sounds of mortar shell explo-
> sions, the shrieking of dying soldiers, the naked bodies of women, tawdry
> and loud movie poster drawings in primary colors—all these were inter-
> mingled chaotically and tortured him.[7]

The second stage, though disproportionately brief and merely
suggestive, is dominated by Yunju, whose outlook undergoes a
radical change. The awakening in her of the primitive kind of
affirmation for life strikes a note of hopefulness nonetheless,
despite the smothering atmosphere of the entire situation. The
moral climate of the postwar landscape is aptly an uncharted map
that must be completed by each individual with proper landmarks
and contours.

About the middle of the 1950s, a group of writers tried to

link the postwar Korean situation to that of world literature, or more particularly, European literature, and in their opinion, the common ground was an existential approach to the predicament of man in this age and space. "The Poems of John the Baptist" (1957) by Chang Yonghak is a case in point.

Almost plotless, the story is largely a tract of existential philosophy interspersed with an allegory-packed parable of a fabulous cave-rabbit that seeks freedom, the description of the inhuman ideological war that even spreads into a prisoner-of-war camp on a southern island, the suicide of Nuhye, a North Korean prisoner of war, and the reminiscence of Nuhye's life in the camp by Tongho, a fellow prisoner, after the latter's release from the prison.

The story is about an effort to recapture the root of existence upturned by the cruel and meaningless ideological war. The cave-rabbit of the parable, lured by the resplendent rainbow-colored light that seeps into the cave from the outside world, forsakes the peace and comfort of the inner cave and is stricken blind and dead the moment he reaches the crack that opens to the outer world. This unfortunate rabbit is a metaphor for man in general in this age and space, and more particularly, of Nuhye and Tongho in the POW camp. "This war in which my flesh has been torn and my blood spilled—was this really mine?" they often wonder. "The utmost punishment one can impose upon his worst enemy is death ... A man cannot receive worse punishment than death however vile and evil he may be! ... But in the camp they cut off limbs, gouged out eyes, and lopped off the ears and noses of corpses."[8] Indifferent to the acrimonious hatred and blood-shed between the opposing ideological factions within the camp. Nuhye dreams of freedom as he looks up at the blue sky. His search for it leads him finally to suicide at the barbedwire fence of the POW camp.

Thus suicide becomes Nuhye's final solution to overcoming man's limiting situation. His death is the expression of will aspiring after freedom in the face of the cruel hate machine called ideology. But could this be the final answer to the fundamental question? In an afterword written several years after publication of the story, the author states that the true protagonist in this work is Tongho rather than Nuhye.[9] Nuhye and the fabulous rabbit die the moment they think they have attained freedom.

Freedom exists somewhere beyond the finite realm. It is something akin to John the Baptist, who prophesies the coming of the Messiah, but is not himself redemption per se. What is important to the author is the course that will be charted by Tongho, who is the disciple as well as an alter ego of Nuhye. The story, however, does not present any conclusive suggestion. The note of a redeeming quality is indeed very faint, if not totally ambiguous.

The image of man as the Walking Wounded can take on still another guise: I am referring to the maimed figure in the social-environmental nexus, suffering from economic indigence, sociopolitical injustices, and other absurdities of postwar society. The fictional works dealing with man groping for a sense of direction in the moral quagmire or at the precipice of existential anguish and despair—samples of which we have just seen—were, rightly or wrongly, labeled the Après Guerre school. Postwar Korea, however, was under such harsh and miserable conditions that neither existentialism nor the tenets of the Après Guerre school could take deep root in Korean literature. Though the key factor in this regard is the dire socioeconomic condition, we can discern another factor that has equally important bearings on the subject: the general social climate. Looking back, we can safely say that the manner in which the Korean War ended had a limiting sway on the typical *après guerre* versions, for the three years of bloody strife led only to a precarious truce that did not bring a decisive victory to either side. It was a cease-fire, not a peace. The ever-present threat of renewed aggression from the North persisting, the sociopolitical climate remained largely that of a quasiwar. Thus Korean society in a way simply could not permit the typically bold self-abandonment of the *après guerre* style with its nihilistic bent. And thus the works that come to terms with the naked truth of society, with all its inherent problems, again occupy center stage. Their approach is broadly "realistic," but the dominant image of man is still that of the Walking Wounded.

For instance, Ha Kŭnch'an's rural scene is quite a departure from the somewhat vain and abstract world of the so-called Après Guerre school. In his "Two Generations of Ordeal and Tribulation" (1957), as well as in his "The White Paper Beard" (1959), Ha portrays atmospheres and lifestyles native to rural

Korea. Caught in his poised and genial style are authentic rural men, women, and children: inarticulate, destitute, yet patient. They are the sufferers of the war's deprivation.

What Ha does for rural people, Son Ch'angsŏp does for city dwellers. What the protagonist, a war veteran, of his "A Washed Out Dream" (1956) finds in Seoul is a suffocating poverty, material and spiritual. Was there once a dream, indeed? If so, where can one snatch a peaceful night's sleep in which one can recapture that dream?

Some suffer more than others in the cutthroat game that is the main business of postwar society, and the worst is usually received by gullible men and women of good faith. That is what Son's "The Superfluous Being" (1959) is about—a satirical portrait of misfit and forsaken men doomed to a life of misery and failure. The men and women who are unable to "function" in this society must become superfluous human beings.

Let us take a closer examination of Yi Pŏmsŏn's "The Stray Bullet" (1959). Here an erratically fired bullet aimed at nothing becomes a metaphor for the image man as the Walking Wounded. Ch'ŏrho, a lowly clerk in a downtown accountant's office, wants to lead a righteous life in spite of poverty. Although he handles large sums of money on paper every day in his work, his wage is pitifully meager. He walks four miles to and from work because he cannot afford the trolley fare. He suffers greatly and constantly from bad teeth, but he cannot afford to see a dentist. His deranged mother, who continuously lets out the cry, "Let's go back!" (meaning back to North Korea, where the family formerly enjoyed a decent life), is a permanent fixture of the cardboard shack that they call his "house." His pregnant wife, who "does not even remember that she was once beautiful," patiently performs household chores even when the expected date of confinement draws near. His sister, a prostitute who caters to foreign soldiers, and his brother, a war veteran with no prospects for a job, are two off-and-on dwellers of his cardboard "house."

One evening the younger brother comes home drunk, and in the ensuing argument touched off by the elder's admonition, the younger one boldly challenges the elder's outlook on life— that a man must never succumb to the degradation of conscience no matter how he suffers from other degradations.

"That's right. We must cast away conscience, ethics, custom, law, and everything else," (said the younger one) ...

"I would have been a rich man long ago, if I could have brought myself to do that," the elder brother countered.

"I know ... What is conscience but a thorn in your fingertip. Remove it once, and it won't bother you any longer ... "[10]

Ch'ŏrho is so poor that he no longer has any zest for life, but he can never adopt his brother's attitude.

The following day, he receives a phone call at work from the police station. He soon finds that his younger brother was caught in a robbery earlier that day. Going home from the police station, he is met by his sister, who tells him that his wife is having trouble giving birth at the hospital. She hands him a bundle of banknotes. Reaching the hospital, however, he finds that his wife is already dead. The money has become useless. He wanders the streets aimlessly and sees a dentist's clinic. On the spur of the moment, he walks in. Four bad molars, but the dentist will remove only two of them, insisting that removing them all at one time can be very dangerous. Ch'ŏrho seeks out another clinic to have the rest removed.

Dizzy with pain and bleeding, he hops in a taxi and directs the driver to take him to the hospital where his wife's remains are, then changes his mind again and tells the driver to drive around to no place in particular. He keeps saying, "Let's go," echoing his deranged mother. The annoyed driver mutters, "My, this man is like a stray bullet." Sinking into a daze, Ch'ŏrho muses, "Perhaps I am a stray bullet accidentally fired by God."

We have seen the image of man in postwar Korean fiction as the Walking Wounded in its varied modes and guises. Though markedly different from one another, what they have in common is that they all are victims of the war and the ruthless postwar society in which all order has broken down. The shattering legacy of the war deprives, distorts, destroys, and finally pulverizes the suffering man. Indeed, the picture is very grim, and the gleam of hope, if any, is not readily discernible.

Another common factor is the manner in which the suffering and brooding main characters respond to the predicaments in which they find themselves; I refer to their personal and individualistic posture. The pain of loss, the bewilderment at degradation and disintegration, the despair and anguish in the

face of an impersonal society that threatens to devour them—
these and others finally do not lead to any awareness pointing
to the means by which their plight may be mitigated. Even in
the works in which social-environmental nexus plays a vital role,
the indictment of the ill remains merely suggestive.

Offhand, this situation can be defended on two counts. First,
writers were too overwhelmed by what went on around them to
record anything but their shock and despair—evidence that
only proves the extent and degree of atrocity and devastation of
the war. The second count is a rhetorical question: Is it not but
the business of modern literature to draw the individual self? Time
would solve the first, but in the second we discern the extent of
the influence of the literary war waged between the "pure
literature" camp and the "tendentious literature" camp in the
earlier decades. This, too, would be modified and qualified with
the flow of time and taste, and the discussion of the changed
outlook is properly the subject of the next section.

III. The Inspired Rebel

A new pattern slowly evolves. A group of writers arrives on
the scene to present a new image of man—man not as the defeated
and brooding figure that is the victim of society and history,
but as the positive hero with wisdom and courage who defies the
encroaching surroundings. The new voice, only faintly audible
at first, gathers momentum as the turbulence of the sociopolitical
arena of the early 1960s unfolds. These writers are supported
by still another group of avowedly dedicated critics who maintain that the affirmation of life is a prerequisite of any literature
that needs no apology and that social participation is a legitimate
function of literature in order to advance that affirmative belief.
A lively controversy ensues between pros and cons, but the main
job of those who stand for *Littérature engagé* is to present a possibility
for socially oriented literature without falling into the pitfall of
tendentious literature.

Regardless of the outcome of the critical controversy, the image of man as an Inspired Rebel emerges dominant. Perhaps,
at first, it took shape as a simple reaction against the passive
individualism of the immediate postwar years, but it was, in time,
fostered into a positive figure whose consciousness expands into

a firm, earthy realization of the possibility of man.

What inspires the rebel? No doubt the hightened social and political consciousness, stirred up in the gathering storm that led up to the April 19 revolution in which an autocratic regime was toppled by students, played a key role. That memorable event vindicated the spirit of justice and self-rule once asserted by the thwarted March 1 independence movement of another age. The resultant self-confidence, pride, and awareness of possibility helped fashion the new image of man. This gave rise to a new kind of literature: indictment and criticism of existing reality came into vogue. The validity of realism was reaffirmed, as evidenced by the works of such writers as Sŏnu Hwi, Kim Chŏnghan, and Hwang Sŏgyŏng, but the works of such writers as Nam Chonghyŏn and Chong Ulbyŏng, which straddle the delicate borderland between satire and exposé, also became popular.

Less readily recognizable, though equally important as a source of inspiration for the literature of this period was the cultural awareness of the people that I touched on briefly earlier—the search for cultural identity. The shabbiness of Korean culture of that day—epitomized in the epithet, ''the chewing-gum culture,'' does not adequately describe the hollowness and confusion caused by the wholesale influx of foreign ideas and way of life in which many intellectuals saw the cause of the national plight. This naturally led to a heightened historical consciousness, and this interest in history in turn was linked to the sociopolitical consciousness in a roundabout way. Thus a flood of fiction, based on history came into being, in which the gist was to see the present in a clearer light. The history of the Korean people under Japanese colonial rule, the heroic fight against the oppressor in the March 1 independence movement, the tragic division of the country, and other such historical events became favorite subjects, as evidenced by the works of such writers as Yu Chuhyŏn, An Sugil, Ch'oe Inhun, Yi Hoch'ŏl, Sŏnu Hwi, and others. In the case of Sŏ Kiwŏn, the search went even further back in history to trace the footsteps of the popular leader of the Tonghak agrarian uprising that took place toward the end of the Yi dynasty.

Sŏnu Hwi's novella, ''Flowers of Fire'' (1957), is generally considered the piece that started to turn the tide in favor of a positive hero. In this work, the author seems to criticize the easy, resigning attitude of the Korean toward the force of history. It deals with the suffering of three generations of a family (Hyŏn, the protagonist, the father, and the grandfather), using as a backdrop the turbulent period from the March 1,1919, independence movement to the June war in 1950. Hyŏn is a son born after the death of the father, who lost his life in the fight against the Japanese in the March 1 movement. He is brought up by his mother and grandfather. The grandfather, a petty grain dealer, is not only an old-fashioned man encrusted with superstition but also a man given to indolent selfishness. Thus he is not proud of his son who gave his life for the national cause; it is his firm conviction that ''saving the country and the people is high-flying nonsense ... You watch out for yourself. Don't ever try to lift a finger for the sake of others, for it never pays to do that. Don't ever rely on others, either,'' Thus the old man even hates the dead son, who had become a Christian against the old man's will and was shot down by Japanese soldiers during the movement and left the burden of the whole family to the old man.

Having no personal knowledge of his own father, Hyŏn grows up under the influence of his grandfather's passive individualism and that attitude becomes part of his consciousness. As a boy, Hyŏn comes home one day with cuts and bruises from a fight against village urchins who ridiculed his grandfather's physical peculiarity. He expects to be comforted and commended for this bravery, but what greets him is his grandfather's stern reproof. Incidents of this kind shape him into a timid onlooker in life. ''Never mind others; I don't want to get involved'' becomes his attitude as a boy in high school. But once in a while this indifference is challenged by the contrary urge innate in him. In college, when a Japanese professor preaches the necessity of the Greater East Asia Co-prosperity Sphere, Hyŏn babbles out his dissent in spite of himself. But immediately he recoils into himself as if he is ashamed of his nakedness. He is taken into the Japanese army, and later he defects to the Chinese Communist army in Yenan, but he cannot bring himself to get involved in the greedy factional bickering among the Korean Communists there.

Thus when he comes back to his hometown in North Korea after the Liberation, his attitude is still ''don't torment others as you would not have others torment you.'' Soon the June war breaks out, but he is still indifferent.

But his indifference cannot last long. Though he wants to

perpetuate the comfort of his shell of individualism, the outside world is in preparation for a stormy tempest overcast by dark clouds. He is forced to participate in a so-called people's trial in which innocent people are summarily sentenced to death in the name of people's democracy. The absurdity and atrocity of the proceedings suddenly awaken in him the will to resist. He realizes that the real "people" should not put up with the murder waywardly committed by the death contractors. He feels he should face squarely and fight against the agent of injustice.

> Thirty years! In what manner have I lived the past thirty years? A series of aversions and escapes ... What pain have you borne and endured? None. Nothing but indignity and cowardice ... shutting yourself in a shell like a clam or shunning the sun like a mole. My life has not been one of living but of vegetating. Now I must start to live for the first time, and I must die to prove that conviction.[11]

With this awareness of human complicity, he engages courageously in a lone but hope-laden fight against the Communists, as his father had against the Japanese army thirty years earlier. He receives a fatal wound in the fighting, and in his dying moment he sees the flowers of fire, the sign of liberating life-force.

Ch'oe Inhun takes a slightly different stance: if Sŏnu's Hyŏn is a creation of a somewhat crude ideology, Ch'oe's Yi Myŏng-jun, the protagonist of The Open Square (1961), is an agent of an intellectual approach to the tragedy of Korean history—the tragic division of the land.

The novel is in memoir form, reminisced on the deck of an Indian ship, the *Tagore*, by a released prisoner of war, Yi Myŏng-jun, who has chosen to go to a neutral country. He was born and reared in South Korea, but defected to the North before the war and finally became a POW, captured by the Southern army during the war.

It was his father who defected to the North first. In this way, Myŏngjun, a philosophy student, came to live with the family of his girlfriend (Yŏngmi), a typical bourgeois family of Seoul in whose indolent way of life he felt restless. Soon the police begin to annoy and humiliate him because it was made known that his father was on Northern propaganda broadcasts to the South. The hatred for the police rekindled his love toward his father, and his fling at a love affair with a girl named Yunae was not totally satisfying. Finally he decides to defect.

In the boat going to the North, he is excited by the prospect of revolutionary fervor, and he thinks he is headed for a "clean open square," leaving the closedness and mustiness of a "hermetically sealed room." What awaits him in the North is a series of disillusionments, however. His father has remarried and indulges in the easy life of the elite Communists—the Northern version of the inane bourgeoisie. The exciting spirit of revolution to which he wanted to devote his youth is nowhere to be seen. He gets a reporter's job on the official government newspaper, but he is soon subjected to "self-criticism" for his "petit-bourgeois consciousness" and "misleading reporting based on subjective views" when he writes a truthful account of the plight of a group of Koreans in Manchuria. He then volunteers to be a manual laborer and gets hurt in the construction of an outdoor theater. The accident gives him an opportunity to get acquainted with a beautiful ballet dancer, and this develops into a love affair on which his hope hinges for a while until she cuts him loose and leaves.

When the Korean War breaks out in 1950, he comes back to Seoul as a member of the People's Liberation Army, but by this time his disgust with both the North and the South is almost complete. His job in Seoul is to investigate and pass judgment on the Southern "reactionaries" rounded up by the conquering Northern army. Among the prisoners he finds his one-time love, Yunae, who is now married to Yŏngmi's brother, Taesik. In his despair from the loss of faith in the two warring political systems, Myŏngjun attempts to find sadistic satisfaction in wreaking vengeance on the couple. But he fails to find satisfaction in torturing them and ends up secretly turning them loose, a traitorous act on his part. Later, during frontline duty, he briefly meets the ballerina, who is now an army nurse, but she gets killed in action while he is captured.

When the truce is signed, he feels he has no place to go, not being able to have faith in either side. The glorious open square he yearns for in which people can lead a decent life in trust and harmony does not exist on either side. A mere apology for such a square does exist on both sides, of course, but it is a travesty, a sham: in the South, the square is "a defiled and miserable one ... in which baseness, greed for power, and perverted sex masquerade,"[12] while in the North it is a square where "the party replaces the people ... and a mere gesture of revolutionary fervor, not revolutionary fervor itself, an imitation of excitement, not excitement itself, and a rumor of conviction, not conviction itself, rule."[13] Thus he opts for self-exile in a neutral country where he knows no one and is not emotionally involved in anything. But his hope is not sustained, and he commits suicide by hurling himself into the blue ocean from the deck of the *Tagore*.

Thus the novel ends, and it naturally leaves us with a question about the validity and viability of the protagonist as a rebel hero. True, to some the denouement might appear weak, and death and despondency rather than life and hope might appear to rule the novel. On the other hand, we must allow that the mark of the novel is to dissect intellectually the ills that beset the two societies. What can an intellectual do under the circumstances? Indeed, the hero's death in the novel is a symbolic death disproving his false hope for a life in an alien country. Death will some day be followed by rebirth, and the proper open square in which the reborn hero engages himself will be none other than his homeland. And appropriately enough, the final note struck by the novel is that of a qualified hope for the future.

The image of a truly positive hero with no apology or qualification is presented in the works of Kim Chŏnghan. Kim is an old-timer who wrote in the late 1930s and early 1940s. Then miraculously, he made a comeback in the 1960s, after a silence of a quarter century, to become one of the more popular and fairly prolific contemporaries. His literary comeback proves the extent of the favorableness of the literary climate of the 1960s toward his kind of writing, a rebellious kind; and the range and the theme of his writing may be seen in his personal life, which has been studded with frequent imprisonment (on seven separate occasions) on charges of antigovernment plots and instigation of agrarian revolt. His stories are about the poverty and denigration of the downtrodden and forsaken and their heroic battle to regain human dignity and decency. As might be supposed, all his stories are rendered with deep affection and insight for the oppressed but with no high-flown intellectual or ideological flair.

For instance, "The Story of the Sandy Delta" (1966) concerns the poverty-stricken denizens of a sandy delta called Chomai Island near the estuary of the Naktong River.[14] In spite of the fact that the delta had been settled by innumerable generations of islanders, the land title had belonged, during the period of Japanese rule, to the Japanese-owned Oriental Development Company. Since the Liberation, however, the title has been surreptitiously transferred to a national assemblyman. Then lately, it has again been transferred to another wealthy and powerful man in the region but without the islanders' knowledge.

The story is given in the form of a composition written by a boy in middle school and submitted to his teacher. The boy's father died in action during the Korean War, but his death was so anonymous that he was not even buried in the national cemetery, nor did his bereaved family receive the benefit of the support for the war dead. The boy's uncle fared no better: he was lost at sea while working for a deep-sea fishery company, but the company did not return to the family either the body or compensation. And a neighbor of the boy, accused of being a Communist because he protested against the government plan to turn the island into a colony for lepers, has just served a prison term.

In fact, the plan to build a leper colony in the delta was a sham plotted by the wealthy nominal owner of the island to drive out the islanders. Failing in this, he designs an even more vile and treacherous plan: on the pretext of reclaiming the land in the delta he builds a dike. Soon the rainy season sets in and the river rises. If the dike gives way at the peak, the whole island will be washed out in an instant. Therefore, it must be drained. The islanders, led by the boy's grandfather, demand that the dike be drained beforehand, but the goon squad hired by the wealthy man stops them. Tension mounts and in the ensuing fight, the boy's grandfather heroically overpowers the roughnecks and succeeds in saving the island, but he accidentally commits a murder by pushing the leader of the goon squad into the turbid current.

We see in the old man and the islanders, and in their plight and subsequent rebellion, a true aspect of the people's history and their force in action as a potential energy to reshape history. Though poor and uneducated, they refuse to put up with the design of history forced on them, and in the end, they nobly rise out of the subhuman conditions by enduring and rebelling.

At least some passing mention must be made here of Hwang Sŏgyŏng as a writer of rare promise who keeps the light burning for the kind of fiction under investigation. One of the youngest writers, he is the most recent colorbearer for the image of man as a rebel in socially oriented fiction. Most prolific in the past four or five years, he is a writer rightly belonging to the 1970s.

When I say that he belongs to the 1970s, I do not mean merely in terms of literary chronology. True, most of his works were published in the 1970s, but what is more fundamental, in my estimation, is his milieu, which is precisely that of the 1970s. I refer to the newly emerging outer-urban cores in the peripheries of larger cities and the small people who are the wretched and pathos-packed denizens of this new environment. The urban-rural dichotomy has been fairly traditional in Korea, although the cleavage between the two became markedly conspicuous in the late 1950s and early 1960s, and quite appropriately, the two worlds are amply reflected in the works of writers of this period. For instance, even within the context of this article, Son Ch'angsŏp, Ch'oe Inhun, Yi Hoch'ŏl, and Yi Pŏmsŏn may be said to stand for the urban, whereas Kim Chŏnghan and Ha Kunch'an are notable champions of the rural. But the emergence of the outer-urban cores is a new phenomenon derived from the sudden shift in population, mostly from the rural region to the urban region. It is a by-product of the development oriented economic program supported by massive international loans in the latter half of the 1960s, and its complications began to manifest themselves most markedly in the 1970s. The outer-urban cores grow in clusters where the migrant rural population ekes out a pitiful living. These people are not at all sure of their identity; they are not yet fully accepted as city-dwellers, and yet they have no idyllic rural home to which to go back. And it is this environment and its people that Hwang makes the heartland and inhabitants of his fictional works.

Hwang's literary mode is that of realism, but what makes him a special kind of realist is the free and casual kind of life-affirming outlook he renders in his characters despite the squalor and degradation of the environment. Take "On the Road to Samp'o" for example.[15] It is a story of three people who meet haphazardly on the desolate road to Samp'o on a cold morning. One is a young day-laborer who has fled from a construction work camp because he was caught in the act of violating the wife of the owner of an eating house; another is a middle-aged man who is on his way back home to settle down after "roughing it" for the past ten years or so, spending about half of that time in prisons, on and off, on various charges; the last is a whore who also wants to go back to her village, fleeing from the whore-master to whom she owes money. They are typical denizens of the outer-urban core, helpless and downtrodden outcasts. But an immediate and unconditional comradeship envelops them, and it is in this spirit that the two men put the party pursuing the prostitute on the wrong path in spite of the lure of a reward. So the three main characters continue their journey to Samp'o, but it is quite obvious that the Samp'o they dream of, the idyllic and euphoric village where milk and honey abound, no longer exists. It will be a grotesquely disfigured place similar to the places from which they have fled. Nevertheless, this motley group is never without hope.

That the new social stratum is a result of an impetuous modernization is easy to see, but what is alarming is the rate at which the new stratum and its habitat grow, and thus an outer-urban environment can sometimes exist in places far beyond the peripheries of large cities. (One may argue that all this is part of the urbanization process, but the word that describes that process more accurately, in my opinion, is "deruralization" rather than urbanization.) Hwang's novella, "The Place for Strangers" (1971), is a good example of this. The locale of the story is a land reclamation work site in a coastal area, but the working people there are typical outer-urban core dwellers—mostly social outcasts, deprived of economic means, neglected by society and government, and sometimes ruthlessly exploited by the socioeconomic machineries. The drama of the story hinges on the struggle between the workers and the construction company that unscrupulously tries to make unfair profits at their expense. The workers finally fail in their struggle, but curiously, they do not fail as human beings. Their leader even strikes a note of optimism in the face of all contrary conditions. He is a new kind of rebel, free from the onus of ideological-intellectual formulations or emotion-charged and schematized indignations of the older writers. The new rebel will not tolerate human devaluation either, but the act of rebelling is so natural to him that it becomes his lifestyle, which he "enjoys" to some extent. This creation of a new rebel is the source of the charm and importance of Hwang as a socially oriented writer of fiction in our days, and it is not an overstatement to say that the texture of Korean fiction in the near future will depend greatly on the future he charts for himself.

The writers and works discussed thus far show the extent and modes of existence for the image of man as an Inspired Rebel in postwar Korean fiction. A sense of justice and a deeper understanding and compassion for the man caught in the plight of the postwar Korean landscape are central to their works. The undaunted will and wisdom to overcome that predicament is the underlying principle.

One or two comments may be added regarding this type of fiction. The works become longer, in general, and for the first time in the history of modern Korean letters the novel begins to be accepted as a congenial form. The bettered economic condition certainly has something to do with it, but the primary reason seems to lie in the nature of the subject matter—the current historical-social-environmental nexus.

Another comment concerns the changing mode of realism as evidenced particularly by the works of such writers as Hwang Sŏkyŏng. The newer version is far more sophisticated than the older version. In fact, the sophistication of style is the hallmark of the writers since the latter part of the 1960s, and this may be better illustrated by the works of the writers that I will discuss next.

IV. The Victimized Aesthete

The emergence in the past ten years or so of a group of talented young writers who write in a markedly different way from that already discussed is a remarkable literary event. Though few in number, they are producing works of exceedingly high quality, and the extent of popula as well as critical acclaim accorded to these writers promises that they will command a wider and brighter horizon in future Korean fiction.

Their milieu is decidedly urban, their stance intellectual. What sets them apart is their special kind of sensibility: colorful, urbane, and almost sensuous. This is more readily recognizable in their style, which freely commands irony, juxtaposition, inversion, sensuous imagery, and other rhetorical devices—a departure from the traditional realism—but this trait in their style is extended into the outlook of the image of man they create. Their perception of the man-society relationship is not very different from that of their contemporaries who are more socially oriented: that man is a victim of society, or history, that he did not make. But they depart markedly in their response to this confirmed condition. They seem to probe for a possibility to mediate the contradiction in a way that is chiefly aesthetical.

Another noteworthy trait of their works is the flair for experimentation, and it is in this that we recognize an overwhelming influence of Western literature on these writers. Curiously, Korean fiction writers in the past were not very susceptible to experimentalism even when they were well aware that it was a hallmark of Western literary modernism that they were supposed to emulate, consciously or otherwise. One notable exception would be Yi Sang, who wrote in the late 1920s and early 1930s, and it is to his world that the works of the new generation are linked, atavistically, as it were. The influence of Western literature on these young writers is indisputable, and one way to account for it, though ''extrinsically,'' would be to investigate the educational background of these writers. For instance, take the three writers I intend to discuss in this section: Kim Sŭngok, Yi Ch'ŏngjun, and Ch'oe Inho. All are graduates of reputable universities in Seoul. Kim was a French literature major at Seoul National; Yi was a German literature major at the same institution; Ch'oe was an English major at Yonsei. ''Biographical fallacy'' notwithstanding, one is bound to see in this something more than mere coincidence.

Let us now examine a few stories written by Kim Sŭngok, the unquestioned leader of this group. His ''My Fifteen *Idées Fixes* Reconfirmed'' (1964) is a rather short piece,[16] a record of what goes on in the mind of a young down-at-the-heels college boy who ruminates over things in general while ''giving the slip'' to a rich girl with whom he has a date. Some of the things he thinks about, his relationship with his elder brother who lost an arm in the war, for instance, richly suggest that he is acutely aware of the victimized condition of his generation, but his response is peculiarly individualistic and aesthetical. Thus he confines himself in his drab boardinghouse room in what he calls a ''hibernant'' stance and enumerates his fixed ideas which reveal the extent and quality of his sensibility. Even his sexual urge is hibernant, and this is why he stays home when he has a date, picturing to himself the waiting and disappointment of the girl, who has no means of reaching him.

The juvenescent world of the Victimized Aesthete is wonderfully caught in his "Seoul 1964, Winter" (1964). Two young men, both age twenty-five, meet one winter evening in a street stall where cheap drinks are served. One is a graduate student at a university, and the other is a petty clerk in city hall who has once failed the entrance examination to the military academy. Two strangers, they strike up a conversation while drinking, but they have no topics in common until they find out that they share an identical flair for useless and senseless yet accurate details such as "the eighth streetlamp in front of the Pyŏnghwa Shopping Center being out of order" or "there being thirty-two persons waiting for the bus at Sŏdaemun stop, seventeen women and five children among them, as of 7:15 p.m." They speedily become friends and fervently exchange their secret information.

When they get ready to leave the stall for a further exploration of the city in the same spirit, a sad-looking middle-aged man asks to go along. He says he has enough money for the three of them. So the adventure starts, but later, the middle-aged man discloses the source of the money. It is from the hospital to which he sold the corpse of his wife, who died that morning. Barred by the curfew, they stay overnight in an inn. In the morning, they find that the middle-aged man has committed suicide during the night.

"The Night Prowling" (1969) is another example in which the pathology of the urban society of the 1960s and man's inept but aesthetical sensibility and boredom in response to that society are vividly caught. The heroine of the story is a teller in a city bank, and she is secretly married to a fellow working in the same office. They cannot make their relationship public because she wants to retain the job for financial reasons (It is a common practice in Korean banks not to allow married women to stay on the job). So they behave as fellow workers at the office even though they are husband and wife at home, and in time she comes to hate this contradiction, which she equates somehow with the boring life in general of her time.

She once had a strange experience. One day, in broad daylight, while she was crossing an overpass in the city, a man, a total stranger, accosted her, and gripping her wrist, he told her that he had some urgent messages to give her. She was led into a nearby hotel, and without much ado they shared a bed. That was his message and they parted. Of course, she resisted unsuccessfully at the time, but later she was not at all sure if her resistance had been in earnest.

And she now thinks that the affair was much healthier than her boring relationship with her secret husband. Thus in her desire to rise above the quotidian, she prowls the night street in search of an adventure, a breakthrough, in vain.

We must not be deceived by Yi Ch'ŏngjun's style: in spite of his more traditional and sedate style, his world is in complete agreement with that of Kim Sŭngok. Of course, there is a temperamental difference. In comparison, Yi's approach is more intellectual, and this is clearly illustrated in "The Maimed and the Nitwit" (1966).[17]

Although it is a short stroy, the content is so complicated that it defies a neat summary. The narrator is a young artist who whiles away his time, failing in love and also failing to produce a work after his own heart. He cannot attain a positive stance in life, and it is obvious that he is an aesthete suffering from the impossible ineptitude of his time and age. His elder brother, a surgeon and a war veteran, also stumbled recently: he inadvertently killed a little girl while operating on her. He ends his medical practice and wastes himself away by drinking, though he is writing a novel in secret. The novel reveals that the true source of his guilty feeling is not so much the death of the girl as his supposed murder of a fellow soldier during the retreat from North Korea. But he succeeds in "getting it off his mind" by writing about it, and thus he resecures his mental balance and resumes his practice, while his younger brother still hangs low since he cannot spot the cause of his ailment. Or rather, he knows the cause, but he does not know the remedy.

The author seems to be stressing the qualitative difference between the elder brother's generation, the war-time generation, and the younger brother's generation, which inherited all the guilt and anguish of the former generation intact yet not its raw energy nor its subterfuge. The former is the "maimed" generation that has a clearly visible wound, whereas the latter is the "nitwit" generation that does not know how to nurse its invisible wound.

There is another plane in the story that may elude the careless reader. It is directly concerned with Yi's literary inclination to "fabulate." Within this story, two different worlds are superimposed: one is the quotidian world where the everyday life of the narrator, his elder brother, his sister-in-law, and his girlfriend take place; and the other is the fabular world woven into the elder brother's novel. These two worlds demand to be merged and reconciled within the framework of the story. In fact, this kind of fabulation is a consistent pattern in the works of Yi Ch'ŏng-jun, and this is precisely what links this writer to some of the more noted fabulators of contemporary Western literature. For instance, to find a similarity between him and such fabulators as J. L. Borges of Argentina or John Barth of the united States is not farfetched.

The writer in this group with the liveliest and most colorful style is Ch'oe Inho. The youngest of the three, he is the most prolific of the group and employs the most sensuous style in his writing. Moreover, his tireless experiments in the spirit of modern Western literature are novel and refreshing. In his small way, he is cultivating a new possibility for the Korean language as a medium of modern fiction (Since the introduction of literary modernism, considerable work in this vein has been advanced for poetry, it seems, but it has not been so evident in fiction). A summary of "Another Man's Room" (1971) will illustrate Ch'oe's literary world but not the quality of his lively style.[18]

A young man repeatedly rings the doorbell of an apartment. Getting no response, he bangs on the door, arousing the suspicion of the neighbors. Finally he pulls a key from his pocket and lets himself in. The room is in disarray and nobody is in. He soon finds a note on the dresser addressed to "My Dear Husband" from "Your Loving Wife" saying that she "is called away because her father is sick and that there is no need of his looking for her since she will be back very shortly." We learn that the man is the husband and that he has come back from a business trip a day earlier than he had planned. Most likely the note without a date was written immediately after his departure a week earlier.

He stomps around the apartment but is gripped with terrible loneliness intermingled with desperation. The feeling finally overpowers him, and he becomes a victim of fantasy and hallucination in which the wall clock, furniture, water faucets in the bathroom, and other things riotously rampage in mockery.

But two days later, a woman comes into the room. Making sure that nobody is home, she writes out another note identical to the former note and then she hastily leaves. At this juncture, the reader is involved in a confusion that is essentially Kafkaesque. Was the man in another man's apartment, or is he really the husband and the true owner of the apartment? One thing is certain: the story vividly catches the quality of alienation that ensnares the life of city-dwellers in our days.

In summary, the chief merit of the writers of this group seems to be their success in bridging the gap between Korean fiction and that of the world. It is for this reason that we may entertain hope for the future, for their versatile talent will no doubt play a vital role in shaping Korean fiction in years to come.

One additional comment in the spirit of literary sociology may be made here. These young writers are avowed "professionals," and they try to make a living solely by writing when most of our contemporary for their occasional dabbling in less serious popular media, but it shows, by and large, the seriousness and degree of their commitment to their chosen profession.

V. Conclusion

I have discussed postwar Korean fiction in terms of the images of man portrayed by the writers. Because of this framework, such other aspects of interest as style and technique, have largely been spared except in passing.

Spared also are discussions of some other fictional types and trends that are no less important. Actually, no literature of a thirty-year period of any country may be subsumed under only three types. Thus, for instance, works that deal with changing manners and mores and those that pictorially capture the hew of our life in a spirit of lyricism that is uniquely Korean have been left out. Of course, there is a reason for this: important as they are, and they occupy a special corner in postwar Korean literature, they form a minority that is not properly a part of the mainstream. However, the three types discussed in this article will sufficiently illustrate the range and pattern of fiction produced during an unprecedented period of turmoil and upheaval in Korea. In summary, I am compelled to conclude that Korean fiction has responded well to the conditions of life and culture, and I hope this anthology will throw some light on the way in which contemporary Korean literature takes the full measure of life in this period.

But what about the future? I have made some hints about the possible complexion and texture of future Korean fiction in the course of my discussion. But they are merely hints, nothing more. Certainly it will depend greatly on what history has in store for us and on the newer literary modes and trends that catch the imagination of writers. Yet one thing is quite certain: judging from past performance, there will be no lack of talent, whatever turn history may take or whatever mutations the artistic language may experience in the future.

NOTES

This introduction appeared, in slightly modified form, as "Images of Man in Postwar Korean Fiction," *Korean Studies* 2 (1978): 1—27.

1. Ihab Hassan, *Radical Innocence: Studies in the Contemporary American Novel* (Princeton, New Jersey: Princeton University Press, 1961), p. 3.
2. Kim Tongni, "Father and Son," *Postwar Korean Short Stories: An Anthology,* 2d ed., Kim Chongun (Seoul: Seoul National University Press, 1982), p. 5.
3. Sol Schindler, "Simple Narration Hallmark of Korean Short Stories," *Korea Herald,* February 9, 1975, p. 4.
4. Song Pyŏngsu, "Shorty Kim," *Han'guk chŏnhu munje chakp'um chip,* ed., Paek Ch'ŏl et al. (Seoul: Sin'gu Munhwasa, 1960), p. 191.
5. Son Ch'ang-sŏp, "Walking in the Snow," *Postwar Korean Short Stories,* p. 50.
6. Son, "Walking in the Snow," p. 58.
7. Sŏ Kiwŏn, "The Uncharted Map," *Postwar Korean Short Stories,* p. 79.
8. Chang Yonghak, "Poems of John the Baptist," *Postwar Korean Short Stories,* p. 36.
9. Chang Yonghak, "Silchon kwa Yohan sijip," [Existence and "The Poems of John the Baptist"],*Han'guk chŏnhu munje chakp'um chip,* p. 402.
10. *Yi Pŏmsŏn,* "Obalt'an" [The stray bullet], *Han'gŭk chonhu munje chakp'um chip,* p. 287.
11. Sŏnu Hwi, "Pulkkot" [Flowers of fire], *Han'guk tanp'yŏn munhak chŏnjip* [Collected works of Korean short stories] (Seoul: Paegyŏng Sa, 1966), p. 378.
12. Ch'oe Inhun, *Kwangjang* [The open square] (Seoul: Minumsa, 1973), pp. 127-128.
13. Ch'oe, *Kwangjang,* p, 126.
14. "Morae t'op iyagi," *Kim Chŏnghan sosŏl sŏnjip* [Selected fictional works of Kim Chŏnghan] (Seoul: Ch'angjak kwa Pip'yŏng Sa, 1974).

15. Hwang Sŏgyŏng, "Samp'o kanŭn kil" [On the road to Samp'o], *Kaekchi* [The place for strangers] (Seoul: Ch'angjak kwa Pip'yŏng Sa, 1974).

16. The three stories by Kim Sŭngok discussed here are collected in *Kim Sŭngok sosŏl chip* [Collected fictional works of Kim Sŭng-ok] (Seoul: Saemto Mungo, 1975).

17. Yi Ch'ŏngjun, "Pyŏngsin kwa mŏjŏri" [The maimed and the nitwit], *Pyŏngsin kwa mŏjŏri* (Seoul: Samjungdang Mungo, 1975).

18. Ch'oe Inho, "T'ainŭi pang" [Another man's room], *Han'guk taep'yo tanp'yŏn munhak chŏnjip* [Collection of representative Korean short stories], vol. 29 (Seoul: Chonghan, 1975).

Father and Son

A man got off the boat. Under his dark and threadbare over
coat he was wearing traditional Korean garments of white cotton. The felt hat he had on was so old, weather-beaten, and
smudged with dirt and sweat, that it was hard to tell whether its
original color of the hat had been gray or black. He seemed to
be in his mid-forties, but he had no beard. One could tell at a
glance he was a peasant. In his right hand he was carrying a small
bundle wrapped with a white cotton cloth. It was rice. He had
had about six or seven pounds when he left home, but since then
he had given away small amounts of it at several different places
in exchange for meals. About two pounds of rice was all that was
left in the cloth bundle.

As he stepped down to the wharf he asked another man getting off the same boat, "What's the name of this place?"

Giving a side glance to the peasant, the man said rather curt-
ly, "Yŏsu." The truth of the matter was that he had asked the
same question over and over to fellow passengers as the boat was
pulling into Yŏsu harbor and again just before disembarking,
and knowing this, the man who answered the question on the
pier was slightly embarrassed.

"It's Yŏsu, is it?" he made a faltering halfquestion. No one
answered this time. Only two or three people gave him a side
glance and hurried away.

It was evening, and the wind blowing down from the Chiri
mountain range was somewhat nippy, although it was early
spring; it was far too early for apricot blossoms.

"How far is Kwangju from here?" asked the man (his name
was Sŏkkyu) again.

Once more no one answered.

"Will there be a bus going to Kwangju today?"

This time two people answered him at once.

"Not likely."

"You'd better check at the depot early in the morning."

The first was a young man in army uniform, and the second was a middle-aged woman in white Korean dress with a silk scarf around her head.

"How far is Kwangju from here?"

"Oh, on foot it'll take four days at least."

"Four days?" Sŏkkyu was astonished.

The purpose of Sŏkkyu's journey was to visit his son Pongho, who was reportedly stationed in Kwangju. The truth was that he had had second-hand information that his son, who had joined the army, was now with an outfit whose headquarters were in Kwangju. The man who gave him the information said that the designation of Pongho's outfit was much longer than X Regiment of Y Division, but he had forgotten the rest. He was Mr. Yang from Hamyang (the county seat). Mr. Yang owned a small match factory there. Since Mr. Yang's own son, Yongbok, had gone into the army at the same time as Pongho it had become Sŏkkyu's habit to drop in on him whenever he went into town, just to talk about their sons.

It all started in early February when Sŏkkyu stopped by Mr. Yang's factory as usual, Mr. Yang was happy to see him and told him that he had heard of Pongho. "P-Pongho, you say?" For a while Sŏkkyu was afraid that he might faint.

Mr. Yang explained that he had just been to the Army Hospital in Pusan where his son Yongbok was hospitalized for an arm injury. The injury was not serious but it called for about a month's rest and treatment in the hospital. Mr. Yang said he had heard from Yongbok that Pongho was with some outfit in X Regiment of Y Division in Kwangju.

Since enlistment, over half a year ago, Sŏkkyu had not heard from his boy, and it had become the cause of his wife's nightly tears and his own deep sighs. He even neglected his farming. And all of a sudden this big news. The world had suddenly become brighter for the couple.

"Why don't you start right away and go see him? Nothing is important till you see our boy, not even the farming," said his wife. That was the way he felt, too.

The excited wife disclosed her plan to prepare cakes and other delicacies for her boy, but the more soberminded Sŏkkyu told her not to go overboard just yet, because two full months had already passed since Yongbok saw their boy last, and also because Mr. Yang had forgotten the last half of the boy's military address. Because of these discrepancies he was not sure if the boy was still there, nor, even if his son was still there, was he certain that he would be able to find him, the address being incomplete.

"Then you go to Pusan first and get the exact address from Yongbok," his wife said.

Well, Sŏkkyu was not exactly dumb, and he had already thought of that himself, but that would mean longer time and more travel money. Besides, the cough he had had since the boy's departure had made him rather weak, and he was not at all sure he could stand the long jouney by bus and boat and then on foot.

He had had two years of primary school education, but that was over thirty years ago, and farming had been his only concern for all these years. Now he didn't have confidence in anything else. Therefore, the idea of having to make a journey from his home in Hapch'ŏn in Kyŏngsang Province to Kwangju in Chŏlla Province was almost like a journey to an unknown world.

"How far is it from here to Kwangju?" He posed this question to several people in the village—people who seemed to know more about the affairs of the world than he did, such as the clerk in the village office, or the village elders. But no one seemed to know for certain. The clerk guessed it to be around five hundred *ri*[1], whereas one village elder judged it to be around seven hundred. Their guesses about the distance between Masan and Yŏsu alone ranged from two hundred *ri* to four hundred, and the distance between Yŏsu and Kwangju was even worse; it ranged from as little as one hundred and fifty *ri* to five hundred.

Being at a loss, Sŏkkyu decided to look up Mr. Yang in town to get a more definite idea about the distance. Besides, it was from Mr. Yang that he had to borrow the money needed for the trip anyway.

But Mr. Yang wasn't at all sure either. According to his "wild guess," it came out to something in the neighborhood of six or seven hundred *ri;* Masan to Yŏsu was around three hundred

---

1. pl. ri. a Korean measure of distance, equal to about a quarter of a mile.

more, and then adding the distance from the village to Masan, the total would be over six hundred *ri*. It would be more like seven hundred *ri*.

Seven hundred *ri*! Sǒkkyu had no idea how far a distance of seven hundred *ri* actually was. For all practical purposes seven hundred *ri* was as good as seven or seventy thousand *ri* to him.

"Let's say it's seven hundred *ri*, how many days would it take?"

To this Mr. Yang said, "Well, let's see," and he began to count with his left fingers. "You must allow one day between Masan and Yǒsu by boat, and between Yǒsu and Kwangju there must be either a bus or a train, and so it will take another day. But of course these boats and buses aren't always there waiting for you and you just might have to wait two or three days before one of those things is ready to move. Besides, they don't always make good time once they get started. They break down often on the way, you know. So I'd say the whole thing would come out to be five or six days at least."

"Supposing it would take that long, what'd the expense be like?" asked Sǒkkyu. In truth, this part of the question was really what he came to see Mr. Yang about.

"The more the better, as they say," said Mr. Yang. Then he added gravely, "Travel expenses are not all you need either. I mean, you would want to give some spending money to your son."

"I suppose you are right," said Sǒkkyu in a tone of great respect for Mr. Yang's opinion.

"I'd say you must have at least thirty thousand *wǒn*[2] in your pocket before you can leave," judged Mr. Yang solemnly.

Sǒkkyu was well aware that thirty thousand *wǒn* these days wasn't really a great sum of money, but to him it was a lot nevertheless; he didn't even have a thousand *wǒn* at the moment. Of course, farming cost some money for such things as fertilizer and wages for the helpers. You could borrow though. In fact, it was Mr. Yang that lent him that money every year. Mr. Yang always made the loan because he was sure that he could get the money back in fall. This year Sǒkkyu could borrow again within the usual

---

2. pl. won. the monetary unit of Korean, equal to 100 chǒn: valued, in 1983, at 1/750 U.S. dollar. In the early 1950's, at about the time of this story, 1 U.S. dollar was equivalent to roughly 10 won.

limit, but if he was to use the money for the trip to visit his son, how would he manage his farming? Money wasn't the only thing, for that matter; now was one of the busiest and most important periods in farming, so setting out on a journey at this time might seriously damage this year's fall crop. Well, so what? What's a little debt when a body is withered from coughing, worrying; when a man's had no sleep and is longing for a glance of his son's face? He felt he would be able to cope with anything after the visit.

"Lend me thirty thousand *wŏn*, Mr. Yang."

It took Sŏkkyu four days to travel from Yŏsu to Kwangju. He walked about twenty *ri* the first day before he went into an inn to stay overnight. On the second day he walked about thirty *ri*; then he caught a truck that was going to Sunch'ŏn.

When the truck pulled into the city of Sunch'ŏn it was long past lunchtime. The bus for Kwangju had already left in the morning, and he started to walk. He walked the following day again, and it was not until he reached the town of Pŏsong-ni that he was able to get a ride on another truck that was going as far as Posong.

The following day, early in the morning, he got a bus ride from Pŏsong to Kwangju.

In Kwangju, Sŏkkyu went into an eating house, and while having lunch he asked the proprietor if he had ever heard of Kim Pongho of such-and-such regiment of such-and-such division. The proprietor advised him to go to the division headquarters and ask. Sŏkkyu then asked if the division headquarters was in Kwangju. To his great relief, the proprietor assured him that it was. He asked how to get there.

Someone at the division headquarters sent him to a regimental headquarters, and there again someone advised him that Kim Pongho was with the Recon Company of one of the battalions in the regiment. By that time it was completley dark out.

It turned out that the Recon Company was located about twenty *ri* out of town, but Sŏkkyu immediately started to walk in that direction. The night was pitch dark, and when he rounded the foot of a hill he could even hear the hootings of an owl. When he finally reached the village, he gave out a long sigh. He went into the village office and asked the man there to put him up for the night.

At day break he left the village office.

The Recon Company was using an old school building for their barracks. The school building was a little way out of the village. Several olive drab tents were pitched on the playground, and the Korean flag fluttered in the wind on the pole.

Sŏkkyu accosted the guard, holding the weatherbeaten felt hat in his hands, and bowing several times he asked falteringly:

"Uh, uh, do you have a boy here from Haman County by the name of Kim Pongho?"

The guard returned a salute and asked where he was from.

"I came all the way from Haman County of Kyongsang Province. Do you have Kim Pongho here?"

The guard pointed his finger toward a little shack that bore a small wooden plate that said VISITORS. Bowing profusely, he went over to the shack.

The soldier on duty there looked up the list and could tell him right away all about PFC Kim Pongho. He was not in the Company area at the moment, however. His platoon was out somewhere and would be back that afternoon.

So his boy *was* with this Company! At first Sŏkkyu could not believe what he heard, so he uttered unwittingly a half question, "That so?" to the face of the smiling soldier. Although it wasn't a question that expected an answer, the soldier kindly repeated what he had said, and told Sŏkkyu in addition that he should come back in the afternoon to meet his son. He was impressed, grateful, and awestruck. How efficient and kind these people were! Holding the felt hat in his hands, he bowed profusely again and moved away.

He found a turfed spot on the rise along the foot of a hill, and covering his face with the felt hat he lay down and dozed off. Half asleep, he heard the chirping of birds, and thought now that even the melody of the birds' chirping had special and blissful meanings.

When it was past lunchtime, he sat up and began watching the gate of the camp. Two or three times when he thought he saw a boy in uniform that resembled his son he got up and ran down toward the gate, but each time it turned out to be a complete stranger. As the afternoon wore on fear began to set in, fear that his son might not show up at all. He got up abruptly and rushed down toward the gate, as if to shake himself loose from that evil idea.

Just then it hapened. He saw his son standing by the Visitors shack. Under the steel helmet the boy's face looked much smaller than his father remembered. Sŏkkyu could not trust his eyes, but all the while he edged in toward the boy. The boy, too, recognized the father.

"Pa!" With this cry Pongho accosted his father.

"Is that you, Pongho?" said Sŏkkyu weakly.

Pongho took off his helmet and bowed to his father very unmilitarily.

"How they treating you, hard?" This was Sŏkkyu's second question.

For some reason the boy kept a sullen silence at this question.

"Aren't you hungry?"

"No, I'm all right."

For a while neither of them said anything.

"Can you leave the camp for a while?"

"No, I can't. I will get a pass for tomorrow afternoon."

From noontime on the following day Sŏkkyu stood waiting outside the Recon Company. Around two o'clock Pongho, dressed as he was the day before, came out and met his father. He said he had a leave of absence from two to four, and his platoon was to leave in the morning for a mountain region where they would be engaged in a guerrilla policing action for about ten days.

Sŏkkyu took the boy to the market place. Pointing his finger at cakes and fruits, Sŏkkyu asked his son which he would like. Pongho said that he had just had lunch and didn't feel like having anything. He merely asked about how his mother and kid brothers were doing, and again for some reason he was sullen and silent.

They went into an eating place and ordered soup and an order of rice apiece. The father ordered a bowl of *makkŏlli*[3] for himself. He spread the cakes and fruits out on the table, but the boy would not touch any of them. He did finish his soup and rice however.

"Why don't you have some of these?" said the father, pushing the things toward the boy.

"You take them home and give them to the kids," said

---

3. cheap, unrefined rice wine

Pongho, pushing them back toward Sŏkkyu. Then another stretch of silence.

After trying with much effort to think up something to say, the father asked, "When do you figure you will be able to come back home?" but the son replied quite simply and in the same sulky tone:

"I don't know."

"Not till the war is over?" said the father after another stretch of long silence.

"I don't know," said the boy, simply as before.

Then they had nothing to say to each other for a long while, and by that time their two hours was nearly up.

"You run along, then," said the father.

"Yes," said Pongho, and got up.

They left the eating place and started toward the camp.

"You go back home, Pa," said the boy, stopping in the street.

"All right," said the father. Pongho looked up in his father's face and unwittingly the father returned the gaze, but averted his eyes hastily (For some reason looking into each other's face for a sustained length of time was embarrassing to Sŏkkyu).

"Well, you run along now."

"Yes, Pa, and you look out for yourself on the way back home."

Pongho took off his steel helmet and bowed as he had done when they first met. Then he turned and began to walk away slowly. All the boy's movements were clearly registered in the father's memory to the minutest detail. Pongho was making his way toward the gate, looking backward over his shoulder two or three times. At first Sŏkkyu had drifted in the same direction unconsciously, but when the boy looked back the father stopped.

He wanted very much to stand there and watch the boy till he went out of sight completely; but for some reason, that seemed too forward an act on his part, as if he were taking advantage of somebody by doing so, although he wasn't sure whom he would be taking advantage of. So he stepped off the road several paces, and hiding himself behind a warehouse, he urinated.

(end story)

A Respite

O Sangwŏn

He lay shivering in the darkness. Everything would come to an end within the hour. His hands and feet were frozen. Frost-caked dirt walls closed him in and he could glimpse the icy sky through a crack in the trapdoor above. He was lying in a hastilydug, underground prison. A faint body odor was in the air. It couldn't be more than three days, he thought. Then he recalled what one of the men had said when they had pushed him down the ladder into this hole: "This fellow will fare no better than the last." Who could that other fellow be? Could he be the same one he had seen outside awhile ago just before they shot him? If not, who could he have been? He began to shiver even more; he was frozen to the marrow.

What group do you belong to? What is your educational background? Your motive for enlisting? What do you think of communism? What are your feelings toward the United States? What? Comrade, what you are saying lacks sense!

You are still classconscious, dear comrade. Of course, we know you cannot help having been born to the class to which you belong, make no mistake about that. But we hate the pride and consciousness of your class. We will give you another chance to think it over. We will hear your answers in exactly an hour, and your answers will decide everything.

These remarks, exchanged during the investigation, came back to him piece by piece. In an hour everything would end. The sound of snow trodden underfoot as he was marched from the investigation room to this underground prison, led by a soldier of the People's Army[1] and followed by another with a Russian

---

1. refers to the North Korean Army.

Tommy gun pointing directly at his back, still sounded in his ears.

In an hour I will be led out to the same place. After a brief verbal exchange the leader of the band will say: "Very well, dear Comrade, walk straight along this river bank without looking back." Then I will hear the sound of snow under my feet as I pace along. No, they might strip me of my uniform before they send me off. (Although my combat fatigues have a few tears they are Americanmade and still good. I will walk along the white river bank, my skin red from the cold. Several rifle shots will ring out and I will slump to the ground. Soon the red of my blood will dye the white snow and everything will come to an end. They will march back to the headquarters, their rifles slung over their shoulders, muzzles pointing down. They will file into the warm office kicking the snow from their boots, rubbing their hands to warm them. After a few minutes they will forget about me altogether, warming their hands at the stove, rolling cigarettes or lazily stretching out on chairs.

It doesn't really matter who dies once he is dead. These things are daily routine. I will be the only one who will die neglected and forgotten, bleeding and clutching snow in my hands.

He felt a sudden cramp in his muscles. Was it the cold? He smelt the odor again. He was't the first, he thought, just a link in an endless chain...

We fight and we die in the end, that's all. There is nothing else. We are for or against nothing, nor are we after anything. We fight as human instinct directs us, and we die as the result.

The front line had pushed steadily northward. Several contacts were made with the enemy. The reconnaissance platoon, of which he was the leader, was far ahead of the other troops, deep behind the enemy lines. Communications with headquarters were lost.

The soldiers in the platoon watched the radio operator anxiously. Friendly forces retreating all along the line! All roads blocked by the enemy. Where should we try to make a breakthrough? Now the number of skirmishes began to increase. He began to lose his men one by one. He decided to take to the mountains, avoiding contact with the enemy as much as possible. Hunger and fatigue. The number of men steadily decreased while the remainder had to fight their way through the cold and snow not knowing exactly where they were heading. Lost in the knee-deep snow of a blizzard, they made their way into a small village. Deserted houses lay half buried in the snow. There was no sign of the enemy. The famished soldiers scattered throughout the village in search of food. All they were able to find was a sack of frozen potatoes. They ate them raw. Then they all slumped down, exhausted. The hunger and fatigue weighed on them. Every toe was frostbitten. At sundown the blizzard became even more furious. The night sets in quickly in the mountains. The platoon sergeant was sitting up, leaning against the door frame but, hearing the storm outside, even he finally fell asleep. It was one of those nights on which one might expect a surprise attack.

But nothing happened.

The fight against the cold, hunger, and snow resumed with dawn. One by one, platoon members fell victim to the elements. He watched the last stare of those who fell. He knelt beside them when they went down in the snow, unable to follow the others. His hands, searching their pockets for possible mementoes to send back to their families, were even colder than their dying bodies. Murmuring "Lieutenant ... " they died, their eyes turning, cold, wandering off into the void.

"Lieutenant, I was born in North Korea ... I am alone, and I don't have anybody in the South ... This is my address in North Korea."

He was handed a frayed piece of paper. He held the dying soldier's hand and squeezed it without a word. What else could he do?

Now only six were left.

They pushed through the snow, leaving the bodies of the dead behind. Fear began to take over. The rugged terrain gave way abruptly to a plain. They could see a highway ahead of them. The platoon sergeant, who had gone on to scout, ran back.

There were innumerable hoof marks, wheel tracks, and boot impressions, he reported. He carried back horse dung. It was soft, proof that troops had passed by not very long ago. There was nothing they could do except wait for nightfall and cut across the plain to the mountain range on the other side. So they waited.

They got to the other side of the highway without difficulty. They made their way along the ditch, taking great care to remain concealed. They slowed down as they drew near the mountains. Just then it happened. The sound of a shot and one of them dropped with a shriek. They all hit the snow.

They wondered from which direction the shot had come. As

he cautiously raised his head to look around, another shot rang out. It was from the left flank. They all faced that direction.

Their predicament was obvious. The enemy knew where they were, but they did not know where the enemy was. They could not remain there like sitting ducks. They stood out in the snow even though it was dark. They started to crawl toward the mountain. Bullets whined around them. One of them shouted "Lieutenant!" with a shriek. He closed his eyes. He was sweating profusely. He crawled forward with his eyes closed. He felt weak and at times he feared he might faint. The dark silhouette of shrubs that girded the foot of the mountain appeared ahead. The enemy fire slowed down. The platoon sergeant was hit just as they reached the foot of the mountain. He dragged him behind some rocks.

He did not realize how far he had dragged the sergeant when he himself slumped to the ground exhausted; it was almost daylight.

It was getting even colder in the cell. He moved a little. He was numb all over from the cold. Soon everything would come to an end. The same rank odor pervaded the damp hole. Footsteps could be heard in the snow. They drew near. Maybe the hour had come. He sat up. A few moments of suspense. Then the footsteps faded away. Nothing. Just someone passing by. Very cold. Did the man turn back on his way here? He felt weak again.

"What was your major subject? Why did you choose to study law? The fact is that you had been soaked in the conventional ideas of your class since childhood . You must discard the habit."

"We think very highly of fellows like you, comrade. I am always prepared to embrace fellows like you."
The draught through the crack in the door brightened the light from the fireplace.

"Comrade, I think you are a fine young man. Go ahead, help yourself to a cigarette." He poked the fire and the embers burned brightly.

"Dear comrade, I think you are the sorriest young man in the world for that very reason. I am very sorry that you won't change your attitude."

"Comrade, why do you stare at me so coldly? You say nothing ... I see, I understand what you are trying to tell me with your silence. I am sorry you won't reform.''

The words came back to him as if in a dream. He stirred a little in an effort to warm himself. His thoughts wandered further into the past.

It was nearly daylight when he and the sergeant finally slumped onto the snow. The dawn was beautiful. The snow-covered scenery was even more beautiful. The snow on the trees glistened in the early morning sun.

The sun was quite high when he finally sat up. The sergeant lay unconscious in the snow clutching his bloody leg. He had more bloodstains on his shirt, at the shoulder, and on his back. The lieutenant propped him up.

The sergeant slowly opened his eyes. Seeing the lieutenant, he smiled a bitter smile. The lieutenant embraced the sergeant, rubbing his cheek against the other's. They were the only ones left.

''It seems it's my turn now, sir,'' said the sergeant quietly. He looked down at the sergeant's face, but he could detect no sign of gloom: only a hard-boiled determination that had survived long years of military service. The sergeant had served with the Japanese army during World War II in the South Pacific and later in northern China. Following the Liberation he had spent two months in a prisoner-of-war camp. Then he had served in the Chinese communist army and subsequently in the Nationalist army before returning to Korea only to enlist again in the Korean army. He was a career soldier and said there was nothing more interesting than life in the army. The moments of mortal risk in battle were the only times he felt he was truly alive, he used to say.

''Men are born to kill each other. What else is history but a record of the massacre of man by man. I like fighting. When I hear battle cries, my heart leaps. When I have placed an enemy in my gunsight, I am overwhelmed with joy. I feel history is being made at that very moment. The meaning of life is fighting and dying fighting.''

That was how he lived. Now he lay dying. He knew it was his turn to go.

In his damp hole he now recalled the sergeant's words. He tried to rise but fell back on the ground. He had a cramp in his right arm. He clenched his teeth and waited for the pain to pass.

Soon everything would end. He thought of the sergeant again.

"Sir, I have made up my mind where to die." Saying that the sergeant had crawled to a sunny spot and propped himself against an old oak.

His serene face with closed eyes showed no trace of sorrow nor loneliness. Only the solitude of the snowcovered mountain reflected in his face. Then he slowly slid sideways and slumped down in the snow. The lieutenant rushed to help him sit up but the sergeant, half opening his eyes, said with a small smile, "Leave me be ... "

The sergeant closed his eyes again. His breath came slowly.

The lieutenant walked on alone in the knee-deep snow heading south. Often he collapsed. He wandered around in snow storms not knowing his direction. His feet were numb from the cold. Fear and despair began to take hold of him. *Am I heading in the right direction? What is my present position?* There was nobody to consult, but he couldn't very well stay put in one place. He staggered on through the snow storm. *How far do I have to keep going like this? When will I get somewhere*? He slept in the snow. With the dawn he walked again. After many slips and falls he was a mass of cuts and bruises. Fatigue and hunger, cold and loneliness plagued him at night. Nightmares awakened him to the darkness and solitude of the night. *Am I going to be buried in the snow like this for eternity*? The night would somehow end and the dawn would break. He got up because he had to walk. The terrain became rougher. Once he sliped over a cliff and fell four or five meters. When he came to, his whole body ached with indescribable pain.

He got up. His clenched fists were shaking violently. He had to climb back up the cliff from which he had just fallen. Its four or five meters seemed an insurmountable height but he had to get up them. He began to climb, his teeth clenched; he sweated profusely, the sky began to sway above him; He clung to the roots of a tree and closed his eyes; the root came loose, snow and dirt blinded him, but he reached the top. Once there he passed out.

As soon as he came to his senses, he began to walk again. Walking southward step by step was the only thing left for him to do. The carbine had become too heavy and so he tied it to his back.

A week passed and he finally conquered the mountain one evening as dusk stepped quietly in. When he awoke the following morning, the sun was high and he was startled to find a small village practically under his nose. He had slept in the snow when a village was so near! A warmth, a new desire to fight on, welled up in him. He slid down the slope to the village, his eyes brimming with tears. He reached the edge of the village. Its houses, with their open doors, looked deserted. The snow in the village was fresh and untrodden. Pig sties and cow barnes ... this must be a place where people live! He stepped through a door ... a pillaged chest of drawers, scattered rags and dirty clothes ... He scooped up an armful of old clothes and held them close. Ah! the human odor! He looked around the room ... it was deserted.

Just then he heard footsteps outside. He jumped up and took cover against the wall. He found a peephole through a crack in the wall. Nothing seemed to stir outside. *Was I just hearing things?* The next moment he distinctly heard people talking. He became alert, expectant. He peered out more closely. About fifty yards away, behind another small house, a group of people were marching along a path. They halted.

There was no mistaking they were soldiers, even from that distance. There seemed to be some American-made uniforms among them, too. *Am I already behind friendly lines? No, that couldn't be ... Wait, what about the other uniforms? They look unfamiliar.* To get a closer look at them he had to move to the adjoining hut. He moved deftly and speedily, using haystacks, barns, and such for cover. From his new position he could observe them much better through an opening in the stone wall. Now he could even pick up some of their words.

Comrade, firing squad ... these two words met his ears. *They are Communists!* He listened more carefully. He could now see a barefooted man, clad only in his underwear, standing in the middle of encircling soldiers. His hands were bound behind.

"Comrade, do you have any objection to what the people do?" said the man who seemed to be the leader of the group.

"A human being is not a tool. What more need I say? However, I can tell you this much: I realized for the first time that I was a living, breathing man the moment I was captured. I am happy. I am happy because I am not a tool nor a machine but a living man and I am going to die like a man. I am unable to describe my joy!"

"Very well." A derisive smile curled the leader's lips. "You walk straight down this embankment. It will lead you to the South. Since that is the direction you want to take so much, I am sure you will be very happy."

The victim turned around. He began to walk slowly and deliberately. Two soldiers raised their rifles. Hearing the sound of cocked rifles, the man walked on, clam and manly, his bare feet treading the snow. With the sound of the rifle shots he would drop, still facing the South.

Now the lieutenant knew what it was all about. He felt that the man walking out there on the embankment was none other than himself. The whole scene began to sway and reel in front of him. Almost instinctively he gripped his rifle butt. *It's cowardly to avoid a fight for the comforts of tomorrow. The man walking out there now is nobody but me. I am now being slaughtered, and I am not going to let that happen* He took aim at the two riflemen. The next moment his carbine went off. He saw the two drop to the ground. He squeezed the trigger again and again. They started to shoot back at him. Sweat began to run down his forehead. Things became blurred. They stopped shooting; now they had him completely encircled. They inched closer. Something hard hit him on the shoulder. Then he heard a shot. He jumped up only to slump down again immediately. He knew he was going to faint, but another shot rang in his ears. He felt a numbing pain in his right arm. He felt a warmness flowing down it. He could sense people approaching him, then he felt a blow on his head. He lost consciousness completely.

How long did he lie unconscious? When he came to he touched his arm with his fingers and looked at them. They were stained with dark blood. He could hear people talking in low voices. The place was filled with cigarette smoke. He could see dusty, cobweb-covered ceiling. It was a room then, he thought. From time to time he could hear someone's footsteps outside treading the snow. Just as those footsteps came close and then moved away, his consciousness returned and retreated off and on for a long time.

Repeated investigations followed. The ultimatum was given. Everything would end soon. The floor of the underground cell was getting even colder. His head was clear now. His muscles convulsed at times with a numbing pain. He heard people approaching. This must be it, he thought. *The trapdoor will soon open with a squeak. A ladder will be pushed down through the darkness like the hand of Fate. Quiet. Nothing happens. Why? Is it that I am just hearing things? No, it's those people all right. They are coming to get me.* He tried to sit up in the darkness. He looked up and a bright shaft of light came down the ladder.

"We haven't got all day. Get moving down there. Come on up!"

He climbed the ladder rung by rung. He had difficulty controlling his knees because they were numb and weak. When he reached the trapdoor they grabbed him and dragged him out. He slumped down on the snow. The cold snow melting under his face brought him round. *Now I must get up and must walk firmly. I must do everything with exactitude till the moment I die.*

Grasping the snow he got up. He walked slowly but steadily toward the office, his eyes shining intelligently.

Brief formalities over the order for his execution were given.

They went out to the snow-covered embankment—that same embankment! How many people had taken this route south? Across the wide, rolling plains he could see a mountain range on the other side. It too was clothed in snow. It was a beautiful winter scene. "Walk straight ahead. It leads to the South. Since you so desire to go that way, I am sure you will be very pleased." He began to walk. Each step made a footprint in the white snow. *Now I must walk with firmness.* Squad, ready! He heard the cocking of their rifles. He could see nothing but white snow ahead. *Now everything is going to end. I must do everything exactly right till the moment I die. I must control myself ...*

He walked steadily on, firm step by firm step. *I am approaching death step by step, but I must not abandon myself to fear or despair. The rolling plain with the white mountain on the other side. Then the sound of rifle shots. But they sound different, like something from another world. It's nothing; I must walk on.* He felt a spasm in the back of his head and around his waist. *No, it's nothing, nothing ...*

The white snow gradually turned grey, then black. The end had come at last. *They will march back to their headquarters, their rifles over their shoulders, muzzles pointed down. They will file into the office, rubbing their cold hands together. After a few minutes they will completely forget all about me, roll their cigarettes and stretch out in comfort. It won't matter who has just died. There is nothing more commonplace than that.* His mind gradually blurred. He was lying on white snow. The sun shone brightly.

(end story)

Poems of John the Baptist

Chang Yonghak

Once upon a time there was a little cave in a deep mountain valley. The sole inhabitant of the cave was a hare. The walls of the cave were resplendent with the colors of the rainbow but the hare was ignorant of their beauty. The walls were delicate white marble slabs whose intricate arrangement reflected the sun's rays into the seven colors of the prism. The hare did not know misery; the beautiful colors were all that he knew.

But then something strange happened to the hare. For no reason at all he began to feel an urge. He began to yearn for something, although he did not know what it was. The ray of light seeping into the cave marked the visitation of adolescence to this nether world and made him ponder:

"The outside world that emits such beautiful lights must be paradise."

It was eye opening. The stone house that had seemed so beautiful to him till now suddenly turned into a shabby den. It might be said that owls started to screech in the Garden of Eden.

But he searched for an exit in vain. He beat the walls in despair, he hurled his body against them in tears of anger, but still nothing happened—they were as solid as rock walls could be. They were the cold walls of a prison and he was the prisoner.

How had he come to live in a place like this?

He did not know. He had never before given thought to the question. He could trace nothing but the seven colors in the depths of his memory. He thought there might be another world, an infinite world, beyond the muddled depths of that memory, but that might well be an illusion arising from his vision of an outer world, a world reflecting that which he had not yet seen.

"I could not have been born here," was his conclusion. "I

must have come in from outside just as the light does now.''

The hare mournfully reiterated the same thing on that eventful day. But all of a sudden his ears stiffened as if in alarm. It was his birthday, but he had been sitting mutely, gazing at the cracklike window without the usual joy or gaiety associated with a birthday. But now an alarming idea hit him and his ears stood upright.

He rose carefully, his heart pounding. He tiptoed over to the small opening. He extended his arm toward it.

Nothing touched his hand. He put it out further. Still nothing stood in his way. By now the pounding of his heart was enough to shake the cave.

With his paw still extended out to the opening he turned toward the room. But he was terrified at the sight. The room was dark; gone were the seven beautiful colors. He fell to the floor in a faint.

For days and nights he could not raise himself from the spot. He ran a high fever. He was paying such a high price for the idea that hit him on his birthday. He had thought he might be able to go out through the opening. What an original and fantastic idea! How ingenious he was to think of crawling out of the opening—an opening that had no apparent connection with the outside world except that light came in through it! Compare him to hares that inhabit the outer world who cannot even appreciate the value of air while they are breathing it every day. It was an astounding discovery. No, it was an *invention*.

But it was equally a hazardous idea. Did not his mere paw make the world disappear?

The fever was finally gone. He started to crawl through the opening, then into the passage. The passage was quite wide in parts but for most of the way it was a narrow crack through jagged rock and he had to wriggle along like a worm. His white fur became bloody from scratches and cuts.

It was like being chased by darkness. Time and again he thought he should turn back. At times going back seemed even further than going forward and, at the same time, each step forward seemed to remove him farther from his goal. He was now caught in that world of sophistry where Achilles could not overtake the turtle. He was not advancing but sinking, he was unaware, How long he had struggled in that fashion and then suddenly he stopped. His ears began to itch; he could hear something. It was the first time he had heard a sound. He started to tremble with joy as though he were shedding his old skin. The low spirits of fatigue and despair were gone; new blood began to race through his veins.

But his limbs did not move as fast as his impatient heart wished. Somehow the foreboding that the outside world might not be the paradise he had imagined also began to set in. He would regret many times that he had not turned back at this point and returned to his old dwelling, but those moments were to come much later. If someone had suggested at that moment that he turn back he would have struck a noble posture and said, "Give me liberty, or give me death."

He finally reached the end of the passage.

The exciting outside world with its rhythmic sounds and magnificent colors would spread its panoramic view before his eyes in a second. Giving his whole body to the thrill of life, he craned his neck around the entrance to the hole to take his first look at the world. Then, just then, a terrible thing happened.

Th-u-n-k! Something hit him between the eyes as though it had been waiting hundreds of years just for this moment. He fell down on the spot.

He came to himself some time later, but he saw nothing. He was blind. The intense sunlight of the outer world was too harsh for tender eyes accustomed to the soft light of seven colors.

The hare, it is said, did not move from that spot till the day he died. He was afraid that by leaving he might lose the entrance leading back to his old home.

A mushroom grew on the spot where he died. For some unknown reason his descendants called it "the mushroom of liberty." Whenever they faced a problem they gathered there to perform rites. They were later joined by squirrels, deer, foxes, bears, and even by tigers. Sometimes it worked, and sometimes it did not—this paying respect to the mushroom. But they say it was the most consoling act in times of difficulty.

They felt, it seemed, that the world would follow suit if the mushroom were to perish.

The sun hung over the roof.

From this angle it appeared to be quite high still, although from back there, where he had seen it before, it looked as if it were about to slip behind the mountain; with it the encroaching dusk also seemed to recede with a sudden brightening of the sky. Sense of time seemed to depend much on where one stands: which was the correct time?

Clock time and the time constituted by where one stands. There is a vacant clearing between these two different times. One feels free when one plays in the clearing however expansive it may be. And I must now admit that it was this very clearing with its two different time borders that paved the way for the splitting of in two my ''self.''

It is not at all clear whether time flows through space or space oozes out of time, but at this angle, with the sun over the rooftop, time seemed to be locked in space. On this time-space relationship seemed to exist the order of the present.

What would happen if space-locked time were to break through the wall on the other side to free itself?

They say that it is possible for us to recapture a once-vanished sound by taking an airplane going faster than the speed of sound, theoretically at least, and catching up with its waves. If, as the laws of physics have it, the process of seeing some object is really a stimulus on the retina created by light reflected by that same object, then it must be possible for us to recapture the past on an airplane of a sort that flies faster than the speed of light. The time plane soars high; one sees time flying backward; time flies back into the past.

In this new order cooked rice would turn into grain; the spoonful of rice would travel back from the mouth to the bowl, then to the pot where it was originally cooked. The rice would soon become grain and put on husks. it would travel through the rice dealer's store, the rice-cleaning machine, then back to the rice paddy. After a few months it would revert back to seed.

Of course there is a certain creative formation in that backward process, too; there is a world created, history made.

Which is the maturing formation, rice transformed into cooked rice, or cooked rice into grain?

Which world is the land of production, the dusk turning into dawn, or the dusk turning into night?

Which history is creative and which destructive?

What is creation and what is destruction?

Which flow is toward the past and which toward the future?

I jumped as I came out of my reverie. I looked up and saw

a large transport plane flying southward in the evening sky of early summer. Though I instinctively looked for shade or shelter, I was aware that my fright was not severe. My heart was pounding a little, but that was all. The shock I received on that frightful day from an air raid was great, but in the time that had since elapsed my nerves seemed to have settled down. I took another look at the roof and the hut. It was a dilapidated frame shack.

I moved a step or two closer to it. Although it had taken me several days since my return from the island to locate the hut, I was now afraid to go up to the door and face the owner. To think that such a ramshackle hut, a cardboard house that might well collapse under a strong kick, should also have an owner like other houses was depressing. On the other hand, I thought there was all the more reason for a house like that to have an owner; without an owner such a house would have tumbled down long ago.

But the fact that the castlelike mansion yonder, at the foot of the hill, also had an owner contrasted so strikingly with the frame house that it somehow did not seem right. *What sort of a game are we playing in this society of ours?*

On the way here I had seen an old man sitting in front of house picking something out of a plateful of rice, barely, and beans. If someone were to paint this scene of the old man working in the twilight, the title "White Hair Picking Out Primary Colors" would have been adequate. Now the descendants of the Renaissance are busy peeling the pigment from the canvases of modern paintings. They are indulging in the alchemy of picking out primary colors. But hasn't the age of geographical discovery passed long ago?

I heard the wailing cries of boys craving to sell tomorrow's paper coming up the street below. Is that the reason a crow laments the wasteful twentieth century while perched upon a tree yonder in the dusk?

Caw . . . . . Caw . . . . . .

I started to take the few steps up the knoll toward the tree, bypassing the shack. I picked up a stone. The crow did not seem to be perturbed but it flew off nevertheless. I threw the stone at the branch where the crow had been sitting a moment ago. The crow flew off to the other side of the knoll and I sat down under the tree.

The horizon is always accompanied by a nothingness that yearns for something beyond.

What lies beyond the horizon? Are there rolling plains and hills like here? Someone there must be yearning to see what we are doing here. Two absurdities are sharing the same sky. Can we raise the horizon to break down the barrier? Or should we build a high wall and seal it off completely? This rolling plain is the only place where we can compose ourselves and attain self-possession. We have no guarantee that there will be a tomorrow, but should we treat today as a complete entity? We must live today sincerely.

Sincerity is what counts most. We cannot live under the pretext of searching for truth. Giving up the truth itself is much better. How foul the air has become from the smell of pretention! To measure the degree of its pollution would discourage us so much that none of us would want to continue to live.

I yearn for a spot under this tree. A while ago, from the other side of the shack, this lone tree with branches extended like tired arms, looking so pathetic—almost moved me to tears. But now I was already yearning for what was beyond the horizon. I'm no fickle harlot. If necessary, I could go back to where I had been and watch the tree again and be in tears. I couldn't care less if you called all this sentimentalism—a nostalgic feeling similar to the desire to hear the hooting of owls on a wet night.

The owl must still be hooting. In my home town of K — there was a lone straw-thatched house at the foot of a hill. That hill could be seen from the ruined stone wall that bordered the town on its northeastern limits. Spending the greater part of my boyhood and adolescence around the ruined wall gave me vivid memories associated with the ruins. Strangely enough, though, the scene around the straw-thatched house, where birds had hovered and sung in spring, had never entered my mind's eye. Then all of a sudden I was watching the tree from yonder, the image of the lone straw-thatched house emerged out of the dense fog of oblivion. The spot under the tree, then, might well be called my other home.

"Tongho . . ." I called out my own name.

But there was no voice to answer my call. Only quiet ruled the gentle slope in twilight. I was uneasy. I felt like leaving the place. I glanced at my own shadow. Grudgingly docile, it did not seem like my shadow. It seemed to be an imaginary person sitting near me.

"Tongho!"

I was startled by the voice calling my name. It did not sound at all like my voice; it was really a pathetic shriek with none of the zest I had expected. Taken by surprise, I was ready to call out, "Who's there?" when my lips were locked by another intruder in my memory.

Was Grandfather's grave here?

It was incredible, but I should guess that the distance from the tree to the ramshackle hut was about the same as that from the straw-thatched house to the old pine tree under which my grandfather had been buried. Well then, what had I been doing in the meantime? Where had I been placing Grandfather's grave? I had completely forgotten about his grave, although the memory of my father's scoldings for picking azalea blossoms from the bush behind the grave had always remained with me. I was not even aware that I had forgotten about it. Otherwise, I would not have been so shocked to hear my name called.

That means I am living only a part of myself. A shadow. Am I still Tongho? Am I still myself? Just a while ago I could answer to my own name. Was that the reason—the fact that I was not wholly myself?

But that was not all. There was an apple tree right by the west gate. The chimney of my house stood close by the apple tree under whose shade Grandfather had lounged all his life, sitting on a straw mat with one leg stretched out, and with his hand rubbing his stomach.

Not even God can now transplant the apple tree back by the chimney. No. God cannot do that. He won't do that. I can believe that much. But what if it stands by the chimney some day in some flurry of confusion? To whom shall I appeal?

The apple tree might some day stand by the chimney and my toes on my knees. Ah! who can vouchsafe that this world of ours is not so rank and festering?

I found myself clutching a stone. I shivered. I was afraid of touching my knees.

Impossible do you say? Of course you have reason to say that. But what if it actually happens to you one of these days? It can happen like any other thing that is happening every day. Then it becomes a fact. A fact can correct a truth, but a thousand truths cannot redress a fact—that is the way of the world in which we live nowadays. The world is huge and solid like a gigantic rock, but it is fragile as an egg at the same time.

I clutched the stone tighter in my hand. I remembered someone mentioning that it is impossible to break an egg in your clenched palm however fragile it seems. What if it breaks? Then must we admit the possibility of having our cheeks, our toes under our ears?

I clenched the stone in my fist with all my might.

Give up! You bastard of an egg!

My brow became wet with sweat. I released my fingers. The egg did not break.

But this might be because I was really afraid that the egg might break. For the breaking of the egg would signify the breaking up of the world itself. Thus I compromised. Something within me had betrayed my fear.

That an egg cannot be broken by mere clenching is founded on this betrayal. For no one has ever exerted all his might in his clench. It is quite natural that no one tries. To live in the world breathing air is the same as living in "the Word." Words not only existed in the beginning but they are also the only things that persist to the end. Human beings are merely their mouthpieces. Movement as a speech organ—this is the whole of the human machine.

It did not break this time, but no one can guarantee that it will not break the next time. What guarantee do you have? The present? But the next instant is not the present.

There isn't anything one can depend on when you come down to it. That's why I merely follow others. Had I ever been my own master, leading myself along the road of my own choice? No! Not even once. I have always followed the telephone poles or waited for the train to leave. But I have never traveled on one of those trains. Still I waited; I followed. Why? For the simple reason that there are telephone poles along roads and waiting rooms in stations.

Life is futile and miserable. Why do we still keep on saying that life is better than death?

Let's stop thinking. There's no end to it. Let's just keep on putting things off, following others, and waiting for what? Life may well be something we have inherited on the understanding that we can put off everything indefinitely. When one dies, he dies with everything pending, everything put off.

I started down to the shack, dropping the stone I still

clutched in my hand. On closer examination I found that the shack was made of flattened-out cardboard boxes. Under its cardboard roof lived Nuhye's mother.

A battle field with C ration cartons scattered over it spread before my mind's eye.

It was a Sunday.

North Korean troops swarmed into the positions held by an American outfit which was faithfully observing the Sabbath. Here and there among the empty C ration boxes one could note leftover turkey drumsticks. The officer from the politburo called them "the Sunday present." They had a habit of simplifying everything, connecting everything to single idea that struck their fancy at the time. Thus they distorted the original meaning the idea once possessed.

"The Sunday victory," "The Sunday retreat,"

Thus words like people, freedom, and even Marxism had been distorted to mean something else.

And so, we the orphans of the Communist volunteer troops had repeatedly made banzai attacks on "the capitalism of fifty years ago" with a turkey leg in one hand and a grenade in the other.

It happened just as I was about to run down the slope along a ridge where a huge pear tree, looking no less than three hundred years old, stood. Thud! Black flames. Bang! The world was torn apart. My fragile breath stopped at that moment, for I didn't know where to escape. My body with its aching stomach rose up toward the sky where bombers were flying high. Just before I went to hide among the thick foliage of the old tree I noticed it too was uprooted and making a parabolic trajectory in the air.

Sometime later I found Tongho a "Sunday prisoner," still clutching the turkey leg in one hand and blood trickling from his wounds.

How often Tongho cried as he looked at the label around his neck saying "P.W." Invariably followed in the wake of these sobs came, the memory of his infancy, when he went about wearing a bib.

He was an infant. He was an infant with a bib. He was an alien infant lost in the world.

I had no reason to think that self, this self, was one and the same self. I could not call myself "I" without hesitation. My feet, my hands, even my job did not seem to belong to me. I merely assumed that they were mine because they were part of me. Thus I became my own guest. I was not really myself. I was wearing a guise. Someone else was being me.

I don't think I was insane. Whenever I was shocked, especially when I heard the drone of an airplane, I went sprawling on the ground with an aching stomach and foaming mouth. Sometimes I attacked a automobile with a club or a stick. But I still regard those states of mind as healthy and normal. For being calm in the face of the abnormal can only indicate a paralyzed nervous system and an ailing mind. There is nothing abnormal in trying to destroy an automobile that can kill a man by running him down.

The pain others suffered brought about actual physical pain in me. When I saw a worm drop from a tree, I writhed in pain. Sometimes I laughed out loud and sometimes I sobbed, but I always had justifiable reasons for doing so.

It was after we were moved to the island that I met Nuhye. We slept side by side and he was the only one who didn't laugh at me. Following our removal to the island my nerves began to calm down, but it was also at this time that I became indifferent to and apathetic toward almost everything. In contrast, Nuhye seemed to be contented with everything. He was willing to do all the dirty work around the camp. Strangely, however, no one could actually order him around. The truth was that it was he who ran everybody. In spite of this he sometimes looked moody and gloomy and that puzzled me. After his death, I sat alone under an overhanging rock and waited for the arrival of the boat that was to take us back to the mainland. It didn't come. It had not arrived when spring passed, and it did not show up when the summer waves washed shore. Fall . . . winter ... another spring ...then when the island was turning green for the second time, I boarded the boat.

But I was not happy at all when the harbor basin on the mainland finally embraced the boat. I felt as though I had left something precious back on the island.

Looking back, I saw the island as though it were a hunter's game bag thrown over the shoulders of the horizon. It was a weather-beaten skeleton of lava without a breath of peace. It was a grindstone of modern history where a cold current and a warm current churned in the blue sea. The dust of human beings was pulverized by its rocks. It was the chaos in which the miscalculation of history was spinning in blood! Ah—did green grow when spring visited those rocks, too?

The sad cries of seagulls lamenting the shoreline ... What kind of cradle was the island?

A footstep drawing near. The island from which a new shadow is to emerge out of fog! It's high time *it* appeared. Today is passing away forever. The sky is so near. The sky looks so far away because it is so near. *It,* **too,** is near!

Turning around, I felt the pressure of the mainland closing in around me.

Freedom was heavy. It was an apprehensive expectation. It was but the doorway to another island, to another prison camp.

I was standing in front of still another door—the door of the cardboard box shack. I knocked two or three times without getting an answer. I hesitated for a moment deciding whether to push or pull. I pulled as one usually does even though the door seemed to be hinged inward. Squeak—it was meant to be pushed open after all. Even so, it pulled open without much effort. I changed my mind, however, and when I was about to push it open a black streak flashed by me from inside.

The next instant it was crouching upon the roof of another shack, looking down at me. A black cat. The sun was down and the world was turning into the haven of the cat. I was now forced to realize my existence in that world.

I pushed the door open. The inside was draped with cobwebs.

"Nuh ... Nuh ...," I was stopped short by a voice that groaned from the sandy floor. The owner of the incredulous voice must have thought I was Nuhye back home alive. The emaciated form, by now half out of a bed of old blankets, did seem like a human being. At least it was alive. But it was merely a form in the past tense. It bore the mark of life simply because it had never been declared dead. The cat had, it seemed, snatched away "the present" from the old woman but a moment ago.

I pushed the panting and exhausted form back onto the bed by its bony shoulders. She was as light as a bundle of straw.

She had the palsy and could not speak. She was paralyzed down one side. One half of her body was resting in forlorn solitude as though she were living on the interest with the principal frozen.

A hand that did not seem strong enough to lift even a pair of chopsticks lay limply on my knee. Her expressionless face did not betray whether she realized that I was not her own son or whether she simply did not have the strength to show her emotion. A lone tear, oozing out of an inflamed eye, ran down her lined face toward her ear. At any rate, the look of the worst famine in sixty years was clearly on her face. I felt I should say something tender, something tearful, of only for the sake of departed Nuhye, but I could not bring myself to do so.

My embarrassed eyes fell upon the brown, blood stained blankets. Then I noticed the spots on her hand were blood stains. Had she hurt herself? Had she coughed up blood? It was no use trying to find out now. She was dying.

Looking about the room, my eyes fell on an army mess kit. The sight reminded me that I was hungry. Just then the thought struck me that the old woman might have had practically nothing to eat for the past sixty days.

"Can I get you anything to eat?" The words brought instant animation to her eyes and a gurgle to her throat. The hand that had been placed on my knee slid off. I felt her whole frame shiver. She was dying of starvation.

So this was another island. The worst. I arose, for my sorrow was overpowering. I had to go out and find food above all else.

I pushed the door, forgetting that I should have pulled it. The cat casually walked in through the opening. As I was going through the door, I heard a squeak; the cat cleanched a mouse between its teeth.

It went around the old woman once and stopped by her head with the half-dead mouse on the mess plate, at the same time pressing the plate against the woman. It stepped back a little and cocked its head.

The woman's hand was now extended toward the plate. Startled by the movement of the hand, the mouse hobbled off in the direction of her feet. Maddened, the cat ruthlessly assaulted its victim. It held the victim in its mouth again and jerked its head, sending the mouse against the wall with a thump. The cat caught the falling mouse in midair and gave it another shake. The mouse tried to escape but the cat flew at it.

The cat seemed to have forgotten that people were around. It seemed to be absorbed in its own game. It seemed to enjoy the sport immensely. It repeated the same act over and over until the mouse finally became motionless. Then the cat coaxed the mouse to escape by giving a few gentle shoves with its nose. The mouse staggered a little as if it had no other choice, but it was no use. The cat possessed an excess of vigor. I finally got tired of the cat's cruelty.

I stopped short just as I was leaving. Somehow the mouse had landed on the woman's stomach and it was now completely motionless—probably dead.

I held my breath. Her hand approached the rodent. It approached the victim as stealthily as a spider approaches a fly. It gripped the victim.

An indefinable foreboding possessed me. The cat was proudly watching the woman.

The next instant I dashed—threw my body—toward her hand with a shriek.

I did not know where she had the brute strength stored in her thin body. She would not let the mouse go. Even while I was trying to loosen the mouse from her grip I was conscious of the infuriated glare of her maddened accomplice behind me.

She was going to eat the mouse—actually *eat* the mouse! I grabbed the mouse from her and threw it at the cat.

"Mother!"

But to call her mother must have been either a mistake or make-believe. Actually, my immediate impulse was to throttle her and finish her off then and there—to kill a woman who had so sullied the human race. In order to make the owner of the castlelike mansion fatter, the people were eating mice. The old woman had been living on mice caught by the cat! That explained the bloodstains on the blankets. While even the watchdog was eating beef at the mansion, this crummy, lousy old woman was . . .

A furious impulse to spit on her gripped me. Once I had experienced similar nausea and rage. It was back on the island. I was in the latrine and, thinking I saw someone beckoning me from below, I looked down and nearly fainted from shock and fright. It was a real hand. A human hand sticking out obliquely from a heap of human excrement as if trying to reach my ankle. It belonged to Nuhye who had died the day before.

"Mother! I am your Nuhye!" A torrent of enraged tears flowed. I buried my head in the bosom of the woman that now seemed to be at the end of despair with her mouse meal taken away from her.

Squeak!

The cat was devouring the mouse. In front of me the old woman was nailed to the cross of death. I was sandwiched in between two deaths. In order not to slip from the precarious pinnacle, I clung to her wrists like a child, repeating "Mother!" The sound of my voice seemed to make me her son, to make Tongho Nuhye. Just because there is a world in which one equal two, there is no reason why there should not be another world in which one plus one equal three.

"Mother, let's go and live in the city!"

Where in me had such sorrow been stored? Compared with that sorrow I was as small as a grain of wheat, a handful of dust in the wind. I felt a hand turning cold. I tried to remove it as if to wake up from my sleep. But my fingers were tightly locked in hers. At last I was trapped; the hand in the latrine had finally caught up with me.

I felt a shiver run down my spine. The chilling blood of the old woman seemed to have trickled into my veins. The face seemed to recover a faint trace of animation at one point—was it merely my fancy? The numbing cold of death was creeping upward, up, up into me.

Was it not I who was in fact dying? How else could one explain the gradual drop in my body temperature? My hand was getting cold like a piece of steel . . . then my arm. The cold would soon creep toward my heart. My nostalgia traveled back to the cave era, to the age of bronze—the glacial epoch—I had been caught by a comrade buying myself an ice candy on the sly. How pitiful had I looked then. But I wondered why the face of the comrade was covered with dreadful pimples. It was all pimples. Southward, southward, we had been marching every night, hand grenades hanging from our belts. Frogs were all around. Why do frogs croak so much? Charge! Thump! Bang! The pear tree drew a parabolic line through the air. Then I was a prisoner of war. Was it a southern island where seagulls were said to sing? The hand in the latrine. Nuhye with his eyes plucked out. The cry, "Long live freedom!" had still to come forth from the clearing and the bloodshot eyes were watching.

I was shoved aside. I stumbled. The old woman was in her death throes. It was as if the chains binding her to life had at last been broken. What amazing brute strength had been hidden in her! She screamed as she writhed. I fell back several times as she shoved me.

An old donkey running helter-skelter downhill in the twilight—it might get caught under the wheels of its own cart any minute.

With a last heave her breast collapsed. Bleary eyes without any focus. From a corner of her half-open mouth a thin line of saliva flowed and trickled down onto the bed—life was draining from her body drop by drop.

Her breathing came harder and harder. It seemed as though she would not be able to stand the everincreasing speed of its rhythm much longer. Death was enjoying its dance of victory in her throat.

It was an agony even to watch her die. I stared at her intently, breathing hard, with my eyes swollen. For awhile I was under the illusion that I too would cease to live when her breathing stopped, when the last maelstrom of her life subsided.

The approaching footsteps of death began to ring in my ears. Death began to wail in my ears. The noise of its wailing made me giddy. I began to give way to fancies and visions.

Visions whirled round in my head. They cried. The room cried. The sky cried. The clearing under the sky cried. The world was full of cries and shrieks. Wait, they are the shrieks of swine. Oink, oink! Black, white, red, blue, and all other possible colored pigs were grunting. On the top of the hill, down in the valley, across from the river, swine were grunting.

A great horde of swine breaking loose from the slaughterhouse now covered the entire earth.

Oink, oink! They covered streets. They plundered. They devoured filth. They loosened pillars. Buildings collapsed. A city boasting one million turned into a ruin in a matter of minutes. Civilization lay dead with its white belly gazing at the heavens. Nothing stood upright. Dead. Death inhabited metropolises.

The horde moved on in search of its next victim beyond the horizon, giving meaning to the meaningless.

A silent march emerged on the ravaged scene—a march of trees. Pines, oaks, elms, dates, paulownias, cherries, zelkovas, all possible kinds of trees released from the dictionary marched onto the scene. Disregarding

alphabetical order, each stood where it chose. All was quiet. It was paradise.
It was the quietude and the sadness of paradise. Once I experienced the
same kind of sadness. It was when a dogcatcher with a sharp hook gaffed
Mary, my pet poodle, and dragged her away. Mary had lost her license
tag. I was nine then. After a good long cry, I turned to the shade of the
acacia trees. Not a sound except the singing of cicadas on that quiet sum-
mer afternoon could be heard. The scene was quite like this. It was deep.
One's native place is deep. It may even be deeper.

But the world cannot remain quiet forever. Bustling began to ripple
from one corner. Paradise, after all, stands on shaky foundations. Owls
flutter off one by one. Men always heal blind birds.

Ape-men invaded the scene swinging from tree to tree. What were they
carrying? Their backs characteristically bent, stone axes around their waists,
they were carrying torches. The same old story. Can't they ever learn?

These offensive fellows will soon talk about Venus and erect an altar
in her honor. Utter a few incantations, the earth will move and self will
awake. Factories will be built and the smoke will give birth to two-story
houses. The Republic will hand out licenses guaranteeing liberty to its
jubilant citizens.

It is snowing quietly outside. Must we repeat this dreadful history?

It is snowing, large and fluffy flakes. It seems as though the whole sky
is falling on us. It is snowing. The snow piles up on the ground. The
whole world becomes white. The snow is like a quilt. But the snow still
piles up. It reaches the caves. It reaches the rooftop. It reaches the sky.
No more air, no more wind. We must rewrite biology textbooks. A new
type of man breathing snow is born. Being forgetful, they will soon forget
that they have lived breathing air.

If that is the case, what did man breathe before he began to breathe air?

A dark figure emerges from the snow. With his horsehair hat pulled
down over the eyes, this young mendicant monk is blind. He advances,
feeling his way with his hands. Without a staff, without eyes, he has come
a long way. He stops a little way off and tears stream from his blind eyes.

Is not this ragged monk the very person who broke open the slaughterhouse
gates and who tore up the dictionary of trees?

"Nuhye," groaned the old woman, and that brought me out
of my reverie. I thought I heard a gurgling sound in her throat.

The room was now all but dark. This was how Nuhye's
mother died.

The ghostly glimmer of the cat was glaring at me from where
the wandering monk of my fancy had been standing. My blood

boiled; I could swear they were Nuhye's eyes.

Nuhye hanged himself on the barbed wire fence.

Everybody in the prison camp called him Silkworm.[1] Thus when not being able to grasp the true significance of his new status as a prisoner, everybody was still in a state of despondency, some thoughtless fellows teased Nuhye, who was always looking up at the sky.

"Mulberry, mulberry, mulberry leaves are falling from the sky."

"Tigers leave fur behind when they die; silkworms leave silk behind when they die. Ha, ha."

But it wasn't silk he wanted to leave behind. He wanted to be a phoenix or a dragon and fly off into the blue sky.

He was not a member of the Volunteer Corps, which was made up of recruits from occupied South Korea. He was a regular in the Puppet Army of North Korea. But even when the camp was in a turmoil due to communist agitation, he did not sing "the Red Flag" but was content to look at the blue sky as he lay on the ground.

In the eyes of the guards the camp was merely a place in which thousands of filthy crows cawed; but inside, underneath, was a vigilant whirlpool of undercurrents that had lost all direction. They were of a race that had not had a war of their own for centuries. Napalm, along with such novel ideas as "a democratic stronghold" "the East and the West," or "the World Peace Appeal Movement," baptized a country which had known nothing in the way of modernization except perhaps shovels and field sneakers. Those country hillbillies were merely bewildered beings covered with cuts and bruises. Sometimes they thought they might turn into city slickers. Sometimes they thought they might be marionettes. At other times they felt they were hypnotized. But they had charged to the sound of the trumpet. When they stopped running to look around, they found themselves in the middle of carnage. Their homes, their schools lay in ruins like match boxes crushed by an iron hammer. What little they had accumulated since the beginning of the Enlightenment Party was

---

1. Nuhye—personal name. It's phonetic sound is close to *nu-eh,* a silkworm; hence the allusions in the text to silkworms."

now destroyed. They were naked; they had become the beggars of the world.

But they grew in the camp. Just as petty thieves grow into bold criminals while serving their time in a penitentiary, they learned to quote from the "Geneva Convention" to talk of "humane treatment." "This war in which my flesh has been torn and my blood spilled—was this war really mine?" they often wondered to themselves. But they teetered between this and that until they came face to face with their clinging attachment to life. It was an attachment to the life that had so far been treated as a mere screw in a huge machine. They wanted to live. They had to live. So they started to kill others. Another war had begun. Killing others seemed to be a reasonable means to their own survival. In this southern island the red flag and the blue flag again fluttered in the sea breeze to soothe the fears of the world Under these two flags they bathed each other in blood in order to survive. The second war within the barbed wire encampment was strictly their own. It was their war to preserve their lives. Therefore, not to take part in that war was to give up one's right to live.

It was a struggle beyond human attributes. In no other war had people killed each other so viciously. The utmost punishment one can impose upon his worst enemy is death. Nothing more. A human cannot receive worse punishment than death however vile and evil he may be. That is what the name human stands for. That is the last belief humans can have in human. In death rests the entire weight of life. One's crime cannot be greater than one's life, and death is the end of everything. Sorrow, joy, ticklishness, pain, blood, sweat, good, evil, and all the conventions on earth end with death. It is consolation, rest, forgiveness.

But in the camp they cut off limbs, gouged out eyes, and lopped off the ears and noses of corpses. Then they dumped them in the latrines. In the name of ideology, the classes, the people!

They regarded life as a plaything. They considered humans worms!

What could one do about that?

You could do nothing. You could do nothing except call it an episode that happened outside the human compass. Under these circumstances Nuhye still lived on, the blue sky his fortitude. Before I knew how and when, I got into the habit of crouching beside him. They did not bother me because they had decided I was a half-wit, but they could use that attitude to ignore. One day Nuhye was summoned to the shade of a persimmon tree.

"Comrade! We do not wish to brand you as an enemy of the people and a henchman of American imperialism, of the warmongers. How about it? Comrade! . . . Say something!"

Then they would turn from threatening to begging. It was natural because Nuhye had been a hero of the people, receiving the medal for the highest bravery during the war.

"Comrade! Don't you mind being called a traitor against the people?"

". . . ."

Dangerous looks began to well up in their eyes. "Answer us! You are a reactionary!"

". . . ."

Still there was no answer. The response had to be one of two anwers but he seemed to regard both as inadequate.

Clubs danced on his head and shoulders as they screamed phrases like "corrupter," "traitor," or "enemy of the people!" I had not realized he was as stolid as an ox. He was standing upright like a fence post. He sank down with a particularly strong blow to his head. Then the feet surrounding him kicked him all at once.

I went up to him after they had left. There he was still looking up at the sky. Two thin tearful lines creased his face.

Looking up at the summer sky I saw clouds coming in fast off the sea.

I lay down beside him and raised my eyes toward the sky. It was a peaceful sky mirroring none of the dark shadows that inhabited the earth.

"How about trying to raise something up there?" I said to console him. "It's so wide and it doesn't even have mountains. Won't it yield a good crop? Wouldn't peace rule there?"

"People would only build fences there if anything grew."

"Really?"

"You had better live long."

"Why? Do you mean you are going to die?"

"No, I have an old mother. You can cut all bonds except

the umbilical cord. If only you could cut it off.''

"You can leave silk behind, is that it?''

"Become a phoenix or a dragon and fly off into the sky.''
Several days passed.

"Silkworm has killed himself!'' The cry that ripped the dawn seemed to be the signal that Nuhye had finally been able to metamorphose himself into a phoenix or a dragon to accomplish his coveted ascent to the heavens.

Nuhye's body was dangling from the barbed wire fence.

But for what had happened the night before, I would not have been shocked by his death. The night before, he had tried to hug me tightly, to crawl into my bed.

"How warm your flesh is.''

His breath, hot and sensual, tickled my ear and gave me goose pimples. To tell the truth, relations between us up to that time had not been close enough to warrant this. I thought there had been an understanding between us; that our dialogue was nothing but romanticism at best or mere nonsense at worst. But now he was forcing me to give ex post facto consent that all had been real with not even a single minute detail to be altered.

"In my dreams last night a beautiful woman hugged me very tight. Like this. . .''

". . . .''

I lay motionless as if I were paralyzed.

"On that very moment I realized that Mother was mortal like any other person. To realize such at this late date . . . Oh, there are so many things that one should realize.''

". . . .''

"Do you know who the woman was? Your flesh is so soft.'' His embrace was nothing short of homosexual. Of course, such activities had been open secrets in our tent.

"I'll tell you who she was. But don't let the others know, because I am not sure at all.''

He held his breath. He seemed to be quite embarrassed even in his excitement. I think he had reason to be.

"Salome. You know of her, don't you? The woman who wanted to have the head of John. It was she who hugged me!'' Saying this he pushed me away. Then he panted. "My fruit has ripened, but I am not ripe to match the fruit. I won't be ripe forever! I have no wings,'' he said.

My body trembled like that of a raped woman.

Immediate retaliation was taken against the corpse of the traitor. The only two reasons that warranted such vicious and cruel acts were that he had been a hero of the people and that they had not been able to persecute him as much as they had wished while he was alive.

They ordered me, of all things, to hold his gouged-out eyeballs and to stand till the sun rose in the east over the sea. I could have feigned a weak heart, but were they not Nuhye's eyeballs?

I had Nuhye's eyeballs in my hand waiting for the sun to rise, while a guard whistled a nostalgic melody far off on the other side of the barbed wire fence. In what way were the eyeballs related to the whistling? Miscalculation, that's the word. We were all living a miscalculation. It was not the old home in Kentucky but those eyeballs that the whistling should have yearned for.

I did not understand why he had chosen the barbed wire fence as the instrument of his death until I read the testament he had left behind. The two different worlds—the inside world in which I had to stand holding his eyeballs and the outside world where the whistling of the guard was soothing his homesickness—were the only two things I knew. I had not really seen, and therefore had not realized, the meaning of the barbed wire fence separating us and therefore, in a paradoxical way, bridging these two worlds. And finally on that early morning a breakthrough was made by the dangling corpse on the fence.

Although he had mentioned that his mother was then living in South Korea and that she had moved from North Korea with the retreating army after hearing her son had been captured, the letter was not addressed to her. In fact it was more a memoir than a letter.

The letter:

They said I was one year old at birth, as is customary in this country.

Five days passed before I was christened, and these five days may be the only true life I ever had. Since the world consists entirely of names, I would never have existed at all if I had died during those five days.

My name was entered on the family register as soon as I was christened. Being thus confined to a corner of a page in the thick register, I became an entity that could never be removed from the book except by an official notification of death.

I stopped suckling at the age of four and rice has been my staple food ever since. Of course, I did not realize that this was the beginning of a collective responsibility. Since I began to articulate myself at about this time, you might say that the process of assimilation was well on its way. I entered school when I was eight years old. Thus I was preparing myself to be an atom in society before I knew what I was doing.

The school was a home of sin and crime. I learned about sin and crime through the punishments I earned. Things went well for the school if it could maintain a standard of discipline whereby a student could be made to lie down thirty minutes for each one-minute tardiness. While I was undergoing such torture, I had to watch other students who had arrived about ten seconds before I did march into the classroom proudly and jovially. Then I realized the cold fact that being late fifty seconds is all right while being late sixty seconds constitutes a crime. The same principle seemed to explain how my family became so rich in an amazingly short time while my early childhood was spent in poverty.

It is still vivid in my memory, that pitiable scene standing holding a bucket full of water in the hallway for breaking a window pane. All the children had gone home and the sun was setting. Nothing stirred in the empty school building except my teacher's eyeglasses peeking out once in a while from his office door at the end of the corridor just to see if I was doing what I was supposed to do. Fow how long was I to go through that torture? I could see a dog chasing something on the deserted playground. I cursed my arms. If I hadn't had any arms, I wouldn't have had to go through the torture. My arms were all numb and they didn't feel like they were mine. I let the bucket go in spite of myself. I cried aloud, flopping down in the middle of the puddle. I feared the still newer punishment that I was sure to get and the sense of aloneness that there wouldn't be any one around to help me.

Somehow I grew up to be a middle school boy. We were supposed to wear two white lines on both our caps and uniform sleeves. To me those two lines symbolized the limits beyond which we were not to step. But at the same time it could mean that we could do anything we pleased within those limits.

One morning, while the whole student body and the faculty gathered for the morning ceremonies, I nearly went out of my mind. I discovered that every student's jacket had exactly five buttons. It was fearful. Then as I grew I learned that there were more and more of the same fearful things surrounding us. Every house had windows and every pencil looked about the same. All eyes were under eyebrows. I saluted most eagerly everyone in the upper class as I was supposed to, and they all returned my salute most casually. That in turn made me salute them all the more enthusiastically. At school I was a model student. One day when I was seventeen, a snake cut across my shadow. Grabbing a pick, I tore after it. It was an act intended to free myself and to find the open road; I was getting tired of the narrow and shadowy confines that the name "model student" offered me.

At last I wrote the word autonomy on a sheet of paper and tacked it on the wall in front of my desk. Of course I had not realized that it was only an estuary in the sea of heteronomy, and soon I became a college student.

I left my hometown to study in a foreign land. One afternoon while I was at the window of my second-floor room, absent-mindedly thinking about home, my eyes caught something moving. Then, realizing what was happening, I nearly broke down. The pine trees of Myoshin Temple on the far-off hill were marching toward me. Gasping, I ducked behind the wall. The Revolution had finally been set in motion. Which side should I support? Which side should I join? Should I dash out crying, "Long live the pine trees!" If so, my date with Kuniko, a Japanese girl, to see a Tarzan movie that evening would be broken. I was much troubled—caught between two choices the Revolution and a foreign girl. Deeply troubled by the dilemma, I decided I would first have a look at how the Revolution was going. I peeked out. Again I was shocked; the Revolution had apparently been called off. The pine trees had retreated back to Myoshin Temple. I let out a deep sigh of relief and decided the whole affair had been an illusion. I thought I would feel much more at ease if such irregularities would never happen again.

I graduated from college with some knowledge of evolution and other theories. But still I had not realized that accident is the true ruler of the world, and that therefore existence itself is sin; I merely saw the image of myself in the mirror, divided into two cells.

I returned to the backcountry where I was born. The bells that chimed in the quiet dawn air from faraway temples led me to a life of complete inactivity. Sometimes I played with deer or chased hares, but I was mainly a poet who produced nothing. I was merely content scribbling poetry that would never be published.

> *I wish I were a bell,*
> *A bell that breaks the stillness of dawn.*
> *I wish this bony skeleton were a bell,*
> *A lank frame devoid of flesh and blood.*
>
> *The blue autumn sky,*
> *The sound of falling leaves, red and gold.*
> *One leaf, then another*
> *From eternity to temporal burden,*
> *Pulse engraves solitude.*
> *The glistening dewdrops on the canonical robe . . .*
> *Are they the rhythms that life left behind?*
>
> *I wish I were a bell*
> *In this season of shadowy glen.*
> *Neither desire nor Buddha I aspire,*
> *Let me only be a simple bell.*

Then World War II ended.

I attempted a rebirth by becoming a friend of the people. I joined the Communist party. I soon found that there were no people in the Party. They were busy creating a people by killing off the enemies of the people. Creating and killing and an unbridgeable gap between them. It meant the isolation of life, too. The fire of life goes out just we become conscious of it. And we call the remaining ashes life. In this distorted mode of life goodness can only exist where an awareness of goodness exists. It is an abyss. It is the same difference, a gap of ten seconds, which had shocked me when I was a small school boy; it is a barrier that blocks the way to freedom.

In order to break the barrier I threw myself into the war.

But I became a prisoner. I was still as lonely as I had been in the north. I drew up a new mode of life in the loneliness and despair.

A slave. The new type of free man was a slave. I felt free being a slave. Finally I came to realize that this third type of slave, who freely accepted shackles and fetters, was the true hero of the modern age. This realization was a great relief to me. For the first time since I was given a name I breathed freely and enjoyed liberation.

But, alas! That also was a deception of a brief moment. It had merely been a temporary agitation. To look back, the history of mankind has been a series of alternations between agitation and cooling off; we were agitated by the Copernican theory, the Bastille, the survival of the fittest, Red Square, and so on down the line. Each time one bitter disillusionment followed closely on the heels of the other.

The modern slave is not a free man but a slave of freedom. Man has to be a slave as long as freedom exists! Freedom, too, was another numerical figure. Freedom was restraint and coercion. It was something to be overcome. Freedom was something created *post factum*!

God, eternity. It was a sacrilege to deal with the life hereafter when these explications had been created afterwards. Life is not an explication but a right, not a superstition but a desire! The only way to make life really alive was to annihilate God, eternity, and all other things connected with freedom.

Freedom should really be something that opens the way to true being, a being to follow, a prophet—a John who will stoop to tie his shoelaces and finally lie down, slain by the wayside.

Now I am lonely again in the wilderness. The moon has already set, but the sun won't rise in the east. I can neither follow my shadow nor linger here in inactivity.

This is the end as well as the beginning of the land. This is the joint where time that has passed and time that will come meet. This place is not broad enough to stand even a pin point on. This is the borderline itself.

But how broad a world this is, this fertile land of production. This is the chaos from which time and space flow. There is no dilemma in this world. Innumerable laws illuminate the still night of poesy without violating each other. Meanwhile, constellations inlay the vault of the night sky. Here there are no kings, no slaves—no anxiety and therefore no compromise. No custom, therefore no depravity. The cause of everything is sufficient unto itself, and it measured against its own scale. Here there is no reason why the sun should always rise in the east. It's always new, always morning, always spring. Ah! the young continent. . .

When will we wake up from the nightmare of Gulliver who drifted to the island of dwarfs? When will we be able to break loose? It's not the Bastille but the shoreline surrounding these islands that should have been breached!

I can wait no longer. I must find myself at once. I reserve one last right to find myself.

I can really see myself, escape from myself, and watch the true world emerge out of the fog only when I am totally liberated from the eyes that have been surrounding me.

Suicide is that attempt; my last chance for hope. If I fail again to see my true self there, it will be a futile act. But then, if life awaits such a futile death, I might as well undergo the metamorphosis as soon as possible.

Septemeber, 1951

The letter was watching me with two phosphorescent eyes. Those two eyes, the eyes of the cat, kept glaring at me like a petrified curse in the pitch-black darkness. A cold sweat broke out on my forehead. It was a struggle in which the odds were heavily against me. I could see only its eyes while it could see my eyelashes as well. What sin had I committed, what sin other than that I was alive? Those two eyes seemed to condemn anything that moved or was alive.

I wondered if there was any way to extinguish those eyes. The glare of the eyes seemed to pierce my body. I was helplessly sleepy. The fatigue which I had brought from the island now seemed to overpower me.

The fear and the sleepiness, and the strand tension which they wove and infinite number of possibilities existed there.

If the tension broke with a cry of "Meow!," the shoreline would break also and the branches of a dead tree on the hilltop yonder might bloom with red flowers. Possibilities were always possible and the number of possibilities were limitless. Existence is what is left behind after all the possibilities are obliterated by accident. Therefore, existence is by definition sin or guilt. Existence is a crime. The whole list of crimes makes up the world. The world is the offspring of crime and man is the criminal.

To live is to commit crimes. They can not sit there because I am occupying the place. The act of sitting down automatically displace other people. Therefore, I am liable to be displaced by them. Each moment an infinite number of possibilities are making their claims. Each existence is shuddering before the possibility that might be realized the next moment. They call that shuddering liberty in this world. Should we wake up or keep on sleeping? The cat was still glaring at me in the darkness. I had killed its mistress. I had killed the old woman. I would be a murderer as long as those two eyes were gleaming side by side in the darkness.

Suddenly the distance between the two phosphorescent spot shortened. I saw my chance; the cat had looked away. The next instant, my fist flew toward it but it arched in the empty air. Those eyes had already slipped under my arm and out through the open door.

I chased it. It gave me a backward glance and fled toward the hill.

I ran up the hill after it, but it had vanished.

"Meow!"

Looking up, I saw the eyes shining down at me from the branches of the tree where crows had cawed in the twilight. Throwing rocks at it did not extinguish the fire. It did not have wings, and I had lost the tree-climbing talent of the ape.

The moon elbowed its way out from among the clouds. The area around the cat seemed to disintegrate, as the glare of revenge and its curse. The crouching silhouette of the cat perched among the branches like a dark fairy.

"Meow!"

The dark, ghostly, and revengeful glare of the eyes was still breathing in that cold, shuddering cry that could have frozen the distant shorelines.

The fire will be extinguished when the sun rises in the morning. I am sleepy and having a hard time watching the eyes.

Wearing Nuhye's silk garments, as it were, I am standing under the

tree as the night wears away silently.
Will the sun really rise over the eastern hills when morning comes?

(end story)

Walking in the Snow

Son Ch'angsŏp

"No, it's impossible!" Mr. Ko was adamant. Kwansik looked up at Mr. Ko as though the answer was totally unexpected.
His eyes had a how-dare-you-refuse-me look. Mr. Ko's face was
expressionless. Both remained silent for some time staring at each
other across the tea room coffee table.

"You're being too harsh! You're going too far!"

"Too harsh? No, I'm not too harsh; you're too cheeky. That's
all."

"I'm desperate. I can afford to be cheeky. But you wouldn't
care if I died of hunger or cold!"

"I can't be held responsible for your death no matter how
you die, whether you die from hunger, cold, or a traffic accident. Why should I of all people be responsible?"

"I never figured you would treat me this way. You can't be
serious."

They became silent again. Both were agitated.

Kwansik would have no place to sleep after tomorrow. For
that matter, his very livelihood was up in the air. Until today
he had been living with a man from his hometown who had
established an unlicensed medical clinic in a slum area. Kwansik had never studied medicine but he had been acting as an assistant on the strength of his being the son of a doctor. It was not
a prosperous enterprise by any means, but they had managed
to survive until the clinic had been closed by the health authorities
a few days previously. The pseudo doctor had disappeared with
all his belongings and someone else was moving into the former
clinic tomorrow. This was how Kwansik came to ask Mr. Ko,
his teacher during middle school days, to take him in for a while.

"We meet for the first time in ten years and you ask me for

such a favor. Is this your notion of good manners and common courtesy? I really don't understand you young people.''

"This isn't the first time. It's the second time.''

"It's the first time we ever sat and talked like this. That time we ran into each other on the streetcar we merely exchanged greetings.''

"Anyway, I never thought you could be so heartless.''

"Before you accuse me of being heartless, don't you think there are certain things you should consider about me? The conditions under which I live; my personality; my personal tastes, my. . .''

"I can't afford such luxuries. I must find a roof to put over my head. Where can I go?''

"What would you have done if you had not run into me?''

"It's a long road that has no turning. There must always be a way out. There must be. I came here because I had confidence in you and in our friendship. You are heartless!''

"Friendship? There seems to be no limit to your audacity! I do not recall any occasions or instances between you and me that warrant the use of the word friendship. I sold knowledge at the going rate and you boys bought it. Since when have we established a close relationship? After three years in North Korea and three more in South Korea as a teacher I have come into contact with thousands. Well, do you supose I have the obligation to be bound by friendship to each and every one of these? You mean to say that I must offer my friendship to those who wouldn't even offer to buy me a cup of coffee? Was I born merely to help others? Was I born just to offer you friendship?'' Mr. Ko was worked up and his voice was shrill. All in the tea room looked up to see what was happening.

Even after he had left the tea room Mr. Ko was furious. The boy's impudence wasn't even funny. What nerve! What's more, the boy seemed to think that he was harsh and even cruel to refuse. That was the most annoying part of the whole affair.

It was around dusk the following evening. It was particularly cold and Mr. Ko sat in the tea room later than usual, thinking of his cold rented room with abhorrence. Just then Kwansik showed up again. He was carrying a bundle wrapped in an old gray blanket. It was his possessions. He shoved through the narrow openings between tables and chairs while guests looked up at him in surprise and waitresses frantically motioned him to stop. Mr. Ko arose, frowning, to meet him.

"Let's get out here." Mr. Ko emerged from the tea room pushing Kwansik ahead of him. "How dare you do this to me!"

"I had no choice. I am sorry, sir," Kwansik dropped his head. His lips were blue and he was shivering. Mr. Ko figured that they could solve nothing by standing in the street. More harsh words would not help either now that things had gone this far. The bundle was left at a nearby bookstore and they went back to the tea room.

As they sat down at a table Kwansik bowed his head once again.

"I am truly sorry it had to be like this, sir. I must use the phrase you used yesterday. I am going too far."

Kwansik scratched his head a few times. "I made up my mind not to inconvenience you like this, but after walking around Seoul all afternoon with that bundle, I had no one to turn to but you. I had no choice. Just a week, no more. I will never forget the favor, Sir."

There wasn't the slightest trace of yesterday's overbearing attitude; he was meek, subservient, imploring. "You are quite an actor," thought Mr. Ko but he could not refuse him as he had done so firmly yesterday.

"I can't afford it really, but if it is just for a week we will manage somehow," said Mr. Ko finally. This was how Kwansik became a permanent guest in Mr. Ko's single rented room. This was the beginning, we might say, of the storm that blew into this withdrawn gentleman's quiet life.

One day Kwansik brought home a dark-complexioned girl who had unusually large round eyes. A small dimple formed on one cheek when she smiled. She said she was twenty-two years old, but she did not look over eighteen. She was wearing a black velvet jumper and green corduroy slacks; the seat and knees of the slacks were threadbare. She said her name was Kwinam.

"She is my girl friend and she is going to be my wife one of these days."

"Don't get fresh!" Kwinam glared at Kwansik.

"She is quite a talented dramatist," Kwansik said by way of introduction, not heeding what the girl was saying. At this,

Kwinam took off her beret and bowed low in Japanese style. She impressed Mr. Ko favorably despite her shabby clothing. When Mr. Ko asked her if she wanted to be an actress, she merely smiled and shook her head.

"She wants to be a playwright. Of course, she wants to take up directing and acting on the side," Kwansik explained. Mr. Ko commented that that sounded like a challenge not at all suited to a girl.

"Why, is not life itself a play?" said the girl coolly.

"My, my!" said Mr. Ko to himself. As a rule he had an instinctive distaste for such words as life and mankind when bandied around by youth, but this time it was different.

"Do you think so? Is life really but a play? I should think life has its sincere aspects too."

"That's only façade. You pretend to yourself that others are sincere but it takes a real actor to make others believe he is sincere. Of course, that is the ultimate goal of dramatic acting."

Mr. Ko was somewhat stunned. Her remarks had something and he could not dismiss them as those of an impudent hussy. She said things that had a freshness about them.

"That means I am no more than an actor myself and not a very good one at that?"

She merely smiled.

"She often tells me to quit my poor and clumsy acting too. She is a hard director," said Kwansik with a loud laugh.

"I know this good-for-nothing here has been trying hard to seduce me, but I know his clumsy tricks and can see through his poor acting," said the girl sharply.

She left after eating a humble supper prepared by Kwansik. Mr. Ko saw her to the gate. She looked so cold in her shabby clothes. Kwansik accompanied her to the bus stop. As soon as he returned to the house he started firing questions at Mr. Ko.

"What do you think of her, sir?"

"How do you mean?"

"I mean to marry her one of these days. She isn't bad at all, is she?"

"Marry her? How can you talk about marriage when you are not capable of supporting yourself alone?" growled Mr. Ko.

"You underrate me. Wait and see."

"I do not underrate you; I am talking about facts. All I am

saying is that a man who is sponging off someone else is not qualified to talk about marriage.''

Kwansik was bothersome to Mr. Ko. He showed no signs of moving out when the agreed-to week had passed.

''It's over a week since you came here,'' Mr. Ko once said to Kwansik by way of reminding him that time was up.

''My, my, so it is? How time flies! Life has been so carefree that I feel much better now. Within a month or two I'll be putting on weight. It is a good thing I decided to come here after all,'' had been Kwansik's cool and breezy answer. Mr. Ko just stood there openmouthed.

Mr. Ko made a living drawing illustrations for a few magazines and teaching drawing two hours a week at a girls' high school. He hadn't anything like a big income to begin with. Now that he had two mouths instead of one to feed, he was barely making ends meet. Kwansik consumed an amazing amount of food; three times as much as Mr. Ko ever ate. Fuel expenses and just about everything else had doubled. But that was not all; Kwansik wore Mr. Ko's underwear and suits without giving it a second thought. Mr. Ko usually left home before Kwansik each morning. Once he ran into Kwansik, who was with a young girl, in the street. Mr. Ko did not recognize him at first, he looked so smart and different. He had had a fresh haircut and was wearing a new suit which Mr. Ko recognized as his own. He had had the suit made last autumn even though he could ill afford it. He liked the cut and color and so had put it away for special occasions. Naturally Mr. Ko glared at Kwansik angrily.

''I'm sorry, sir. I had to see someone and so had to look decent today. I'll go right home and take it off.'' Saying that, Kwansik scurried away to join the girl, who was standing a few paces ahead. That evening Mr. Ko spoke sternly to him about the suit. Kwansik scratched his head a few times, but he looked quite unconcerned.

''You're making a federal case out of it. It's only a suit, dammit! I'll give you a dozen of those when I get my hands on my million.''

Mr. Ko could not counter this. This incident concerning the suit was followed by many a scene over underwear, socks, and other such things.

Kwansik had another strange habit. He would ask Mr. Ko embarrassing questions. He would ask why Mr. Ko had not married, for instance.

"It's none of your business."

"I'm worried. What's the point of living?"

"You mind your own business—if you have any business, that is."

"I have a scheme. I know a woman with a mint of money." Mr. Ko merely turned his back.

"I'm going to introduce you to her."

". . . ."

"I can never figure you out," he continued, "Sometimes I feel I'll go crazy if I don't get married soon."

Sometimes Kwansik was even more brazen.

"Sir, I want to show you a good place. A damned nice place. I bet you haven't been to any of those places. Five hundred *wŏn* apiece for a throw. One thousand *wŏn* is all both of us need."

Mr. Ko could stand it no longer. He was being insulted by this youngster. He was infuriated.

"Shut up! There is a limit to everything! Are you trying to ridicule me? Get out of my place if you don't want to respect my feelings, my character, my personal tastes. Get out!"

"Take it easy. I'm not trying to ridicule you or anything," said Kwansik. After a while he put his hand out. "I'll go there alone if that's how you feel about it. I want to borrow five hundred *wŏn*," Kwansik said sullenly.

Mr. Ko gave him the sum without any hesitation; he was glad to be rid of him even for a short time. Pocketing the money, Kwansik strode out of the house into the darkness.

This shameless youngster became more annoying to Mr. Ko. He was even becoming oppressive. But he could not drive him out of the house. Kwansik wasn't the sort of person to obey like a lamb either. This he knew well. He had nothing to blame but his own irresoluteness. He was exhausted.

Kwinam came to the house often. Kwansik brought her along most of the time, but sometimes she dropped in alone. She always wore the same clothes, the black velvet jumper and the green corduroy slacks with the frayed seat and knees. Then there were the men's socks she always wore which sometimes had holes large enough to show her toes and heels. At times when she stayed overnight she would mend her socks while Kwansik prepared their supper. On such nights Mr. Ko suffered most, for he had to relinquish his bedding to the girl since his was much cleaner than Kwansik's. Even so, the girl was hesitant to use bedding at first. She said the quilt was too dirty. Mr. Ko had to cover the upper edge of the quilt, the part that touched her neck, with a towel. She crawled into bed with everything on except the jumper. Then she undressed under the quilt. After some wriggling she produced her slacks, then her woolen underwear.

"Hey, are you completely naked? No kidding!" Kwansik asked the prankish question. He was already in bed, but he had been intently watching her undress, craning his turtlelike neck.

"Don't be fresh! Go to sleep."

"I'm not sleepy. Can you blame me? Remember, there are two unmarried men in this room, Kwinam."

But it was Kwansik who fell asleep first. He fell asleep easily like so many healthy people do . He would even drop off to sleep in the middle of a conversation. By the time Mr. Ko would get through with his nightly task of completing magazine drawings, she would be fast asleep too. Somehow he would eye the underwear by her pillow. It was woolen underwear to be sure, but it was army underwear in extremely bad shape. It had patches on the knees and elbows. Mr. Ko would watch her sleeping face and recall her life story as she had once related it.

She was born to a Korean father and a Japanese mother. Two years after the Liberation in 1945 when she was fourteen, her mother deserted the family and went back to Japan. She had a brother who was nine years old. Within a few months of her mother's departure, however, her father died suddenly. He was assaulted and killed by some person or person unknown. People figured it was the doing of the leftists since her father had been quite active in the liberal youth movement. As she recalled, things had happened so suddenly that she hadn't even been sad. She merely felt as though they were the poor orphans in some fairy tale. They were cared for by an aunt. Since the aunt was well-to-do they could continue their education under relatively happy circumstances. But the outbreak of the Korean War in 1950 ended all that. The uncle had left Seoul alone just before the Communists occupied the city, and the aunt was killed during an air raid while the children were in a shelter in a neighboring house. Her brother was now delivering newspapers, living in the night watchman's room at a newspaper company and attending a commercial high school in the evenings.

Mr. Ko pressed his lips to Kwinam's while she slept. She moved her head on the pillow. "I did that thinking of you as my own daughter. I'll buy you some warm underwear as soon as I get a bit of extra money," Mr. Ko mumbled wistfully to himself. He rearranged the quilt covering her. He pushed snoring Kwansik to one side to make room for himslef to lie down. But his wistful, pensive mood did not last long. No sooner had he lain down beside Kwansik than the youngster began to twist and turn. Many times during the night Mr. Ko woke up with a numb leg from Kwansik lying across it. But he decided not to mind all this just to give the girl a peaceful night's rest.

One day the girl said she wanted to ask a special favor of Mr. Ko. She wanted to stay at the house for the time being. She said she was very tired of snatching a night's sleep here and there. She had been staying with one of her married cousins until recently but it had become obvious that she was not welcome. Since then she had been dropping in on friends, staying with each for a night or two. Now she had just about run out of friends too, she said. Mr. Ko willingly agreed to let her stay, for he thought she might be a welcome change in the drab life he and Kwansik had been living. He urged her to get her things right away but she had practically nothing to call her own except for a beaten-up suitcase. She wanted to leave that at her cousin's, however, for she might need a pretext to go back there one of these days. "Who knows, and I'll be needing some excuses," she said.

That morning, right after Kwinam had gone out after breakfast, Kwansik sat down opposite Mr. Ko and said:

"I'm going to marry that girl. You just wait and see."

"Why do you always make such a fuss about getting married? Moreover, I don't think Kwinam is a suitable match for you."

"There you go again. You'll never know. You'll never know what's what in life," said the young man impatiently.

"What do you know? Do you know so much about life?"

"I know what I want to do and I know what I need. I know these things very precisely."

"Is that all?" said Mr. Ko somewhat sarcastically.

"That's exactly where you are wrong. The world has changed. People no longer care if they are despised. The important thing is to grab the meat."

"You are becoming quite a philosopher! You grab all the meat you want and leave me alone!"

"Being alone will not help you to function in this world, I can tell you that," said Kwansik.

Mr. Ko was silent. The word function came to his head unexpectedly. "What function do I have in this world," he was asking himself. "Am I fully functioning as a man, a person, a painter?" he asked himself. He could not help seeing his own shabby image looming before his mind's eye.

One day Kwansik brought another woman to the house. He said she was from his hometown in North Korea. He said, by way of introducing her, that she had a wholesale cosmetics store in the East Gate Market. In her flashy outfit she still didn't look any younger than thirty. The gold rings on her fingers were too big and heavy. She wore thick makeup, which did not serve to hide her plain looks. She brought expensive friuts and cakes. She spoke with a broad North Korean accent.

"Mr. Ko, I hear you're from Hwanghae Province?" she said, and added that she had considerable respect for people from Hwanghae Province. Then she looked at, almost examined, his facial features in such a way that Mr. Ko was embarrassed. She said that she knew much about Mr. Ko through Kwansik and that it was a rare thing for an educated and honest gentleman like Mr. Ko to remain a bachelor like this at his age. "That by itself is enough to make me respect you," she said.

"I don't know what Kwansik has been telling you, but I command no respect."

"Of course you do! You are just being humble. You are over forty years old and you are still a bachelor without a house of your own. This can only mean that you have no worldly ambitions and that you are a man of integrity. Gentle and honest people aren't treated right these days!"

Mr. Ko gave her a cold look and half turned away from her.

When it came time to prepare supper she produced a roll of ten thousand *wŏn* notes from her pocketbook. She dexterously counted out three thousand *wŏn* and handed it to Kwansik.

"You run along and get some good things to eat. Boys aren't too good at such things, I suppose. That's right, you can go along and help him with the purchases," she turned to Kwinam.

"I've never spent so much money. I've never even held that much money in my life," countered the young girl with firm dignity. Mr. Ko had never seen Kwinam react this way. The woman gave the girl a contemptuous look and said nothing. She went into the kitchen herself when Kwansik returned with the groceries. She prepared supper and borrowed all kinds of dishes and bowls from the landlady without even first consulting Mr. Ko. She voraciously attacked the food she had prepared and proved herself quite equal to Kwansik with respect to gluttony. After the woman had left, Mr. Ko reproved Kwansik for his indiscretion in bringing such a woman into the house.

"Don't be a wet blanket, Mr. Ko. It's about time you got married. She's got some thirty or forty million *wŏn* to her name. That's more than enough to get something really big cooking, you know," counseled Kwansik.

"She would make a better match for you than she would for me if that is the case," retorted Mr. Ko sarcastically.

"That's because you don't know her. You don't know what kind of a woman she is. That bitch doesn't trust me at all." Then Kwansik went on to say that from the way she looked at Mr. Ko he judged that she was well satisfied with him. Then he repeatedly recommended that Mr. Ko marry the woman it being an ideal match in every conceivable way. Mr. Ko found some funny aspects in the situation—a young brat recommending an older man to get married and all that. As last he dismissed the boy saying, "You are a funny fellow."

When he finished washing the dishes that evening, Kwansik again extended his hand toward Mr. Ko. He wanted to borrow five hundred *wŏn* for "you-know-what."

"Why don't you get the money from that rich woman? Five hundred *wŏn* is a lot of money for us, you know," said Mr. Ko.

"Money must circulate. You can't make it unless you spend it."

"For the life of me I can't fathom your basic attitude toward life. You're slovenly and dissipated. Especially when Kwinam is around."

"Leave your preaching till I get back. I feel like going to such places all the more because she is around. Only if she would listen to me and reciprocate my feelings toward her," and he tried to put his arm around her waist.

"Don't you dare! I'm no whore!" She shoved him away with both hands. Mr. Ko gave him the money.

"Remind me to pay you back one of these days."

He left the room almost triumphantly while Mr. Ko frowned after him. He frowned not only at lad's reckless attitude but also because he was disappointed in himself.

"That kid doesn't seem to have any moral sense at all," murmured Mr. Ko half to himself. Kwinam countered, "It's alright so far. It's alright as long as he doesn't get to love vice for itself."

"What is alright?"

"I mean it's about time people did away with their habitual hypocrisy."

"Do you mean to say that you condone depravity?"

"Isn't hypocrisy also depravity? Why can't you break through the wall of conformity—you a painter, an artist? Unless we throw away the mask of hypocrisy life can never be anything but a poor melodrama."

Mr. Ko stared at her in surprise, yet he felt refreshed and even elated. It wasn't the paradoxical logic of her remarks that caused this reaction he knew, but he was aware that there was something undefinable, something strong, humane, and touching in what she said.

That night Mr. Ko was unable to concentrate on his drawing. He kept turning to look at Kwinam, who was fast asleep. Kwansik was back from his adventure and snoring in his bed. He drew Kwinam's sleeping face. He drew again and again until he had a satisfactory result. While drawing Mr. Ko realized what a lonely life he was leading. He looked down at the girl's face again. One of her arms lay on top of the quilt and so he fondled her hand. He knew well nothing would ever come of it. He slipped into a fit of loneliness. At last he lowered his head and pressed his lips to her soft mouth. Turning in her sleep she withdrew her hand. "I do this as a father to his own daughter," he murmured to himself. As he was getting into bed he kissed her lips again, and this time she woke up. He was somewhat embarrassed.

"I did that as a father would to his own daughter," he whispered. She merely smiled, closed her eyes, and rolled over to the other side.

From that night on he kissed her whenever she fell asleep before he did, all the while thinking of her as his daughter. Sometimes she awoke, sometimes she didn't. At times she pretended to be sleeping even when she wasn't, but when she did take notice, she invariably smiled and said nothing. Only once did she say. "It's alright with me if this repays you for what I owe you. Nothing is free in this world."

Kwansik increased his exhortations that Mr. Ko marry the cosmetics woman. He insisted that she was more than willing to marry him. It would be good for all concerned, he argued: no more magazine illustrations and drudgery for Mr. Ko; a good and honest husband for her; something on the side for himself as the matchmaker. Mr. Ko said that he did not understand why Kwansik should feel good when other people were getting married.

"Why shouldn't I be happy when I see you marrying into the purple?"

"What are you saying? Seems to me it's more like being hired out as a stallion. I don't want that kind of marriage."

"You are incorrigible! What are any of us but merchandise? As long as we are to be sold, we should make sure we are sold into wealth. Besides, I have a stake in this marriage. I can cook up something big with that woman's money as bait."

"That's why I keep telling you to marry her yourself. Then you can have everything."

"You can't be serious! Don't forget she is a woman who has built up a business all alone. You can't fool her. There are many would-be gigolos who want to marry her, but she says no! right to their faces."

"Why is that? I thought she was out to trap any man."

"Let me tell you why. She can read men's minds like she can the palm of her own hand. She knows those guys are out to get their hands on her dough. I like to think of myself as a guy with special ways with girls, but I'm beginning to think that this woman and Kwinam are somewhat beyond me." Kwansik shook his head slowly.

"If that is the case she wouldn't let you touch her money even if I married her, would she?"

"You just let me worry about that part. When I get all the good-for-nothings out of the way I can work on her as a long-term project."

"Why should a sharp-eyed woman like her prefer a man like me?" asked Mr. Ko dumbly, just to see how the lad would react.

"That's where you are wrong. You are the very type that such women prefer. They don't have to be on guard to start with. Not that such men are actually dumb. They just don't happen to have material ambitions, and they are quite incompetent in practical affairs. They only talk about culture and cultural values and such things. Yes, you are the very type such women prefer."

Mr. Ko said nothing. He was beginning to fear Kwansik. At the same time he detested seeing the values in which he belived ruthlessly cast aside by Kwansik. He merely sat there astounded. Kwansik seemed to have taken Mr. Ko's sudden silence to mean a change of heart.

As soon as the breakfast was over, Kwansik said, "There is no need for second thoughts. I'll go see that woman right away. Better still, I'll bring her over if I can. You just do as I tell you." Saying so, he ran out of the house. Kwinam laughed loudly but Mr. Ko could not even crack a smile. He was surprised at himself for not stopping Kwansik. "Am I secretly hoping to be railroaded into this marriage?" he wondered to himself. He looked at Kwinam and he was embarrassed. Of course, Kwinam could not see the workings of his mind. She was busy memorizing lines for her part in a play that was soon to be produced by a newlyformed group of young actors and actresses. It was unusually warm for winter, but still the gray sky showed through the window. Mr. Ko could not help laughing at himself. Finding a warm spot on the hot floor, he lay down to continue with the newspaper he had been reading. A story with a three-column headline drew his attention.

BEAUTIFUL COSMETICS DEALER SLAIN
Was it love? Was it money?

The story said that a beautiful, unmarried cosmetics dealer in the East Gate market named Pyon Yongju (age thirty-one) was shot to death yesterday morning at about six thirty. The murderer is belived to be a youth called Im. Im had long wanted to marry her but was always rebuffed. Recently Im had borrowed about three million *wŏn* from her to finance a business, neighbors testified. The slain woman had come to Seoul during the January fourth evacuation and had built up a prosperous business in smuggled cosmetics, the paper continued. It also said the culprit was at large, but that his arrest was expected any time, etc., etc. Mr. Ko showed the paper to Kwinam. Since Mr. Ko did not know the name of the woman Kwansik had brought home the other day, he was not certain, but for some reason he thought it might be the same woman. She was far from beautiful, but newspapers are newspapers and sensationalism is of their essence, he thought to himself.

"I have no doubt. It's her. Something tells me it's her," said Kwinam.

She was right. It was nearly lunchtime when Kwansik came in tense and agitated. He said they were going to cremate the body that afternoon.

"Let's go there together, Mr. Ko. You tell them you are her fiancé. Kwinam, you come along too. You must testify to that. Only her distant kin and some friends will be there. I think we can get a good cut of what she left if we play it right," said Kwansik.

"Shut up, you bastard!" shouted Mr. Ko as he resoundingly slapped Kwansik's cheek. It was the first time he had ever struck anybody. While a teacher he had never so much as lifted a finger at a student no matter how angry he was.

"I've got to go see," said Kwansik after awhile. Kwinam got to her feet.

"I'm going too. I like funerals, the best of human rituals. I'm going to enjoy this funeral," she said.

"Go! Go! Go get cremated with the body! And don't come back!" Mr. Ko's voice was a maddened pitch. He could not control his upsurging rage. Kwansik and Kwinam went out. Mr. Ko could not sit still. Possessed by the wrath welling up within him, he arose several times only to sit down again. He felt as though he had been terribly insulted. He went out of the house to simmer down. It was snowing outside.

He walked for awhile against the blowing snow. Soon he could see the Han River below him. Snow was piling up on the frozen surface of the river. Climbing the pathless hillside beside the river, Mr. Ko walked on in the snow.

(end story)

One Way

Sŏnu Hwi

I have no way of knowing Hŏ Myŏng's whereabouts, but something tells me that he's not dead. He can't be dead. I don't know exactly why, but I've never doubted for a moment that he'll turn up one of these days when he's least expected.

I am supposed to leave the country tomorrow with my wife. Being newlywed, I am still in the throes of my honeymoon. And so with a guilty feeling, I have come to this place to spend a few quiet moments to reminisce over the misfortunes of my friend.

He and I were sitting at this very table on that day when I saw him last. Like today, the place wasn't crowded. He had led me into the semidarkness of this bar after running into me on the street outside. Both of us were glad to see each other again, for it was our first meeting in a long while and we had the Korean War behind us and between our meetings. I had been back in Seoul only a week after serving with the Supreme Allied Command for the Far East in Tokyo, where I had worked as a military mapper since the outbreak of the war.

I drank whisky and soda while he drank gin with occasional gulps of cold water as a chaser.

"Of course you weren't aware of it, but I have been well posted about you," he said, "Actually what you were doing in Japan helped me a great deal."

"Helped you? How so?"

"Well, I was working for a joint Korean-American Special Intelligence outfit."

"As a civilian? What about your military service?"

"Got through with that a long time ago."

"When?"

"A year after the outbreak of the war."

"Are you still engaged in intelligence work?"

"No, I quit that three years ago too."

"What do you do for living?"

"You can see for yourself," he said as he showed me the emp-ty palms of his hands. "By the way, are you back for good or just for a visit?" he asked.

"A short visit. First time in five years."

"Living abroad is alright, but try not to forget your home."

"Of course," I said. Then I had to confess the real purpose of my quick visit this time. "In fact, I came back here to pick a wife."

At this he raised his eyebrows and said in a loud voice in English, "That's fine!" With that he emptied his glass and call-ed for another drink. When it came he said, "That calls for a celebration," and the new drink disappeared in one gulp. Then he stared into my eyes and I noticed a strange light shining in the well of his not-yet-so-drunken eyes.

"Why? Does it sound funny to you?" I asked.

"Not at all, not at all," he said, waving his hand.

"By the way, are you married?" I asked.

He took his time answering. He asked for another drink. After awhile he said, "I was." A shadow of pain flashed across his face.

"Was?"

"Yes, she's dead."

"Dead? When was this?"

"It's almost a month now."

"No kids?"

"Kids? Kids did you say?" he said, somewhat evasively.

"Yes, kids. Are there any?" I pursued him rather sharply. An awkward smile came to his lips.

"Wife and a kid, you might say I killed them both myself."

"Killed them yourself? How do you mean?"

"Of course I didn't actually kill them, but the way things worked out, it amounted to the same."

I could say nothing now and I merely watched him in silence.

"She became pregnant when we had been married two years or so," he went on, "and you can imagine how happy and ex-cited I was. But soon her doctor told me that she was in no con-dition to have a baby. Naturally I tried to talk her into not having it. But, as might be expected from a woman from Hamgyong Province—where she was from—she was as obstinate as a bull. Finally we decided to concentrate on building up her health and I put her under the care of a doctor. At any rate, four months passed.

"Then one day I was summoned by the Army Intelligence Bureau. I was asked, when I presented myself to the Bureau, whether I knew a certain young man said to have recently crossed over to the South from North Korea. The name was not familiar. I could not identify the young man when he was called in. His thin figure was ghastly, but he had a pair of strangely fierce eyes. When we exchanged a few words, however, a cold shudder ran down my spine; the young man was a member of the special intelligence unit that I had sent into North Korea about a year before the armistice. I was so shocked to see him that it was all I could do to sit up straight on the chair.

"You know what it means . . . I failed to identify one of my men, with whom I swore to share everything, even death."

"That's because he had changed a lot."

"No, what had changed in the course of those three years was not he but I. I had married and settle down while those men were undergoing hell fire. Mind you, I sent them there."

"Anybody is entitled to get married."

"No, it's different with me. Many of my men lost their lives. Many more of them risked their lives under impossible conditions. They were acting on my orders and I was responsible for them. And what was I doing? Enjoying the comfort and warmth of my marital bed!"

". . ."

"In effect, the same kind of disgraceful attitude on my part resulted in the death of my wife and the baby she was carrying."

One day, a year before the armistice when he was still heading the intelligence outfit, Major Garner, an American advisor to the unit, came into his tent, which overlooked the East Sea, with a young girl. She was wearing army fatigues and blue sneakers. She was incredibly slender but she had shiny ebonyblack eyes. Her black hair, casually falling over her thin shoulders, was richly beautiful.

Major Garner introduced her as Miss Yu Hyeok telling my friend that she was a living witness to the barbarity of the Red

Army.

Two scars were visible on her neck when she removed her blue scarf. Barely missing the artery and the neck bone, the bullet wounds, one in front and another at the back of the neck, were still fresh. The one at the back was larger and uglier than the one on the front.

She had been discovered half dead among the heap of bodies left behind by the Communists in the Hamhung Penitentiary when the American forces moved into that city. Released from the hospital, she had declined the offer of a rich American who wanted to adopt her, saying that she preferred to work for the Korean army. She said that was the best thing she could do under the circumstances—her parents and brothers had all been murdered at the same penitentiary.

Major Garner remarked with a smile, as he left the tent, that she had a fiery temper.

"I have been photographed and taken around a lot as though I am a freak or something," said Miss Yu putting her scarf on again. "Of course, I shouldn't complain, for I have been able to see a lot of places, including Japan and America." Then she added with a smile that she had graduated from a high school in Wonsan.

Thus she settled down with his outfit, working in the dispensary.

"The armistice was signed not long after that. It hit us like a thunderbolt. The Americans were celebrating the occasion with parties . . .," he said.

"Sounds very much like the Americans," I commented.

"But knowing how we felt about it, they did not invite us to their parties."

"It was the same in Tokyo."

"But things started to change. The dispatch of agents to North Korea stopped abruptly one day contrary to our plans. The American Advisory Group didn't seem to care what we did any longer. I got hold of Major Garner and asked him what American intentions were. He was very sympathetic to our position—he was a damned nice fellow—but he suggested that we wait for the decision from headquarters. He said we should at least wait out the ninety-day trial period of the armistice first."

"Yes, I remember the magic ninety-day period myself."

"Finally the idle ninety-day term was over, and another month passed before deactivation orders came through from headquarters. I raised hell and demanded immediate action either that I myself and other agents be dispatched to North Korea or that those agents already in North Korea be brought back. But you know the Americans—they draw a sharp line between personal feelings and duty. One day a one-eyed bird colonel showed up and made it very clear that we were to discontinue our activities."

"Quite businesslike."

"I could do nothing except divide what money we had among our men to send them home, and I also left to appeal through other channels."

"What happened to the girl?" I asked.

"She wouldn't eat anything for several days after the orders to deactivate were issued. She would go down to the beach alone. On the day all were paid off, she came into my tent and started to cry silently." He finished his drink in one gulp and went on with his story. "I offered to take her in. I had an uncle living in Suwŏn and I suggested that she go there."

My friend then went to Taegu and then to Seoul in search of ways and means to support or rescue his agents in North Korea. But the flow of history passed by rapidly and cruelly. Perhaps his was too small an injustice to be noticed and remedied by the huge wheel of history. He, too, became tired and his zeal waned. He passed from tense alertness to indolence by way of self-consolation and oblivion. He took to writing hack columns for papers and magazines. At the same time he became interested in politics and moved among the celebrities. His unusual career impressed them and he mixed among them easily. In time he even began to feel that the armistice wasn't so bad for him after all.

In the meantime he married Yu Hyeok. Both of them were very happy when she became pregnant. The expectation of the birth of a new life was a strange sensation to him, for he was used to only the destruction of life. But his wife seemed to be even happier. He could notice an unusually soft and peaceful look on her face when she was dreamily and absentmindedly staring in space. Naturally the doctor's concern about her condition did not mean much to her.

"After about four months of that, a former agent miraculously made his way back, as I mentioned earlier.''

The man who returned and came over one hundred miles of mountainous paths on foot was Ch'oe Hangi. He had been a young art student when he came to South Korea during the Janurary 4 evacuation (1951). He said he had been dismissed from a fine arts college in P'yŏngyang because he drew abstract paintings.

In fact, he kept on painting in his spare time even after he joined the Special Unit. No one could understand his paintings. He was more concerned with color than with form; he said he translated sounds and music into color. Of course Hŏ Myŏng could not understand his paintings, but he was ready to respect creative talent. Ch'oe claimed that he distinguished the sounds of various musical instruments by colors. The piano, for instance, was red, but it came in different shades and tones according to different players. Tchaikovsky was the easiest to paint, and Mendelssohn's music had the most even color. Jazz music naturally had vivid and strong colors.

Once Hŏ Myŏng suggested to Ch'oe that he give up training as an agent and concentrate on his art studies, but Ch'oe declined on the grounds that no one could teach him anything and there was only one man, a Frenchman, who could understand his paintings. Besides, he said he could exercise, for some reason, his sense of color best among present friends.

That was Ch'oe Hangi, and he made his way back alone to South Korea three years after he had been sent into North Korea.

''Through him it was known that our agents had been hit hard and that they had been nearly wiped out a year after the armistice. As I was listening to his account of the disaster I shuddered in shame. When I pictured them in my mind, struggling against cold, hunger, and death without supplies and communications, I nearly went mad. Three years of self-consolation and indolence weighed me down and now I was burdened with self-reproach and mental anguish. Anyway, the surviving agents gathered together and selected three messengers to return to South Korea. One was to take the coastal route, the second was to try the main route with forged identification papers, and the third was to take the mountain route. Ch'oe was that last man and he was the only one who made it. I brought him home and asked him to stay with us to recuperate.''

One evening after supper, when they were listening to the radio, Ch'oe's face suddenly hardened. Bringing his ear closer to the set, he kept turning the dial back and forth. After a while he raised his head with a disconcerted look. When asked, he said that colors did not register in his mind.

"They don't?"

From the next day on Hŏ Myŏng took the young man along with him and made the round of tea rooms where one could listen to good music. He also called on his friends, where they could listen to the piano or the violin. But nothing helped him. He said his mind was a sheet of blank paper across which black lines flitted. Hŏ had bought Ch'oe a complete set of painting materials but the young man would not touch them. He grew weaker and more despondent every day, and Hŏ Myŏng became more and more concerned and worried about the young man. Actually, it was torture for him to see the young man sitting alone absent-mindedly skipping several meals in a row.

Then one day he said his mind didn't even register those fleeting black lines—it was a completely blank canvas. He left the house one morning and did not come back for several days. He returned to a worried house on a plank—dead. He had hanged himself in Namsan Park.

"That was how he died," Hŏ Myŏng went on with his story. And the blank canvas of his mind must have taken me over, for coming home from his burial my mind was absolutely devoid of any feeling. It was completely blank at first. Then gradually pain began to set in.

"Then I came to realize that I had to cut out the past three years of idleness from my life. It would have been a lot easier to do so if I had been single. My wife and the expected baby stood in the way. I calculated and this was where I had made the mistake."

Hŏ tried to induce his wife not to have the baby. She wanted to know the real reason, but he kept saying that he was concerned about her health.

But she was too intelligent to be fooled. "I am going to have this baby no matter what happens. You don't have to worry," she said to him quietly but with determination. "I know what you are thinking, but what can one do now? How will you get there to begin with? What can you do even if you can get there?

Besides, what will I do without you? Am I not entitled to live like other wives?''

He left the house without a word. He saw nothing as he plodded heavily along the street. He could hear only rifle shots and the roar of big guns on a battlefield he had long forgotten. His mind's eye could picture the desperate scene of his men being hunted, wandering through ravines and gorges with empty stomachs. He recalled the time his outfit first began to operate.

They were supposed to drop a radio operator with the equipment first. With ''We will follow right away'' as a farewell, the airplane with the radioman took off. But the plane came back with the man. The pilot reported that they could not spot the prearranged signal from the ground. The plane tried the following day but the result was the same. They kept trying and on the ninth day they succeeded.

Then there was another impressive operation in which they sent in a large group of agents by sea to a point along the North Korean coast. That had been Major Garner's show. First they had been carried north aboard a naval vessel and later they changed to a landing craft. However, they were ordered to stay far away on the horizon while Major Garner rowed to the shore with an American noncom in a small boat. Nearing the shore the major had put on his flippers and reaching the shore alone, explored the entire area to survey its safety. Only after that had the others been allowed to go ashore.

Now he reproached himself. Major Garner and his men were foreigners and it wasn't even their war, but they were risking their own lives for the safety of our men. You might twist it and say that the major was doing such things for the sake of the effectiveness of the mission rather than for anything else. But still
. . .

Besides, it was even further proof that Hŏ Myŏng should have respected life more, for life was greater than any order or any mission. He should have had constant consideration for the safety of his men. Did they not look up to him for a decision when they were in a spot? He could still remember his men, their eyes filled with complete trust.

''We will follow right away.''

They had left with only those words as a promise. There had

been a solemn communion of logic there. Distance had not mattered. There had only been an exaltation in which they were willing to sacrifice themselves for a common cause. They had sworn to die together.

"We will follow right away."

(Right away!) But three years had passed. Most of them were dead now and those who survived were wandering in the woods among beasts. And what was he doing?

Hŏ Myŏng walked among the crowd with a maddened heart. It was the crowd made up of people he knew so well, and their language was that with which he grew up; but now he felt himself to be an utter stranger among them. He felt as though he was a criminal who had been living abroad for three years.

He felt sorry for his wife; he had made her part of his disgraceful record. But suddenly some unnamable presentiment struck him. Anxiously he hurried back home. His wife wasn't in, but the dinner table was set for one and fried eggs, his favorite dish, were waiting for him.

"Of course I didn't sleep a wink that night, and when I was called the hospital the following morning, the operation was already over. I cried and asked to be forgiven. She merely smiled, a sad kind of smile, and kept fondling my hand. She died the following morning before dawn broke."

He stared blankly at the oppsite wall when he got through with his story. Then he finished his drink in one gulp. I wanted to say something to console him, but I could not find the words. Bringing the glass to my lips, I pretended to be busy drinking and kept my eyes close.

"I am sorry I bothered you with this gloomy story," he said, washing his mouth with a gulp of cold water. Then with affected joviality he said, "First time in five years and we aren't doing well at all. Come on, let's have another drink."

"What exactly are you planning to do?" I asked him in a low tone.

"Well, now that I have sold the house and all, I must go and do what I set out to do."

"Go where?"

"Where? Where my men are, of course. You haven't heard this song, have you? This was what we used to sing in our outfit:

Hear the cries calling us to the north
Where we must gallop among deer.
Hear the roar of tigers in the woods
O Brothers, let us together go forth.

"There is a clear path ahead of me and it would be foolish if I digressed." He was well drunk by now, but in his eyes I saw a determined look that nothing could change. "I must start right away," he went on, "I must make it somehow. I might have to go to Japan first—I might bother you in that case. Or I might go to Hong Kong. I must find a way to get into North Korea at any cost. I am still confident that I can do it. Dont' think I'm doing this as a means of self-abuse. I am looking for a way to live, and going there is the only way to live for me at this point. I will only be a living corpse here. The life and death of my wife doesn't have anything to do with this. This will be my last drinking bout too."

I offered to pick up the tab, but he would not let me. Instead I walked him home to his boarding house.

Coming out of the alley, I looked up at the sign on the street corner. It said in large block letters:

ONE WAY

The moon hung in the middle of the sky and clusters of rain clouds were moving fast across it toward the north.

(end story)

The Uncharted Map

Sŏ Kiwŏn

It was during the summer of last year, when he had absolutely no place to turn to following his discharge, that Hyŏngnam accidentally ran into Sangdŏk, his closest buddy from the army. They had spent a little over a year's time together in the same company. The commander of the company was a man who had made captain in six years. The company commander joined the army immediately after the Liberation in 1945 as an enlisted man.

He loved to give disciplinary talks to his men, and his favorite admonition had to do with the arrangement of individual bedding. "Well, men, when I was an enlisted man, we used to arrange and stack our bedding neat and trim just like laying brand new bricks fresh out of the factory. But look at yours—it's disgraceful!" He always wound up his speech by saying, "Well, this may look like a small thing, but this is the way you mold your characteristics (meaning character), understand?" They say that an upstart usually despises the poor more than an ordinary man does, and true enough, this guy was really trying to make slaves out of enlisted men.

Under the leadership of this man, Corporal Hyŏngnam, an ex-art student, and Corporal Pak Sangdŏk, an ex-law student, became close friends. Somehow they survived the severest battles while the company commander (who used to boast that the enemy bullets evaded him) was killed in action. Their platoon was almost completely wiped out, and the company had to be commanded by a stuttering noncommissioned officer. Sandŏk had been discharged from the army about half a year before Hyŏngnam. When leaving, Sandŏk had said to Hyŏngnam that he should look him up if he should ever be pressed for a place to sleep in Seoul. On a piece of paper he wrote down his address in Seoul and he went so far as to draw the ground plan of the Korean style house, and pointing out with a red grease pencil a small room by the front gate, he said, "You can have this room anytime and as long as you wish." Then he added, "You know, I am a lucky man. This house used to belong to that guy's concubine. My own was bombed and nothing is left. That guy used to hold the title to this house, but now that both he and the concubine are dead, it became mine. Not bad, eh?" It was Sangdŏk's habit to call his own father "That guy." He looked so casual when he spoke these words, which tickled Hyŏngnam so much that he could not help but laugh heartily. Paradoxically, Hyŏngnam sensed the existence of a warm affection between father and son in this apparently disrespectful appellation. And he liked Sangdŏk all the more for that.

By and by Hyŏngnam's time in the army was up. Dressed in a blue uniform issued to discharged enlisted men, he was loaded on a truck with others and driven into Seoul, passing through Ch'ŏngnyangni, and was finally unloaded by the East Gate. The moment he set his feet on the hard pavement, the past three years of his life receded into the foggy background of his memory. It was as though army life had been the content of a story he had heard from his mother when he was a mere toddler. It was hard to remember the army as a piece of reality he had just experienced. He was dizzy and the bustling main street just inside the East Gate looked so foreign to him. First he decided to look up his aunt who was supposed to be living somewhere in the Yŏngdŭngp'o area, but it dawned on him that it was impossible to locate the house with the kind of address he had in his memobook. Then he thought of looking up some of his former classmates, but he knew very well that he couldn't look up any of them in his present condition—not too far from that of a beggar. Of course what Sangdŏk had said was in the back of his mind all along, and somehow he knew that Sangdŏk's would be the place where he would finally wind up, but he was saving this, as it were, as a last resort; he wanted to explore other possibilities before he had to fall back on that. This was why he didn't make a beeline to Sangdŏk's house. Then he ran into him on the street. They embraced each other before shaking hands. Then in a mocking manner Sangdŏk gestured as if to strangle Hyŏngnam, saying, "You SOB, whyn't you come to my place right away? Let's go now! You don't have to tell me, your looks tell me enough about your condition." To this Hyŏngnam answered with a smile, but tears flowed from his eyes.

Sangdŏk's house was much larger than Hyŏngnam had imagined. Although delapidated in many ways, still it was a sturdy-looking wooden house. One of the rooms and the roof over the front gate had been shelled and left unrepaired; this was one of the things that Sangdŏk had overlooked in his explanation of the floor plan. That was not the only unexpected thing, however. Sangdŏk was living with a girl. Sangdŏk introduced her Hyŏngnam as Ch'oe Yunju but he always addressed her as Madam Ch'oe. Then Sangdŏk told Hyŏngnam how he had met her.

One Sunday last winter Sangdŏk had gone out to see a movie. In front of the movie house there stood a girl with a suitcase, blankly watching the signboard. She wasn't exactly tall, but the brown overcoat was very becoming to her svelte body—that was Yunju. Sangdŏk had ventured to invite her to the movie by accosting her: "Will you join me in seeing this movie?" The girl, who had looked rather gloòmy up to that time, beamed happily all of a sudden at the invitation and gave him an emphatic "Yes!" like a school child. She looked to be twenty-one or two, and the elegance of her apparel told him that she was of a good family. Thus, believing that she was too good a find to lose, Sangdŏk had invited her to his house after the movie. But this time she made no answers. She just kept biting her lower lip.

"I know I am rude, but I cannot help asking you."

"No, no, it's not that. If the invitation is for me to live with you for good, I might consider . . ." she said and blushed. By nature Sangdŏk was not a man to be easily startled, but at this he had to gasp for breath.

She had been driven out of her home, she told him. She was going down to Pusan to look up one of her friends, but on the way to the railroad station she was attracted to the French movie, and she was having a debate with her pocketbook about whether she had enough money to spare when she was invited in by Sangdŏk. She also told him that she was not too keen on the idea of visiting this friend in Pusan.

"Well, I am an orphan myself and I have no relatives to speak of. This house is all I have in the world, and the job I have now is not a steady one and doesn't pay much. But if you think you can put up with this kind of life, I don't see why we can't live together,'' Sangdŏk had said, and this was how he and Yunju had gotten together. Although Sangdŏk had not asked why she had been driven out of her home, he said he guessed that it was a love affair. Then he added, with self-scorning laughter, ''I wouldn't be surprised if she was kicked out by a man after living with him for a few months. These broads are all like that, aren't they?''

But Hyŏngnam could not despise Yunju. He had always hated this kind of illicit union, but somehow he could not picture her as one of those illicit partners. Maybe the first impression she made on him had something to do with it. Whenever she was spoken to, she looked at you fully, her big, round, long-lashed eyes wide open, and those eye looked so clear and innocent that somehow you were made to face your own squalor. He liked her, but he never forgot to treat her as a lady and the wife of a friend.

Of course other things occupied his mind too. Whatever meagre income Sangdŏk had from his three-days-a-week teaching job at an unaccredited middle school was by no means enough to support this family. So Hyŏngnam felt that he had to earn his own bread at least, but with his background as a sometime art student it was almost impossible to land a decent job. After two months of heartbreaking search he thought he was lucky when a movie house gave him a job drawing signboards. It wasn't the large one you see in front of a movie house that he was supposed to draw, but the small poster-size one you come across around th corner of main streets; he was to draw eight of them a month, four different scenes at the price of five thousand *won* each.

So the living-room of the house became his workshop. A large canvas now leaned against the wall: a cowboy was kissing a blonde girl against the background of green meadows; on the floor by the foot of the canvas were several palettes made of plywood, and on them were some paint brushes and paint of various colors, which sometimes dripped onto the floor. Now Hyŏngnam was dissatisfied with the fingers of the blonde girl that rested on the shoulder of the cowboy. So he picked up a fine brush and soaked it in paint. Then he recalled what the manager of the movie house told him over and over: ''The secret of movie signboard drawing is to make it as sexy as you can, understand!'' While he was working, Yunju sat around, closing and opening the windows to control the heat and gas from the open charcoal burner.

On the days he didn't teach Sangdŏk didn't get up till almost noon, and then it was his routine to have lunch and go out to a go house downtown to play go games. Hyŏngnam's work kept him at home all the time, and thus he spent more time than Sangdŏk with Yunju. He didn't think it particularly pleasant, nor was it especially burdensome to him psychologically. He wasn't exactly a sociable type and was a very bad conversationalist. Besides, he treated her as the wife of a friend and tried to draw a strict line there. When he had first been introduced to her, he addressed her as Mrs—. She had burst out laughing, and Sangdŏk had said, "What the hell do you mean by that? Our relationship is nothing of the sort. Call her Miss Ch'oe." From then on he had avoided the use of direct address, and somehow he managed to carry on a conversation without having to refer to her directly.

After awhile the bulk of their living expenses was earned by Hyŏngnam's drawings, but it made Hyŏngnam feel good because he felt that it was a chance to pay back his indebtedness for Sangdŏk's friendship and hospitality. Sangdŏk's offhand manner about this pleased Hyŏngnam, too; Sangdŏk was not the kind of man who would worry over a little monetary help from a friend and feel indebted to him. And especially he liked the way Yunju took in the whole arrangement; she never took a shallow, adulating posture toward him because of the new financial arrangement. He was grateful to them for this, and he thought he should be discreet all the more not to convey patronizing attitude toward them.

As ill luck would have it, Sangdŏk lost his job; the school where he taught was closed down. He was only a part-time teacher working for three hundred *won* an hour, and it wasn't a steady position to begin with, but the incident must have been a hard blow to Sangdŏk, for he repeated angrily over and over that he would never become a lousy school teacher again.

The new school year had already started and it was too late to look for another teaching position, but Sangdŏk seemed to have no intention of looking for a job. In other words, Hyŏngnam became the sole bread winner of the house. The situation was a very delicate one, and one bad move on Hyŏngnam's part could have aroused misunderstandings and troubles between the friends. So he said by way of encouraging his friend, "Well, take a good long rest first. Never look for a job in a hurry, they say. A good one will turn up all by itself in a little while." And the go games became Sangdŏk's only occupation. Otherwise, he just wasted his time. He bought a book entitled *The Outline of Go*, but after skimming a few pages he threw it in the closet never to open it again. That evening, too, he came home late.

He pushed open the front gate singing some degenerate beggar's tune in an obviously drunken falsetto. Then Hyŏngnam recalled that when they were in the army and Sangdŏk got drunk he used to sing out the melodies of symphonies or concertos at the top of his voice. What a change!

"Madam Ch'oe, can I have some water to wash my hands? You know that SOB bugged me by first telling me to take black stones and then to have a two-stone head start. So I was upset and lost four straight games!" he said, and holding up his open palms for Hyŏngnam and Yunju to see he added, "Look at my hands. They are really dirty." According to his theory the hands of the guy that held the black stones in, got dirtier than those of the one who held the white stones. Of course he seldom came home with his hands clean. Sangdŏk's excuse was that he liked to play the game with people who played better than he did— ("That's the only way you can get better in this game.")

Anyway Sangdŏk was very drunk that day. Lying on the floor of the bedroom, he bellowed:

"Thanks to 'that guy' I have a roof over my head, but what good is a house with holes all over? Hey, Hyŏngnam, how about selling this off to have a rousing good time for a few days? How's that idea grab you, eh?"

Hyŏngnam was used to Sangdŏk's drunkenness from the army days, so he didnt' take him seriously, but merely answered with a grin. But somehow he felt that Sangdŏk was implying something, and it discomforted him. Again controlling himself, he tried to shrug it off by saying, "Lay off, man, Miss Ch'oe is laughing at you." And then giving a playful eye to Yunju for a moment, he tried to calm him down as he would humor a fretful child. Yunju's eyes were smiling but not her mouth, and she gave a long gaze at Sangdŏk first, then looked away and faced the wall. In her cold profile Hyŏngnam could definitely sense a feeling of contempt for Sangdŏk. And this in turn, for some unaccountable reason, gave Hyŏngnam a vague feeling akin to hope. It was a pleasing feeling, which embarrassing, if it had been known to others. But it passed away quickly because Sangdŏk bellowed again.

"Hey, Hyŏngnam, I know you waste money too. I know you shacked up last night in an unmentionable place after a few shots of cheap hooch. You know it isn't good for your health, and besides, how are you going to make your four hundred thousands that way?"

So Hyŏngnam had to play along as usual. "Okay. As soon as I make my pile I'll get the hell out of this place, don't worry. Wait till I make my first one hundred thousand. Then I'll build me a cardboard frame house."

"If you want to get out, get out! Dont' think I'll starve if you do. You think I'd care if you built a palace? Ha, ha, ha," said Sangdŏk, his eyes glaring as though he were very angry, but his laughter showed that he was only pretending. Hyŏngnam laughted out loud too. The hearty laugh made them both feel good and dispelled all possibilities of vexed feelings. Hyŏngnam knew well that he shouldn't plume himself on the fact that he was supporting the family for the time being.

But the strange feeling persisted. He could now definitely tell that Yunju was backing away from Sangdŏk; moreover, it was obvious that she was making a creeping approach to Hyŏngnam.

One objective evidence for this was that, without knowing when it began, he started addressing her as Miss Ch'oe and it came very natural to him. Of course, he still hesitated sometimes, but it wasn't because he lacked the self-confidence of addressing her in this fashion. But rather, in an occasional unguarded moment when he unwittingly faced her glossy, faintly bloodshot, and in a way very sexy eyes, he was forced to imagine her in bed with Sangdŏk the night before, and then he lost his voice.

It was true that Hyŏngnam had resumed going to whore houses lately, but to blame it all on Yunju was ridiculous. While in the army he and Sangdŏk used to visit one of those crummy frontline bawdy houses about once a month for the purpose of what they called "excretion." Therefore, there couldn't be anything new in this now, but for some reason Hyŏngnam liked to think that his desire was provoked by Yunju. Sangdŏk did not

visit those places any longer; he had no need for them. He envied Sangdŏk in this respect. He thought Sangdŏk was right in
pointing out that his visiting of whore houses was the result of
the bravado gathered on the strength of cheap hooch. By now
he was thoroughly disgusted with himself, with the whoring, with
the mechanical bodily movement, and with the empty feeling he
experienced on the way home from one of those places. On these
nights, not being able to sleep, he felt a strong urge to abuse
himself, which ended with a dragging down of color reproductions of European masters from the bookshelf.

It was almost an unbearable pain to see the works of Braque
or Rouault. Though he did not wish to see them, his hand mercilessly turned over the leaves of the book to see the bright color
reproductions of the masters. What happened to his ambition
as a student in the College of Fine Arts, and his desire to create,
and all those intoxicatingly beautiful images? What filled his mind
now were the shrill sounds of mortar shell explosions, the shrieking
of dying soldiers, the naked bodies of women, tawdry and loud
movie poster drawings in primary colors—all these intermingled chaotically and tortured him. He now opened the Klee collection. "The Sun and the Moon." The delicate white hands
of the moon were turned the other way, while the setting sun
was trying to help the moon rise higher and higher.

"In bed already?" a man's voice was heard outside the room.
Startled, Hyŏngnam pushed the book to the corner of the room,
closing it hurriedly. The sliding door opened, and in the dark
frame of the opening Sangdŏk's grinning face appeared. Over
his stocky shoulder Hyŏngnam could see the frail crescent looking like a lone fish swimming in a dark blue acquarium.

Giving a quick glance at the book in the corner, Sangdŏk said,
"I see what you are up against. Listen! Why don't you sleep
with Madam Ch'oe? Just once a week will solve your problem.
That's just about the right frequency for your health. I am more
or less tired of her, but just to keep you company I'll pick Satur-
day nights. You settle on Sunday nights, all right? And quit going to whore houses. Those places aren't healthy."

So it was a proposal for joint ownership of Yunju.

"What the hell you talking about?" protested Hyŏngnam,
embarrassed and upset.

"Don't tell me you have already forgotten that we took turns with one girl in Ch'unch'ŏn! Nothing to get upset about." "Miss Ch'oe is different from those girls!" "Girls are girls, what's the difference? She is nothing to me. I'm not going to live with her all my life. I thought I was doing you a favor by this offer."

In a way it made sense, Hyŏngnam thought. Still, he knew he should turn down the offer resolutely. But instead, in spite of himself the words he actually uttered after a few moments were, "But would Miss Ch'oe agree to it?"

"You are too naive and you overrate her. Just do as I tell you. She is not in a position to refuse you, and I know that all women have nothing but the instinct to love."

For some reason Sangdŏk was quite eager to talk him into accepting the offer. "Maybe Sangdŏk is right, I may be a sentimental bastard overrating Yunju," thought Hyŏngnam. But as the image of Yunju's face loomed large in his mind, he began to pant. "Would she accept me? Of course she would refuse! She would even angrily strike my cheeks! It would be a terrific scene though. For it would disprove Sangdŏk's theory! But then she might accept me. What then?" His head became foggy with all sorts of delusions. But at the same time he was conscious of a vague but passionate desire writhing like a beast within him.

At last it was the first Sunday night after the incident. It passed midnight, but Sangdŏk was not home yet. Recently, Sangdŏk often stayed out all night playing go. But tonight it seemed to Hyŏngnam that Sangdŏk was living up to his offer. And Hyŏngnam knew well that he would go into her bedroom sooner or later. So he walked over and went into the room, opening the sliding door noiselessly.

She was sound asleep. He could smell her body odor, and it seemed like that of a woman with whom he had slept all his life. He turned on the light. She made a faint and sleepy smile for a moment, and while he was still standing there rigidly with his hands in his pockets, she exclaimed, "Get out!" Then after a pause she added, "You might try to use force. But then I know you are not the type." She looked so pale, and Hyŏngnam was conscious that his body temperature was dropping. A chill ran down his spine. He was so happy to face her refusal; it was almost an intoxicating kind of happiness. It took a tremendous effort on his part to keep himself from crying out "I love you, Miss Ch'oe! I love you all the more for that!"

"I knew you would say that," he said instead.

"Why did you come in then?"

He kept silent.

"Anyway I'll have to discuss this with him (Sangdŏk). I thought you two were friends, but I don't know now. Anyway I think I have the right to confess this to him. Now get out!" Her voice was hoarse like an old woman's.

Looking straight into her eyes, he backed out slowly, turning off the light on his way out. And he said to himself over and over, "Hey, Sangdŏk, I won! You lost!"

Sangdŏk's theory was wrong, and his own sentiment was vindicated. But he could not help that this feeling of triumph was adding fuel to his burning desire for Yunju.

The next morning, Sangdŏk came early, and his expression did not hide his curiosity about the outcome of the night before. Yunju asked him into her room right away, and Hyŏngnam knew what she was up to. After a while Sangdŏk's hoarse voice said, "Hey, Hyŏngnam, come in here a moment."

He went into the room, but he found an unexpected scene there. Sangdŏk looked very angry at Yunju, while she was entreating him with her eyes.

"Now listen, Madam Ch'oe," he was harshly saying to Yunju, "Hyŏngnam is the only friend I have. You might say we are one person. If you humiliate him, it's the same as humiliating me. If you could understand this, I don't think you could stick to an old-fashioned notion and refuse him." As he went on like this Yunju looked down to hide her face. Sangdŏk was angrily glaring at Yunju. But in his cruel eyes, Hyŏngnam could easily detect Sangdŏk's triumph. It was clear that Sangdŏk was feeling satisfaction and superiority in the fact that Yunju had refused Hyŏngnam and moreover in the fact that she lost no time in discussing with him. Hyŏngnam wanted to cry out "You bastard! You made that offer knowing all along that it would turn out like this just to humiliate me!" But he knew that to say it out loud in front of Yunju would be wrong. So instead he said, "All right, it was my mistake. Let's drop this subject." He could see now that behind the guise of Sangdŏk's large-hearted laughter and bravado there was the real Sangdŏk, infinitely puny and petty. He thought he could pity Sangdŏk for that. Sangdŏk was now threatening to throw Yunju out of the house if she intended to keep on refusing Hyŏngnam. Yunju said nothing.

"O Kay, Sangdŏk, that's enough. I was in the wrong, and I admit it. Let's forget it," said Hyŏngnam. He thought that by now Yunju might be disgusted with Sangdŏk, and for some reason he liked to think that both he and Yunju had been victimized by Sangdŏk, and that they were now forming, through a tacit understanding, a joint front against him.

Ever since this incident Hyŏngnam patiently waited for possible changes in Yunju's attitude. But nothing really happened, and she was the same as ever. It might be that in her mind the humiliation she received from Sangdŏk had been offset by what she inflicted upon Hyŏngnam, thereby achieving a certain emotional balance within herself. Besides, she might have reasoned that if she was not in the position to leave the house at once, she would gain nothing by displaying her discomfort. And Hyŏngnam became sympathetic and drawn toward her all the more for that. To him it was a feat that not all women could perform. He concluded that it was not so much a cold-hearted calculation as a natural intelligence that was at the root of her attitude.

Sangdŏk became lazier than ever before. Every morning he got up around noon. This particular morning, too, he came out of his room around noontime with a swollen face from oversleeping, scratching his mushy hair. Yunju set up the wash basin filled with hot water for him. Of course it was part of the routine, but for some reason her service for Sangdŏk got on Hyŏngnam's nerves this morning. And the way Sangdŏk washed his face and pimpled neck, splashing water all over the place, his overbearing attitude as though he were naturally entitled to being waited on by Yunju, was disgusting to Hyŏngnam. To him Sangdŏk's behavior seemed to say triumphantly "Now remember, Yunju is mine." To him, Sangdŏk looked very puny and petty. At these moments Sangdŏk seemed to have completely forgotten that he had to borrow pocket money about twice a week. Sometimes, when he saw Sangdŏk going out to the go club with nothing but a pack of cigarettes saying, "I practically live there, and they don't charge me anything any longer. Surely, I have contributed enough money to buy a house," it only seemed to him that Sangdŏk was putting up a bold front. Thus Sangdŏk disgusted him, but at the same time he looked pitiful to him.

A few days later Hyŏngnam drew his monthly pay. Setting aside ten thousand *won* for pigments and other material, he gave the rest to Sangdŏk to use for the house. By so doing he thought he was giving Sangdŏk a chance to manage his pocket money without begging every time.

"What's the idea of giving me the money?" said Sangdŏk, eyeing the bundle with displeasure. Up to that time, the routine had been that whenever Yunju needed money to buy rice, fuel, and other commodities, she asked Sangdŏk for money, and Sangdŏk in his turn asked Hyŏngnam. "You can give it to Madam Ch'oe, can't you?" he added.

"Yeah, but what's difference? Maybe you have misunderstood me."

"There's nothing to misunderstand. We all know that you earned the money. Then why go through me? It's unnatural," Sangdŏk said. Then he added, "Besides, it's the wrong way. Madam Ch'oe is not my wife, and I've told you so many times. So from now on you can give her the money yourself."

To this Hyŏngnam had many objections, but he merely said, "Alright, let it be so." He could hate Sangdŏk for that, but more than anything else the whole situation was very saddening. Why did he have to support them breaking his back drawing movie posters? In order to repay his former debt? All right, he could stretch a point and gladly work for them. But he was in no way obliged to live under this kind of strained feelings. Was it his love for Yunju that bound him to this house? He could find no ready answers. He handed the money to Yunju as Sangdŏk had told him, saying, "Please try to get by this month with this. Sangdŏk's pocket money has to come out of it, too."

She dropped her eyes to the old newspaper that wrapped the money. It was the social news section with some sensational headlines. "I thought I would give it to Sangdŏk, but I just now thought to give it to you. I think it will make no difference," he added.

"I know why you are giving it to me. By giving it to me you are trying to imply that it's not for nothing you have supported us thus far, isn't it?" She said, enunciating each word very articulately.

"Miss Ch'oe! What are you saying?"

"You want to buy me with this money, don't you? With one

third of this money at least." She now looked up and met his eyes squarely.

"You mustn't think so badly of yourself! Miss Ch'oe, you've completely misunderstood me."

"It may be too dear a bargain for you, but then it may be too cheap a one (At this point Hyŏngnam tried to interrupt her, but she kept on). Believe me, I have no illusion about what I am. All right, the contract is done! I'll take the money. I don't know if the price is too dear or too cheap. I am not in a position to haggle, am I?" Saying so she made an effort to laugh with twitching lips.

"Ch'oe, I am in love with you! Don't you know that?"

She kept silent.

"I meant to tell you that for a long time."

"Nobody ever loved me. Nor does anyone now."

"But I do!"

"Forget it. The only place love exists is in the movies. You saw the humiliating scene I had to go through because I once foolishly believed that Sangdŏk loved and cared for me."

"I don't see why a young girl like you talks like an old woman!"

"You love me? Ha, ha, you make me laugh. But if you insist, let it be. I can't stop you from insisting. Anyway, I'll take the money and agree to accept your demands."

"Does this mean that you still love Sangdŏk?"

"My, you are the jealous type, aren't you? Well, I love neither of you." Then she laughed hysterically.

"I see," groaned Hyŏngnam, his face flushed. He was outraged; she had not only mercilessly rejected his confession of love but also countered him with derisive laughter. He felt a strong urge to give her a good beating, but he controlled himself.

"The bargain is done. All right! That will make things simple enough from now on. Everything on a cash basis. Well, well, I'd better be careful with my calculation." She kept saying such things as her mouth twitched.

Hyŏngnam waited for Sangdŏk to spend the night out. Waited for was not the right expression; rather, he vigilantly watched for the opportunity to prey upon her. It was no longer so much his desire for Yunju as the wish to prove his manhood by trampling on her. It became an obsession with him and he felt that unless he violated her he would be pinned on a dangerous pinnacle forever.

On the other hand there was a tiny voice in a corner of his mind that said it did not believe what she had said about cash dealing and so forth. The voice reasoned that Yunju was trying to draw Hyŏngnam into this bargain herself, and by taking advantage of Hyŏngnam, she was trying to get back at Sangdŏk, whom she had loved. It could mean two birds with one stone for her, for by sharing the bed with two men, two close friends at that, she could have two revenges at the same time. For Sangdŏk it was for the wronged love, and for Hyŏngnam for money. According to this reasoning it was evident that Hyŏngnam would be the one who would get the worst of the deal. What should he do then? His mind swayed; should he treat her with absolute indifference under the guise of a gentleman? But at that moment Yunju's long, thin lips flashed in his mind's eye, and her sharp derisive remarks that she might be too dear for that kind of money rang in his ears, and he was instantly back on the dangerous pinnacle, where he felt he had no way out unless he conquered her. Now he felt that violating her was the only action left to him if he wanted to live his life with any sincerity.

But at the same time he had to smile grimly and bitterly, for he had to admit that all this reasoning and patchwork of logic was nothing compared with the simple desire to sleep with Yunju.

The chance arrived unexpectedly soon. But his resolution to treat her as an ordinary whore receded the moment he embraced her body. "I'm not buying you! I love you!" he muttered pantingly. She was emotionally inert. He eagerly hoped that in time she would respond with erotic excitement. But it was like self-abuse against a dummy. It was a humiliation that he had no way of revenging it.

A few days passed, and it was a nippy spring afternoon. Sangdŏk had gone out to the go club. Hyŏngnam, who had been reading the synopsis of a movie in his room, felt hungry. He knew Yunju was taking a nap in her room. For a moment he thought about waking her up and telling her to get lunch, but since he had never done that before he hesitated. But the little devil inside him was saying, "Wake her up and order her. You have the right to do so."

He came out of his room and stretched. The paper lattice

window of Yunju's room was full of sunshine. Then he began
to mentally draw her naked body as he had seen it a few nights
before. The little devil inside him urged him to go ahead. He
walked over to her room and opened the sliding door noisily saying, "Miss Ch'oe, I want you to give me my lunch."

Yunju, who had been asleep with her arms outstretched, asked
with her eyes what he was up to, but around her mouth there
was a scornful smile. "My, you are a bold one, aren't you? Order-
ing me around. It's not like you at all," she said coldly.
Hyŏngnam knew that now was the time to be firm.

"That was out of force of habit. From now on I am going
to be different. I intend to act manly," he said.

"Manly? You've bought my body, but please don't act like
an old-fashioned husband. It would have been different if you
had come right out and said, 'You take my orders because I'm
supporting you!'"

Hyŏngnam could not help feeling some powerful emotion
akin to the admiration that one felt in the presence of a noble
lady who had all the right in the world to be proud. Was it the
downy hair around her ears that made him unable to hate her?
But he should not give in now, he thought. Be firm.

"You think I'm treating you as a wife? No. I give you orders
because I'm the breadwinner of this house, as you say."

"Is that so? Now you are talking," she said. Then after a
pause she added, "But something tells me that you are just putting all this on. However, even if you were right, let's draw a
line in this business. I'm a woman and I'll put up with doing
housework, but don't try to browbeat me into doing anything.
I think sleeping with you for a few hours at night is enough for
the kind of money you spend for me. Don't you agree?" To this
Hyŏngnam could make no retort. His face was flushed, and the
more he tried to hide that from Yunju the redder it got, until
even his facial muscles got distorted. He had to turn around and
leave the room.

It became apparent to Hyŏngnam that this time Yunju had
not told Sangdŏk of what had happened a few nights before when
Sangdŏk spent the night out. So he himself confessed to Sangdŏk.
But unexpectedly Sangdŏk did not show any dismay. On the contrary he looked very happy to hear about it and seemed to be
truly congratulating his friend. And it was all very confusing to

Hyŏngnam. He could not figure out what sort of life they were leading in that house. Of course one thing he could be sure was that he was not gaining anything from that life.

But why couldn't he make a clean break of it? Was it Yunju's attraction? That couldn't be all it was. He admitted that it was partly Yunju that made him unable to leave; but he was also aware that he was drawn to Sangdŏk in a strange way in spite of all the shortcomings of his personality. Might be that he was simply drawn by the strange power of that sordid and grotesque life. If one could be allowed to coin a phrase, "a dismal contentment" would aptly express his feeling toward the life he led there. This might be the result of the mixed feelings that he had lately toward Yunju; he felt compassion for her, and she had become less and less talkative lately; but at the same time he derived pleasure from watching her cower and act as if she had rancor against something. What did this change in her behavior mean? Was she bearing a grudge against Sangdŏk because he had not shown jealousy toward Hyŏngnam? Hyŏngnam did not want to believe this, for that would mean that Yunju still cared for Sangdŏk. Then what? Was she experiencing despair? Was she just another young woman though she spoke and acted like an out-and-out realist who had no room for sentimentality? Hyŏngnam then felt a strong compassion for her. He wanted to rescue her from this inhuman condition. Then he wondered why he hadn't thought of it before. If he could get her a job, that would settle everything, and that was easy enough. In the back of this idea, and therefore in the back of his mind, however, there was a happy and warm scene somewhere in a tiny but sweetly adorned room where he and Yunju were having supper together. And he knew it was impossible to be realized, and if it was impossible, there was no other way but to keep on living this way.

Spring was short-lived as usual. With the coming of summer the number of colorful parasols on the street increased. One day Yunju came to where Hyŏngnam and Sangdŏk sat together talking and asked them to refrain from making nightly visits to her room. "I'm not faking sickness or anything, because I'm well aware that by receiving you gentlemen, who take turns with such precision, I remain on your pay roll." Then after glancing at the two men, who sat rather embarrassedly, she gave out a low giggle.

Hyŏngnam thought that she might be pregnant. It was her habit to notify them when she had monthly courses, but this time something in the way she said those words told him that it was different. Sangdŏk asked her if she was pregnant.

"No, but what if I were?"

"Well, I never thought of the possibility, but if you were, that would be something," said Sangdŏk. Then after looking at Hyŏngnam, who sat very rigidly, he said in a mocking tone as if to turn the whole thing into ridicule, "Let's have a family meeting, and I trust you all will let me have the honor of presiding." At this point Hyŏngnam shouted. "Stop it, stop it!" but Sangdŏk went on. "The first item on the agenda is the right of succession to this family; that is to say whether or not to recognize the infant to which our Madam Ch'oe is going to give birth as the rightful heir to this house." His tone was completely theatrical by now.

"Stop it! This is a serious matter. You know damn well we cannot afford to have a baby under these circumstances," said Hyŏngnam.

"Is it a motion? All right, there has been a proposal that we need no heirs in this house," Sangdŏk went on in his mocking tone. Suddenly Yunju stood up. She glared fiercely at Sangdŏk for a while, then turned around and began to cry, covering her eyes with her hands

"What's the matter? Is our Madam Ch'oe crying?" said Sangdŏk still in his mocking tone.

Hyŏngnam had never hated Sangdŏk more than at this moment. He said, "Stop crying, Miss Ch'oe. You'd better leave the house before anything serious such as conceiving a child really happens. Leave the house. Why can't you do it? Go to a whore house, that would be infinitely better than this place. What attraction does this place have for you? Leave this house and start living like a human being!"

"I know. I know that well enough, and don't preach to me!" she kept on crying. But her tears seemed neither those of sorrow nor those of rancor. It was a self-cleansing kind of crying in which she was purging whatever impure elements she had within her.

"Don't you see it now? Don't you understand it now?" repeated Hyŏngnam, but he knew he was saying this more to himself than to Yunju. She left the room and went into the kitchen. It sounded like she was going to prepare supper.

Hyŏngnam and Sangdŏk sat mutely together smoking cigarettes. After a while Yunju came back into the room and said, "I'd better be honest with you. That's right, I'm pregnant. There's a baby in here," and she pointed a finger at her lower belly. "What!" the two men cried out at the same time. Then Sangdŏk got up and, pretending to punch her belly, said, "Where? In there? My baby is in there?" He said that in an excited tone, and his face lit up with a broad beaming smile.

"Who said it was your baby?" said Yunju, and at that moment, Sangdŏk's face turned white and his facial muscles began to twitch,

"How do you know it isn't mine?"

"It's not yours, nor anyone else's."

"Then whose?"

"Mine!"

"Don't be foolish! Who's the father?" persisted Sangdŏk.

"You've often seen a child walking between his parents holding their hands in each of his, haven't you? Well, if you two gentlemen hold the child's hands from both sides, what am I supposed to do? I can't very well hold its foot, can I?"

"You think I am not man enough to have a baby, is that it?"

"I didn't say that."

"Then what do you mean?"

"Don't you see?"

At this moment Hyŏngnam, who had been sitting mutely, broke in, "What's the use of arguing now? Let's figure out a way to solve the problem."

"Solve the problem your eyes! We will have the baby!" said Sangdŏk in a fierce tone.

"What?" shouted Hyŏngnam.

"We will see who it takes after, you or me?"

But no sooner had he said this than Yunju sharply broke in. "What right do you two have in this? You have no right to tell me whether to give birth or not to, understand!"

"Suit yourself," said Sangdŏk, "but even if you had your own way, the result would be the same; I know you will have the baby."

"What is this? Are you trying to have a say in this?" said Yunju and laughed out loud.

"Wait a minute. Sangdŏk," said Hyŏngnam, "You don't know what you are saying. What will Miss Ch'oe do with a baby?"

Then she turned on Hyŏngnam and said. "And you, you sound like you have the money to take me to an abortion doctor," and she doubled up with laughter.

"What do you intend to do then?" asked Hyŏngnam.

"I'll have the baby." she said proudly.

"You are mad." groaned Hyŏngnam.

Just then, Sangdŏk said, with his fists clenched, "The baby will look just like me, ha, ha, ha."

"Both of you are mad, stark raving mad!" said Hyŏngnam.

Because of the setting sun the roof tiles of the house in front were giving off a deep indigo glare. "I am going to leave this house," said Yunju after a pause; "The baby does not wriggle yet, but I feel it, and the feeling is a rich, replete one. I have made up my mind; I cannot let this baby become your toy also. Sangdŏk, it's too early for you to be glad, because I am not doing this to please you. You have no right whatsoever over this baby." She said this slowly, articulating each word carefully. How could she go out and give birth to a child without even knowing who the father was, thought Hyŏngnam. And he felt an urge to scream at Yunju to think it over, but she went on calmly: "The baby is mine. Of course I know one of you is the father, but I have no way of knowing which one, so it only amounts to saying that neither of you is the one. The only sure thing is that I will have the say-so in this." In her tone there was something like an obsession that went beyond all sense and logic.

"You mean you are leaving right away?" said Sangdŏk menacingly.

"Why not?" countered Yunju.

"Think it over, Miss Ch'oe. Be discreet," said Hyŏngnam. Yunju got up with a bored look and went into her room, arranging her loose hair.

"It's getting dark, you know!" shouted Sangdŏk behind her back. But she did not answer. And her silence made Hyŏngnam realize how painful he would feel when she had left the house for good. For some reason he had been optimistic that everything would come out all right in the end, but now it seemed that a catastrophe was imminent and all his hopes were shattered to pieces. All kinds of confused thoughts rushed to his head: "She's a fool. What does she want? She wants to have a baby? All right, let her have one in the house. I can father the child. In fact, it may very well be mine. At least I love Yunju more than Sangdŏk does."

The light went on. Yunju came out of her room wearing a white blouse and a blue flared skirt. She was carrying a suitcase.

"I thought I would give you supper before leaving, but now that you are hurrying me out. . ." she said in a mock angry tone. Putting on her shoes, she gave a curtsy, lifting the flare of her skirt just a little as a ballerina would in answer to an encore applause. Then she turned around to go.

"What are you going to do with a fatherless child?" said Sangdŏk with a distorted face.

"That's none of your business," said Yunju sharply, turning around.

"Listen, Miss Ch'oe" Hyŏngnam broke in.

"Don't try to stop me. If I could be sure who the father was, I might have followed your advice. But you know how it is, neither of you is the father. Good-bye, gentlemen!" She turned around and started walking toward the gate. Her speech and action up to that moment was so perfect that Hyŏngnam had no time to interrupt. Her last line, good-bye, gentlemen, hit him hard, giving him a hot lump in his throat.

"I don't care any more," said Sangdŏk, and to Hyŏngnam it sounded like the groan of a wounded beast. There was the sound of the front gate, opening and shutting.

"Miss Ch'oe, Miss Ch'oe!" Hyŏngnam rushed after her without even putting on his shoes.

(end stroy)

The Last Parting

Pak Yŏngjun

Yŏngi looked at her watch. She was sitting in a tea room across the street from the station. The train would be departing in exactly twenty minutes. She repeated what she had already done several times—she mentally apportioned time to the various things she was going to do before the train left. Two minutes to walk to the station; two minutes to purchase a platform ticket and walk down the ramp; and three minutes to seek out Sangu among the crowd—a total of seven minutes would be enough, she calculated. That meant she still had thirteen minutes to kill in the tea room. She ordered another cup of coffee.

Her mind was full of misgivings about how tense she would be at the end of thirteen minutes. When the second cup of coffee arrived she let it sit, for she knew that the wait would be even more unbearable if she drank it too soon. She felt the cup and the coffee was just right for drinking, but she did not pick it up. Instead, she looked through the window at the big round clock atop the station tower. Twelve minutes to go.

Then she thought of Sangu, who would be impatiently waiting for her to show up. They had agreed to meet half an hour before departure time, so by now he would be thinking all sorts of wild things. He was probably accusing her of fickleness and inconstancy. He was probably in a state of extreme nervousness—a state of mind directly resulting from her not showing up to take part in what he had, melodramatically, called the "Last Parting."

The term forced a smile to her lips. She loathed it. Every moment, after all, is a beginning as well as an end. Sangu had found a job in Pusan and he wanted to go. "Alright, go ahead then, why torment yourself and everybody else with an end—with a parting?"

However, because Sangu was prone to the melodramatic, the parting, she thought, would be handled dramatically. So she was preparing for the last parting in a tea room less than two minutes from the station, in spite of the fact that she knew well that Sangu would be frantically looking for her among the crowd on the platform. The final scene must be short. Nothing is more boring than a prolonged parting. She now wished she could arrange everything so precisely that she would barely have time to say goodbye with a wave of her hand. She would spot Sangu in one of the carriages, say good-bye to him, and jump off the train as it pulled out. Yes, that would be melodramatic enough for him, she thought. That way they could part without the extras.

She looked at her watch again. Nine minutes to go, and two more minutes in the tea room. She allowed one minute to get up and pay for the coffee, so one minute was entirely her own. She closed her eyes; she wanted to spend this last minute quietly.

With her eyes closed, she thought of the end as such—the end of all things. She wanted to deny it. The end exists only as something relative; it can never exist as an absolute. Take death for instance. You die but your body remains to decay into dust. Sangu would come back someday even though he goes now. Why must one talk about a last parting?

She opened her eyes and saw that it was exactly eight minutes before train time. She arose, walked over to the cashier's desk, paid for the two cups of coffee, and went out onto the street.

Once in the station building she looked for the window where platform tickets were sold but couldn't find it. She went over to the information booth. The clerk there told her that all available tickets had been sold.

"I must see someone off. It's quite important," said Yŏngi impatiently, sensing her carefully planned schedule was falling apart.

"I suggest you go to the assistant station master's office."

She rushed over to the office indicated by the clerk. Only five minutes left till train time. The assistant station master gruffly informed her that no more tickets could be issued since they were oversold as it was. She could not back down now. She tried to talk him into selling a ticket, telling him she was teaching at such-and-such a school and many other irrelevant things. Finally he told her to go and see the woman on the other side of the office. "She handles them. See if you can get one from her."

But the woman was already involved in a heated argument with a man having the same problem. The man was exclaiming loudly that just one more could not possibly hurt. Meanwhile the woman countered with equal emphasis that she was not allowed to issue tickets beyond the limits prescribed by regulations.

Only three minutes were left till train time. Yŏngi decided it was useless to wait around. She hurried over to the ticket gate. No one was there except a ticket examiner shivering in the cold. Rushing up to him she produced her billfold with her ID card. She held up her billfold and said she had to go in to see someone off. He said she couldn't go in. She didn't want to listen to him because that would completely wreck her plans. Stopping here would leave her with no excuses when Sangu drew his conclusions about their relationship. Thrusting her billfold at the ticket collector she forced her way through the gate. From her desperate look he must have sensed the urgency. He returned the billfold and told her to hurry back.

She ran. The train would not actually move till the bell stopped ringing. Looking through carriage window, she ran toward the front of the train. The bell stopped ringing when she was about halfway. Then the hissing of the locomotive letting out steam. The train started to move. She ran as fast and as far as she could. Soon the train picked up speed and left her behind with a broken promise.

Catching her breath and watching after the fast-disappearing train, she noticed a woman waving at someone in the train with one hand while wiping away her tears with the other. She now faced the woman directly. Of course there was no way of knowing whom the woman was seeing off. But curiosity, rather than sympathy, was aroused in Yŏngi. The woman was so saddened by the disappearing train it was as if it were leaving on a journey of no return. It could go no further than Pusan. Why must one grieve over a temporary parting as if sending someone off to the grave?

A faint whistle wafted back along the silent platform. Yŏngi now thought of things passing out of sight. Everything moves in a fast succession of beginnings and endings. Motion itself passes out of sight like the train. It flows on like water. Sangu, too, seemed to be a being that flowed away from her. She raised her arm and waved at a train which was no longer in sight.

"Why did I wave," she wondered. Probably due to the sad feeling one has on seeing the past float away. The woman nearby probably felt the same way. Anyway, it was not at all unpleasant sentiment, she concluded. She left the platform thinking it might be one of the privileges of mankind to be able to experience such feelings.

Passing through the gate she was possessed by an impulse to prolong her sad-sweet state of mind. She loathed the noises of the city which signified nothing but dreadful hardboiledness. She slowly climbed the stairs leading to the station cafeteria. She wanted to soak in her sad-sweet sentiments in a nook of the station, securely guarded from the drab, matter-of-fact outside world.

The cafeteria was deserted like the dry bed of a river during a severe drought. Water would flow over it again when it rained. The dry bottom of a lake, floor of the sea exposed by the ebbing tide—these were far better than a desert, she thought. They had possibilities. Besides, the vaultlike ceiling of the cafeteria was so high. It reminded her of what a Greek ruin with colossal marble columns must be like. Wasn't the ceiling of the waiting room high too? It takes a place with a high ceiling to send people off into a trance, she thought.

Although it was already December, each table had a vase with chrysanthemums. The erect flowers looked like they owned the place.

She had the whole place to herself, so she had no cause for reserve. She made a bold choice of a table; she took the center one. She was all alone in the huge restaurant. No one would notice even if she sang at the top of her voice.

She felt relaxed in this large room with its high ceiling. There was nothing to distract her from savoring the sentiments she had had down at the platform. She ordered a cup of coffee.

But soon people began to trickle in, people who were leaving on the next train, people who would flow away according to the train's timetable. For a moment she entertained the idea of remaining there and having the whole place to herself again after all these people had gone. But she got up. She did not think she could stand the noise of their chatter any longer. Not even for a minute. One has no business standing on the floor of the sea at high tide, she thought to herself.

There wasn't even a postcard from Sangu although a week had already passed. He spoke of a last parting. Did he mean that he was to be understood literally? Suppose he had concluded that she had not gone to the station to see him off. Was that such a critical issue as to warrant complete silence? Besides, Yŏngi had gone to the station. Sangu was not writing to her nevertheless.

She was sitting in her office at the school looking out of the window. It was snowing very lightly. Change of heart, change in quality—these phrases came into her head abruptly. Ice is a different form of water. Snow is a form of ice but it is much softer. Why do we have hard hail in the hot summer when we get soft snow in the cold winter? Some changes are obviously beautiful while others are ugly. When things change, however, there must be due reason, she thought.

Two weeks passed without a letter. She could not make up her mind if his change of heart was a noble one, but she could not deny a change had taken place.

Soon she found herself scribbling things on a sheet of paper. At first it was meaningless but soon she noticed she was writing Sangu's name over and over. While writing "Sangu," "Sangu," "Sangu," she was reminded that the fountain pen with which she was writing was in fact a present from Sangu himself.

A red fountain pen with a silver cap. He had said, "I am greedy," when he presented the pen to her. He meant he was greedy because he had chosen a present that would last for a long time and would remind her of him constantly. But now the "greedy" person turned out to be the possessor of a love that was much more short-lived than the present itself.

For no reason at all Yŏngi thought of the station with its constant flow of people. People arriving and departing. She recalled the station restaurant with a sense of yearning. The ceiling as high as the sky. The sad-sweet atmosphere of the late chrysanthemums. Losing herself in her thoughts, the phone rang.

It was from Mr. Yi who worked in a bank. He had been trying to win her favor for a long while now. He asked her if she had any definite plans for Christmas Eve, and when she said she did not have any, he asked if she would spend the evening with him. The station restaurant flashed through her mind, so when the question of a place arose, Yŏngi named the station cafeteria without hesitation.

"Christmas and the station cafeteria—what a combination," Mr. Yi remarked in admiration when they met on Christmas Eve. It was a novel idea, but he seemed to attach particular significance to it because she had suggested the place.

"All we need now is snow to top it off," he said in a buoyant tone of voice.

She decided to let him enjoy himself. After all, was he not entitled to be amused?

"I wish we were going away some place," he said when the food arrived. He really seemed unable to contain his exuberance.

"I agree, I wish I were going away on a trip," she said. She meant it. She wanted to lose herself in the rush. When the meal was finished Yi said:

"Would you like to go see the new south annex on the station building?"

Yŏngi had read about the annex in the paper but had not yet seen it. She said it was a good idea. It was of modern construction with long rows of windows illuminated by soft fluorescent light. It was a charming building. Enough to incite one's desire to wander. They looked at the timetable.

"I see. This building is exclusively used for Inchon passengers," said Yŏngi. Then she continued after a pause, "Would you like to go to Inchŏn?"

"You mean that?" he jumped at her suggestion. Of course, he would have liked nothing better at the moment, but he could not help thinking she was joking.

"Of course, I mean it."

A broad smile spread over his face as he hurried over to the window to buy ticket for Inchŏn before she could change her mind.

"If we should miss the last train coming back to town, we can always take a taxi," he said as if to reassure her.

Yŏngi made no comment. She did not want to think about what could happen after they reached Inchon. She merely wanted to go some place. Water heads toward the sea. On the way, it might tumble over rapids or it might meander through plains. If the obstacle is large it goes around it. But one thing, it never thinks about what is ahead. She now wished to flow on like river water.

The loudspeaker blared. They walked down to the platform and got on the train, their hearts filled with the excitement of going away. They wished there was somebody to see them off. Soon the bell rang and the train whistle shrieked.

Yŏngi thought of the day Sangu left town. Sangu went away without knowing that she had come to the station to see him off.

With the hissing sound of escaping steam the train slowly pulled out. Yŏngi had the momentary illusion that there was someone on the platform to see her off but she did not look outside. Even if there had actually been someone there, she would not have wished to look. She merely wished to go away with no ado.

"It's Yŏngdŭngp'o already. Look at all those lights," said Yi. After awhile, when the train had left the city limits, he exclaimed:

"Look at the lights in the farmhouses. Aren't they like fireflies?"

But she was not listening to him. She was vaguely aware that she was alive, that she was going somewhere and fast.

"It might just be impossible for us to get back to town tonight," said Yi half to himself.

Hearing this she snapped back to herself. She felt all this would come to an end at Inchŏn. Now she did not want to go to Inchŏn. She did not want all this to end.

As the train was pulling into Oryudong station she arose telling him she was going to the toilet. But she got off the train instead. She started to wave at the train as it pulled out into the dark. Yi, just as Sangu had on that day, was riding on a train without knowing Yŏngi was outside waving. When the tail lamp of the train had diminished to a mere dot in the darkness she thought, "I am, after all, destined to see people off." She gave another wave toward the now faraway train.

Walking toward the small, dark station building she thought to herself, "I hope this station, too, has a large cafeteria with a high ceiling."

(end story)

Time for You and Me Alone

Hwang Sunwŏn

It had been two days already.

The only view was of endlessly crooked mountain ridges and gorges. Nothing seemed to stir, not even the wind.

Captain Chu's body began to sag, though he was supported on both sides. Rather, he was being dragged along on the shoulders of his two companions. A bullet had torn through his leg two days earlier. He and his companions had managed to get through the encircling enemy lines with only a rag binding his thigh to stanch the flow of blood. The bullet had, mercifully, missed both the bone and the nervous system, but an awful numbing pain had set in since that morning—was the leg becoming gangrenous?

It wasn't a journey with a set distance or goal. They were merely heading southward. Captain Chu was well aware that a definite sense of distance and a goal could help the wounded a great deal. Once he had seen a soldier with a bullet hole in his lower abdomen make it back to friendly lines over a distance that would normally take a good half-hour walk, covering up the wound with his shirttail, slumping down only when he knew he was in the hands of friends. The sole reason he was able to struggle on with such a serious wound was that he had been aware of the whereabouts of friendly lines. In other words, he had an immediate goal to gain.

They, however, were denied that definite goal. But the captain dared not tell Lieutenant Hyŏn and Private Kim that they should leave him behind even though he could no longer walk and consequently was only a burden to them. To be left behind alone meant sure death.

Thus when the private suggested carrying him on his back,

the captain didn't hesitate a moment but let himself be carried without saying so much as a word.

The private was seventeen years old, a mere stripling, but being a country boy he showed considerable prowess in carrying the captain on his back. Then it was the lieutenant's turn to perform this duty.

Before he turned his back to the captain, however, the lieutenant gave a quick glance to the pistol which hung from the captain's side. The three had already cast aside their knapsacks, helmets, rifles, and, indeed, even their jackets, long ago. The only weapon left was the captain's pistol.

The captain could easily guess what the lieutenant meant by that glance. In all fairness he couldn't blame the lieutenant. Ever since he became incapable of going on alone he had indeed become a burden to his companions. But the two had not had the heart to desert their superior. It boiled down to the fact that they were waiting for him to make good use of the pistol in order to expedite their own flight.

But the captain simply ignored the lieutenant's glance. He merely took off his trousers and boots and entrusted his weight to the lieutenant's back.

Of course, Lieutenant Hyǒn was no match for Private Kim, but still he was heavier and stronger than Captain Chu and could carry a man on his back for a considerable distance. Both officers had originally been with the Student Volunteers Corps.

What they had eaten during the past two days was quite meager: mostly various kinds of herb roots and occasional spring water to quench their thirst. Moreover, the scorching early summer sun did not help them any.

The streaming sweat flowed into the eyes and mouth of the carrier. Since he had no free hand, the only thing he could do was to close his eyelids tight in order to squeeze out the sweat, spit it out, or shake it off with quick, jerky shakes of his head. Gradually, each step became shorter and they had to take turns more and more frequently.

The captain could feel the unpleasant, sticky and damp sensation of the carrier's back through their wet tee shirts, but oddly enough, it was through this sensation that he felt assured of his remaining alive.

The lieutenant, who had just taken a turn at carrying the

captain on his back again, thought of the same thing he had been
thinking over and over. It was the scene he remembered from
a brief dream he'd had two nights earlier just before the enemy
began to make that horrible noise with tin pans and flutes.

The sun was burning down from a greyish sky, and under
that a brownish and barren wasteland spread to the horizon. For
no reason at all, he had been standing in the middle of this
wasteland, and the dust was so deep as to bury his legs halfway
up to his naked knees.

He was much troubled. There was something on his calves
that he cherished. On the night before he joined the army his
sweetheart had seen his naked and hairy legs and had asked him
to take good care of the longest hair on each shin because she
would like to think those were her own. And now those two hairs
were in danger of being buried under brownish dust.

That was not his only problem. There was an ant hole just
in front of him in the dust. For some strange reason he was under
the impression that he had to watch that ant hole though no one
had ordered him to do so. An endless line of brownish ants crawled out of the ant hole. Just outside the hole, however, stood a
huge brownish ant which was biting off the heads of the ants crawling out of the hole. The place was filled with the bodies of ants
in no time at all. In the next instant they weren't the bodies of
ants any longer; they had turned into brownish dust. This vast,
barren wasteland might well be made up of their bodies, he
thought. The jaundiced sun was still burning in the greyish sky,
and he was doomed to watch the ant hole without budging.

This scene in his dream kept coming back to him. He was
painfully conscious of the weight of the captain pressing him
down. There was one way, only one way, to get rid of this unpleasant burden, if only the captain would give up his reluctance
to face reality. If he would only realize. . . Otherwise, all three
of them would surely meet their deaths on a nameless mountain.

He felt a burning thirst.

Then he thought of the letter he had received about five days
earlier from his sweetheart. She had written, ''The blooming
flower of my lips never wither, for the joyous memory of the past
that you have given me waters it constantly.'' Once he had
whispered into her ear after a particularly long kiss that her lips
were a flower, not of a single petal but of many layers of petals,

for there was no end to the joy of exploring it.

There was a noticeable change in the letter too. She used the familiar 'you' form along with his first name; previously she had always used 'Mr. Hyŏn.' This change could mean only closer ties between them. He now remembered that while reading the letter, he had looked at his hairy shins and been conscious of a girl's smiling eyes fondly gazing down on him.

Carrying this man on his back in the scorching heat, he now tried to quench his thirst with memories of the past and of the touch of his sweetheart's lips. He also tried to see her loving and smiling eyes directed toward him, and in following her imaginary eyes, his sweatstained eyes seemed to brighten up considerably.

They came up to a crest in the ridge. It was the private's turn to carry the captain.

The terrain was such that they could either take a short cut by going down into the gully and making the steep climb on the other side or make a detour by following the long but easy ridge line.

Lieutenant Hyŏn proposed crossing the gully, which was reasonable. They were in a position where they had to think about saving their strength even if it was a matter of only a few steps.

But the private's idea was different. If they lost their way and direction in the thick bush down in the gully they would only lose time and energy, he reasoned. While they were still hesitating, the captain spoke up:

"Lieutenant, let's follow Private Kim's advice."

The lieutenant snatched a glance toward the pistol at the captain's side. His dream flashed back again.

The jaundiced sun was high in the greyish sky and the endlessly barren wasteland stretched out under it. He was standing in the middle of it sweating profusely. The ant hole just in front of him was still producing its endless line of brown ants, and the huge brown ant by the entrance to the hole was still biting off the heads of the emerging ants. It was as if the huge ant was mechanically working his mouth and the ants in the line were automatically putting their heads into it. The bodies of the ants were turning into brownish dust. The dust deepened accordingly, and the hairs on his shins were being buried under it.

He fretted, but there was nothing for him to do but stand

by the hole and watch.

Then suddenly he found another fresh hole, not far from the deadly one, that was connected to it by a secret path. This new one, of course, had not been part of his dream. It was the result of a conscious plan. But the foolish ants kept coming out through the old hole and getting their heads cut off.

Lieutenant Hyŏn, though he wasn't carrying the captain on his back, then felt a cold and sticky sweat cover his entire body.

Just before dusk they caught a snake, roasted it, and shared it. When they had finished eating, the lieutenant got up and left as if to go and relieve himself. After a little while the captain spoke to the private:

"You run along, too." It was the first time he had ever mentioned such a thing.

The private looked up at him as if he did not understand.

"Lieutenant Hyŏn's gone. Got tired of waiting, I suppose."

"Got tired of waiting?"

"Yes, got tired of waiting for me to kill myself."

Indeed, the lieutenant did not come back.

"I said, you run along too," said the captain avoiding the private's eyes.

Private Kim thought a little, but looking up once at the setting sun, he silently offered his back to the captain.

Now that there was nobody to relieve the private, they made very little progress. They had to rest frequently.

When night set in, they slumped down completely exhausted.

They thought of the packages of crackers in their knapsacks which they had thrown away earlier to lighten their load, but they seemed to do so merely from habit; in fact, they had passed beyond the point where a person was capable of feeling hunger.

They also thought of Lieutenant Hyŏn. How far had he gotten by now? Private Kim thought it was cruel of the lieutenant to desert them like that. But the captain had the vain hope that the lieutenant would perhaps reach friendly lines soon and arrange to have a rescue party sent out for them. Of course, neither of them spoke of what they were thinking in so many words.

The captain could not fall asleep until long after the private had done so. His wound no longer bothered him. He simply had the strange feeling that once he fell asleep he might not wake up in the morning .

Then, for no reason at all he began to think about the woman. It was quite odd that he should think about her at this particular moment.

It was the woman he had bought for a night in Pusan while he was on a three-day pass. It was after particularly hard fighting in which he had played a key role in securing a hill.

Without being asked, she narrated an experience she had had in Seoul around the January evacuation. She had been working as a hostess in a bar. One day a girl ran into her house around dusk chased by three American soldiers. She had let the girl escape through the back door, and she herself had borne the unpleasant and animal-like lust of the three soldiers. She wasn't even capable of distinguishing one soldier from another; she had fainted and it was not until daybreak that she came to. Oddly enough she had run into the girl that day on a street in Pusan. Of course, it was the girl who had stopped her and who burst into tears of joy at the unexpected encounter. The girl wanted to know if there was anything she could do to help.

When she finished telling her story, she said she was very grateful to that girl and overwhelmed by the girl's graciousness, for, after all, most girls would snub a woman like herself under the circumstances.

While the captain was listening to her story, a laudable enough anecdote, he felt a sudden urge to twist her heart. So he asked her if she would willingly do the same now and lie as in a faint till dawn broke just to experience such gratefulness and graciousness again.

The woman lit a cigarette in the dark and said quietly and simply that she didn't know, but she didn't think such things happened just because one wanted them that way. All she knew was that she had stepped into the shoes of the girl without realizing what she was doing, that people often did things on the spur of the moment which they themselves might wonder about later, that she might or might not react in the same way if she were in the same situation again, and that it all depended on the circumstances at the time.

And now lying on the ground in the darkness on a nameless hill, the captain was thinking over what the prostitute had said that night. Now that he gave it a little thought, he could think of many instances in which he himslef had acted in a similar way. Many times the complexities arising from hard fighting had caused him to react unexpectedly in many unforeseen situations.

Then a new thought flashed through his head. When he had asked her that spiteful question, had he not really taken it for granted that she would act the same way in a like situation? Had he not really expected her to do the same because she was a sullied woman?

Now with death just around the corner, lying flat on a nameless ridge line in the darkness, he felt he had no right whatsoever to expect the woman to act one way or another. By the same token, he thought no one had any right to pass judgment on his own conduct during the past fighting and to have expected him to perform his duty one way or the other in the diverse situations engendered by battlefields.

Suddenly he felt an urge to protest to somebody, anybody, but all around him he found nothing but ever-deepening darkness.

He, too, soon fell asleep.

They set out again on their journey at the crack of dawn. They were forced to stop and rest more frequently. The private, too, shed his fatigue trousers and combat boots. He was well aware of the difficulty of treading rocky mountain paths barefooted, but the weight of those boots had become quite unbearable.

Soon the soles of his feet were cut and bloody, but it was impossible to carefully pick one's way and protect one's feet.

Nothing was in sight but endless peaks and immobile gullies and gorges. Hadn't this godforsaken region ever been inhabited by humans? Instead of the sound of friendly artillery, which they had so anxiously awaited, only a deep and endless quiet and the labored breathing of the private met their ears.

Nevertheless the captain was all ears. He could not afford to miss the sound a pin drop, he thought.

Once the captain suggested taking a rest and having a drink of water. The private did not know what the captain was talking about, but directed by the latter, they came upon clear spring water trickling from a crack in the rocks.

The entire distance they covered that day was less than three miles. During that time they had only eaten three or four raw frogs they had caught.

The private's knees became more and more bent and his back was so bent that he now seemed to be crawling.

The captain felt death coming closer and closer as the private's slouch became deeper and deeper.

Rounding a bend on the ridge late in the afternoon, they saw a crow overhead. They found the path abruptly cut short by a deadly cliff. They nearly stepped over its edge.

Turning away from the edge, the private looked down at the far-off bottom of the cliff. There he saw several carrion crows eagerly pecking at something.

It was a human body, and there was no mistaking that it was the body of Lieutenant Hyŏn. It had the same tee shirt, fatigue trousers, and the boots that the lieutenant wore when he had deserted them the previous evening.

The crows pecked at the face of the corpse. Then the ferocious birds looked up at the two men on the top of the cliff, flew off, but soon returned to their repast.

The eyes had already gone from the face and only two gaping, dark holes remained. The two stepped back a few paces and slumped down on the ground. Seeing the body of the lieutenant, the last bit of strength they had seemed to drain out of their bodies.

After awhile the private got to his feet and scrambled to the edge from where he threw rocks down the cliff. Every time he threw a rock the crows fluttered up from the body but they returned immediately with a few dissatisfied and ominous caws.

The private came back to slump down again. He gave a quick glance at the captain. The captain was lying down with his eyes closed.

The private could feel death closing in. It was odd to feel it now, for he had not felt it in the severest fighting on the battlefield. Tomorrow those carrion crows would peck out their eyes. He thought he would much rather die first than see the body of the captain picked over by those crows.

He wanted to cry but he hadn't the strength to do so.

The private was awakened by the captain's voice. When he opened his eyes, he could see the starry sky above.

"Listen to that," said the captain in a hoarse whisper. "It's artillery."

Fully awake now, the private sat up to listen. Indeed, faint of artillery rumblings like that of distant thunder could be heard.

"Whose guns are they?"

"Ours, 155s, I believe."

There couldn't be any mistake if the captain said so. Just as the private was going to ask, the captain spoke up:

"But it's far. A good fifteen miles."

It was no use then if that was the case. Private Kim resumed his prone position, disappointed.

Captain Chu now felt that he was slowly dying. He could feel it in an absolutely lucid state of mind. Then he squarely faced the idea he had so carefully avoided. He would now put the pistol to good use. If he had killed his doomed self long ago, things would have turned out well for the others, he thought. Lieutenant Hyŏn might not have stolen away and fallen off the cliff to his death. "At any rate, it's not too late to help," he thought. For all his exhaustion, Private Kim still stood a chance of making it back to friendly lines if he were given a free hand. He turned to the private.

"The artillery is to the southeast. Go down the left side of the cliff. Run along. It's an order," he told the private. That said, he slowly and limply pulled his pistol from its holster.

Then, just then, he picked up another sound, quite distinct from the rumbling of guns. At first he doubted his ears.

"What's that sound?" he said to the private after awhile.

Private Kim raised his head and listened.

"What sound, sir?"

"It has stopped. I can't hear it now," said the captain. Then he heard the sound again. "There it goes again. It's coming from that direction." But still the private could hear nothing "It sounds like a dog barking," the captain said.

A dog! Despite his exhaustion, the private came to his knees and crawled to the edge of the cliff. If it was a dog barking, there had to be a house and humans in the vicinity.

"It's over that ridge," said the captain.

But the private still could hear nothing. He backed down to the spot where he had lain before. He slumped down.

"The private is a good soldier and a real man," thought the captain. He wanted to do something for the boy now, and he wanted to do the same for himself if he could. But now the private was mumbling to himslef.

"Tomorrow there will be more crows. Then we won't have any eyes."

But even before he finished saying that he heard the cocking of the pistol right by one of his ears. Startled, he turned around to see the captain aiming the pistol level at him in the darkness.

"Carry me," ordered the captain in a hoarse but strong voice.

The private did not know what was up, but at gun point he had no choice but to offer his back to the captain.

"Walk!"

The private felt the muzzle of the gun touch his right ear. They went over the ridge and descended into the woods.

"Halt!" The captain listened for awhile.

"Turn left a little!" Then after awhile he said, "Wait!" Then, "Go ahead!"

Thus, the private blindly followed the captain's commands, to the right, to the left, halt, go ahead. All the while he was struggling, however, the private could hear nothing. The captain, at the point of death, might be losing his mind and hearing things, he thought. "If so, what's with me now?" He had never borne a grudge against the captain till this moment, but now a furious rage began to well up in him against this man.

But he had to keep on walking; the pressure of the gun behind his ear never slackened. His progress, weak and shambling as it was, seemed to be spurred by gun point.

Finally they reached the foot of the hill.

"To the right." Then, "Straight ahead."

Then the private began to hear something. He slowly realized that it was a dog barking. But he could not guess the distance.

His throat was dry and each step was like falling into an ever-deepening abyss. He felt like giving up and flopping down. But he couldn't afford to; the gun behind his ear pressed harder and harder. He could see nothing. He wasn't even aware of taking each step. Then just as he became conscious of the silhouette of a house, a man and a barking dog ahead in the darkness, he felt the slackening of pressure at the back of his ear. He sagged down to the ground under the dead weight of the captain.

(end story)

The Bandmaster

Chŏn Kwangyong

It is always a trifle embarrassing to start a new job, having
to meet new people and everything.

And it was Mun Ho's first job after months of idleness. His
past record as a musician and his age now earned him the title
of band leader. Of course, he leads all the music, has the choice
of what numbers are to be played, and so on.

Although there were half-a-dozen huge electric fans whirr-
ing and rattling, the hall was unbearably hot and sultry. The
newly opened beer hall was packed with people and it was so
noisy that it was impossible to overhear the conversation at the
next table. The clinking of beer bottles, glasses, and dishes mixed with shouts and laughter. Waiters wearing black bow ties and
with well-combed hair hustled among the tables while hostesses
dressed in white hovered round the tables exuding female efficiency. Fresh out of high school, they looked clean and untar-
nished by the affairs of the world. Wearing identical artificial pearl
necklaces, white sandals, and even pearly beads of perspiration
on their brows, they were like a host of mermaids swimming
in the stuffy atmosphere.

The eye-catching red and blue neon signs and fluorescent
lamps dimly lit the spacious hall. Emptying several bottles of beer
at one corner of the hall, the members of the band went up to
the stage and took their places. Of late, Mun Ho could not control his shaky hands without taking a few drinks. His drinking
had become somewhat wild as if to drown his personal desperation and frustration; it had ruined his health and now it was start-
ing to paralyze his fingers, his last lifeline.

He had been acclaimed a genius twenty years ago when he
gave his first public recital at the Hibiya Hall in Tokyo, Japan.

But now he was barely able to control his fingers even with the help of alcohol.

Mun Ho, slightly tipsy, took his position and grasped his cello. Automatically, he tuned his instrument with the bow. Five feet six, he looked well with the cello. Feeling seedy and wretched inside, he still looked fine on the surface; as a man of fifty years of age he was well built.

He led off the band. The cymbal followed and soon the light-hearted rhythm of the trumpet, saxophone, and clarinet drowned the noise in the hall. All turned lustreless, drunken eyes toward the stage. Mun Ho was feeling much more at ease now; the drinks had helped. Anyway, the awkwardness he had felt during the first of the evening performance did not bother him any more. He was even pleased with himself.

Stormy applause followed the end of the number. Jubilant screams mixed with the applause.

The next number was in accompaniment to a well-known singer whose recent records had been hits. Even the noisiest group listened attentively. Clapping and shouts of encore followed her song.

Mun Ho was very pleased. Now he even enjoyed what he was doing. When the band drummer had called on him a few days before to talk him into joining the band, his first reaction was that he could never lower himself to playing in a beer hall, the modern version of a saloon. But now he felt completely at home and found he could concentrate on the score, his instrument, and the resultant music.

Of course this was not his first such job. He had played band music a lot before, but that was to American troops. His audiences being foreign, he had not cared—no one would recognize him; besides, the financial rewards for playing to American troops were substantial.

The years in his thirties were the happiest for him as a man and as an artist. His outstanding musical talents had won him the unanimous acclaim of music critics and he had commanded the love and respect of the string quartet to which he belonged. During the autumn before the Liberation he had conducted his first orchestra in Pinkiang. That was the moment he had waited for so long. In fact, that was the only moment in his life to which he turned nostalgically even now when he was a wreck as an artist.

The Manchurian fall was chilly. That evening, on the stage of Theater M—on Kidaiskaya Main Street, over a hundred musicians clad in tuxedoes and white ties waited for the appearance of their conductor. The house was so full that even the aisles were crowded with people. Everybody eagerly awaited the appearance of the conductor.

Suddenly, a storm of applause broke out; tall and handsome, Mun Ho had entered the stage from the left. As he made his bow at the center of the stage facing the audience, the house resounded with renewed applause. How many times Mun Ho had relived that moment since then, soothing his ears in the sweet applause, sipping the bitter drink which he had taken to!

Tchaikovsky's *Pathétique* was the feature of that evening. The house was completely silent as if it had been empty till the last note of the last movement reverberated and fainted away. It was an intoxicatingly exciting moment. Amid the thunderous applause and shouts that shook the theater, he proudly gripped the hand of the first violinist.

That evening after the performance, Mun Ho drove along the banks of the Sungari in ecstasy. The future seemed to be an open road stretching toward a bright horizon. In a Russian restaurant he dreamed of his triumphant return to his homeland and subsequent travels through European countries. Fondling a vodka, he sat up all night to plan his glorious future. Perhaps those had been the years of indiscreet passion and zeal, he thought many times in later years, but those had certainly been the happiest years of his life.

Finishing, Mun Ho and the other members of the band stepped down from the stage leaving their instruments leaning against their chairs. As Mun Ho was wiping perspiration from his brow, someone gripped his hand. "Hey, what's become of you?"

It was Kim Kŏnu, his high school classmate. Kŏnu had admired and respected Mun Ho's musical talents very much while they were students together. He had jokingly insisted that they preserve Mun Ho's hand as a national treasure after his death. When they ran into each other again as grown-ups after the Liberation, the first question Kŏnu asked Mun Ho was whether he had insured his playing hand. Taken aback, Mun Ho did not know what to say. Disregarding Mun Ho's embarrassment,

Kŏnu pulled him by the hand and led him toward his table. Still embarrassed, Mun Ho sat down at his table.

"Let's have a glass of beer," said Kŏnu as he handed Mun Ho a glass.

"It's been a long time" said Mun Ho feeling uncomfortable because Kŏnu's other friends were sitting at the same table.

He emptied the glass. The cold beer felt good on his thirsty throat, but he thought he should get up and leave, for he figured it rude to sit with customers—a band musician sitting at a guest's table. He got up.

"I must leave. I am not through with the evening's performances yet."

"You call that a performance? What a comedown. Let's drink some more," said Kŏnu in a drunken voice. The words pierced Mun Ho's heart, but Kŏnu emptied his glass with one gulp and poured Mun Ho another glass of beer. "Of course you cannot live on art these days. Money talks, you know."

Mun Ho had heard that Kŏnu held an important government position and that he was a very influential man, but he had not looked Kŏnu up when he might have been able to use some of his influence to advantage. Especially after he had started to work as a bandmaster for American troops, he had shunned the people he knew. He had been reluctant to tell even his close friends his whereabouts. When he ran into fellow musicians on the street, he cut them short with one pretext or another.

The state of affairs in the field of music following the Liberation was like that of any other field in the country—chaos. The fight between left wing musicians and right wing musicians was bitter and furious. Mun Ho, not being interested in political affairs, did not take sides with either group, but his noncommittal attitude alienated him from both camps. The result was that he was neglected by musicians despite his musical talents. Even the subsequent organizing of orchestras was factional business and so Mun Ho became an obscure bystander. He was consulted whenever they wanted to perform some difficult pieces for the first time in the country, but he was never admitted to their company. Thus he never had had the opportunity to conduct an orchestra in his homeland. Then the Korean War broke out.

While everybody was leading a miserable lives as refugees, a group of musicians got together to entertain American troops, and soon this became his main occupation. When he started to think about doing some serious musical work, it was already too late. He was considered to have degraded himself, and he became the butt of the derision of fellow artists. To make matters worse, the armistice decreased the number of UN troops in Korea, and life for professional entertainers became more and more difficult. Soon he lost his job as a musician; being a classical artist he could not hold his own among hot and swinging jazz musicians.

When Mun Ho returned to the stage from Kŏnu's table, he felt tired and exhausted. He asked the drummer to lead. He fiddled on his cello mechanically, but he really did not know what he was doing. Memories of Harbin, Tokyo, the parallel, liberated Seoul, refugee life, front line outfits crowded his mind.

He knew he had no cause for regret, but he also knew that he had no hope for the future. When a man has no hope or ideal, he might as well be dead. Suddenly he felt thirsty. Alcohol was the only friend he had.

Mun Ho visited Kŏnu's office the following day Kŏnu had given him a name card and asked him to look him up. The name of the insurance company was engraved on the marble front of the building. Examining the name card again to see if he had the right building, he went inside. Since Kŏnu had asked him to visit his office around closing time, he thought Kŏnu would surely be in his office waiting for him. He pushed open the door to the president's office.

A girl came out to receive him. Behind her there was a wooden partition and he could not see the inside of the office.

"Is the president in?"

"No, he is not in, sir," her eyes rested on his shabby bow tie.

"That's strange. I am expected at this hour."

"Ah, then you must be the maestro."

"Yes."

"Please take a seat over here. He said he would be right back. He is in a tea room now with another visitor."

He followed the girl into the anteroom and sat down on a comfortable sofa. On the opposite wall was a framed calligraphy reading "The Unified Korea." The girl brought him a wet towel. Wiping the sweat from his brow and neck with the cool towel, he lit his pipe. He drew back deeply. He felt good and comfortable.

There were three telephones on the desk. One of them was snow-white and it attracted his attention. He realized that he had not used a phone for years. His wandering eyes rested on the statistical charts pinned to one wall. He got up to walk over to the charts. Then he noticed for the first time that the floor was covered with deep, wall-to-wall carpet. Stepping on it, he recalled the taste of good living.

He looked at the charts. "Number of Policy Holders by Province," "Monthly Collection Chart," and so on. But they did not interest him except that the red lines on one chart made it look much like a sheet of music.

He walked over to the window and, lifting the blind, he looked out. For a moment he felt dizzy and then realized that the office was on the third floor. There was a line of parked cars on the street. They were of different colors and their metal tops made them look like toys. "That's right, I could make a good xylophone out of them by tapping the tops one by one," he thought.

The setting sun was hot on his brow. He turned round, letting the shade fall. He saw his image in a wall mirror. He moved closer to. He stood face to face with his image. He could now see quite a few gray strands in his wavy hair. His bald patch seemed to have grown larger. Perhaps it was the angle at which the sunlight fell on him, but he noticed the lines on his face were deeper than ever. Well, I really am getting old.

One of the phones rang. Of course he did not know which one it was. Hanging up the phone, the girl told him that Kŏnu would be right back. He walked over to the sofa again and sat down to relight his pipe.

"You are not indispensable at the beer hall," Kŏnu said as he pushed Mun Ho into his car. Mun Ho was feebly insisting that it was time for him to be at work. "Forget it. You don't have to be a slave for that kind of stinking money. Everybody is out for his own grab, so why don't you try for your own?" Mun Ho sat back weakly. "Mun Ho, let's do the town tonight and you think over the offer I mentioned in the office awhile ago, alright?"

Mun Ho was going to tell Kŏnu that his doctor had told him not to drink because of his blood pressure, but he thought better of it. In this world of vicious struggles for existence, he felt he should be grateful of Kŏnu's kind offer to help.

Meanwhile, for the tenth time since last night, Kŏnu was mentally going over his plans for Mun Ho. He would set up a music institute; he would put Mun Ho in charge; the institute would be self-supporting through collection of tuition fees; his insurance company would be entitled to tax exemptions since it would be sponsoring an educational activity. . .

"Let's begin life all over again," said Kŏnu and they clinked their first glasses. Kŏnu emptied his glass in one gulp. Mun Ho followed suit. "I won't say much more about it. You don't really have to know anything about business. You just have the title of comptroller. Now that my business has snowballed, I am in dire need of someone I can trust. You can never trust crooks. You hire them as executives and the next thing you know they are trying to take you in or take you over. Rats, that's what they are!" said Kŏnu and he turned toward the *kisaeng*[1] girls, "Ladies, more drinks. Let's make it a lively party."

In a corner of Mun Ho's mind was the thought of the band at the beer hall while he sat here and drank, and he felt somewhat guilty. It wasn't big band and the absence of one man could really hurt. "I see what you mean. Don't think I am not grateful to you either, but. . ."

"No buts. And cut that grateful stuff out. I am doing *me* a favor, too, you know."

They drank. They felt quite merry.

"Ladies, let's have some songs," said Kŏnu pouring drinks for the *kisaeng* girls. "You are in the presence of a maestro. See if you can impress him with your favorite songs. Quench your thirst before you start, however."

Mun Ho kept drinking while the girls sang.

"Now it's your turn to sing, President Kim," one of the girls said and the others clapped their hands approvingly.

"I am here to entertain a good friend. Do you girls think I would refuse to sing? But, mind you, my songs aren't cheap." Kŏnu got up and started to sing "O Sole Mio," one of his favorite songs. Once, a long time ago, he had wanted to be a singer but his father, who was an official in provincial government, was against it and insisted his son take the examination for public officials. So he took up law instead, but failed the bar examina-

1. a Korean professional singing and dancing girl; a professional entertainer.

tion twice. Thus he became a petty official in the provincial government during the days of Japanese colonial rule.

But he had made remarkable headway since the Liberation. He soon became a bureau chief in the central government, but got himself involved in a bribery scandal and had to quit. That was how he went on to become president of an insurance company.

"Money talks, boy, money talks. You can be a member of the cabinet if you have money. You can be a national assemblyman if you have money. I will run for the National Assembly myself when I make my pile, just wait and see," Kŏnu was full of bravado now.

Contrasting his own weak approach to life with Kŏnu's high spirits, Mun Ho was even envious of his friend. He sang a couple of songs himself and he tried to dance a little with some of the *kisaeng* girls. Then he passed out.

When he awoke the following day it was well past noon. He recalled some of the events of the previous night, singing and dancing, embracing girls, and such things, but everything was blurred and he did not recall how he got back home. His th. oat was burning. He felt sick in his head and stomach.

He heard his son practising the violin in the next room. Memories of thirty years ago rushed back. He too had been a young student practicing the violin but his own father was dead set against his becoming a musician.

"So you want to be a good-for-nothing fiddler, eh! Support yourself if you want to be a fiddler, understand?" his father had growled at him thirty years ago when he was preparing to enter college.

"You are old-fashioned, Dad. A man is happiest when he does what he wants."

"How dare you talk back to me like that?" was his father's infuriated reaction.

"Life is short and art is long" was the cherished ideal of the students of his day. In rebelling against his father he had felt the pride of a torchbearer. But he had run into one practical obstacle; his father vowed that he would not support him unless he took up medicine. The owner of a large estate, his father could be quite obstinate once he made up his mind. Even his high school teacher made a special visit to his house to plead for him, but in vain. Thus, Mun Ho entered a premedical school the following year. In his second year he threw up in the postmortem room and so he quit school and went back to his music without telling his father.

He thought about this many times later in life. The beginning was indicative of his whole career, he would think to himself. Since it was a career of his own choice, however, he had never regretted the change. At least he never said so if he did.

The sound of the violin in the next room began to get on his nerves. Perhaps his father had been right. Only one in a hundred can become a real artist. The rest are fiddlers and bandsmen like himself.

He now recalled the dialogue he had had with his own son a short while back. It was the first day he went to work at his present job in the beer hall. As he was leaving the house with his instrument under his arm, his son came out of his room and said, "I am ashamed of you, Dad." He knew what was going on because he had overheard the conversation between Mun Ho and the band's drummer.

He called out to Chunsik, his son, and told him to bring a pitcher of cold water. He drank nearly half the pitcher in one breath. The cold water running down the throat felt good.

Chunsik was a high school senior and he wanted to go to the college of music, too. Had he not had enough of the life of a musician living with his father? What attraction could it have?

"Chunsik, do you really want to study music?" he asked.

"Of course," his son answered readily.

"What about your school work? You think you will do well enough to pass your examinations?"

"They say that instrumental performance is most important."

He noticed his son's way of thinking was quite different from his of thirty years ago. He had thought a great artist needed a sound grounding in the humanities. The young people of today seem to think that the most important thing is to pass examinations.

"You must first believe in art. You must also have the theory; otherwise you will only be a good-for-nothing fiddler." He was saying these words more to himself than to his son.

"What about you, Dad?"

You didn't have to say that, Son. I know you despise me at heart.

"Well, it was different in my days. Under the Japanese, art was the only hope. There was something romantic about it and it was something we had to cling to. But now that we have our own country back, well, there are so many things to be done, so many things."

". . . ."

"You either passed the government examination and led the easy life of a government official or you became a doctor to lead another form of easy life. That is why art then seemed far superior than it does now. It's all different now." Mun Ho stopped short. His speech sounded hollow and he knew that it was nothing more than his apologia. "You boys now have so many other things to do. Of course there is nothing wrong with being a great artist, but..."

"I want to give it a try though."

"Giving it a try is not enough. You must believe in it?"

"How can I show that I believe in it?"

"It's a thorny path even when you are willing to give your life for it," half mumbling he turned away from his son. Neither of them said anything for awhile. Chunsik was watching his father carefully.

"I am seriously thinking about changing my profession," said Mun Ho presently, still looking away. "There is an offer for me to be comptroller of a large corporation." Chunsik did not say anything, and he could not tell what his son's reaction was. "It's an insurance company a friend of mine owns. When you start your college education, we will be needing more money and. . ."

The next moment he was surprised when his son broke out sobbing. "I am not really ashamed of you, Da. If you start to work for a company, what will happen to your career, your art, and the hardship you have borne so far? Why do you want to throw it away?" he blubbered.

Something hot pierced his throat. "I only said I was thinking about it."

"Don't ever do that, Dad. That will be the finish of your art."

Mun Ho did not know what to say in answer. He knew he did not know the most elementary aspects of business, finance, or statistics. Friendship was alright, but it was too good an offer—

to be paid a large salary for doing nothing. It could not last long. It's too precarious a position.

Suddenly he felt his instrument finger go numb.

When twilight started to set in Mun Ho departed for the beer hall with his instrument under his arm. His knees were still shaky from the drinking spree of the night before. He did not even notice the noises of the street.

His mind raced back. He started to learn the violin as soon as he entered middle school. One evening he went to see the art festival at a girls' middle school in the neighborhood. There he saw pretty girls dancing on the stage to enchanting violin music. He later learned that it was Dvořák's *Humoresque*. Later in his life he heard and learned to play better music, but none moved him more. It was on that night that he decided to devote his life to music. When he left the auditorium, the cool autumn air felt good on his flushed face.

Later his music teacher recommended that he take up the cello, for it seemed to suit his character better. That was how he became a cellist.

Whatever happened to those rosy dreams, those passions and ideals, and that single-minded patience, he often wondered.

The evening was drawing to an end. They played the last piece. It was getting late and there were many vacant seats in the beer hall. He played the cello halfheartedly. Even for beer hall music it was better to have a packed house.

He felt something go wrong with his instrument. He looked down and saw that the G string had snapped. He stopped and picked up the drooping string. He had replaced other strings many times, but it was the first time that the G string had snapped. It was the string that knew his life story well and it was the string that had the most contact with his fingers. Now the snapping of the string seemed to symbolize his career as a musician. He managed the rest of the piece with the three remaining strings.

After work Mun Ho and other bandsmen went into a saloon. Like all day laborers, each had his daily earnings in his pocket. They all drank till they were drunk.

Mun Ho invited the drummer to another joint when they were through with the first one. They drank more.

"Well, I got nothing to complain about. Life doesn't always

turn out as one plans. So what? I work a day and live a day, don't I?'' said the drummer in a drunken voice. Knowing Mun Ho's life story, he probably said this to console Mun Ho. ''Who knows? tomorrow you may strike a. . .''

''No, that's bad. I wouldn't want anything to happen to me like that. I want a society in which tradition and order prevail. . .''

Mun Ho fell off the chair. The drummer helped him up and led him out onto the street.

The curfew sounded.

The doctor said it was cerebral hemorrhage. The left side of his body was paralyzed. On the way back home the night before he had fallen into a ditch and sustained head injuries.

He returned to consciousness a day later, but he could not move. He merely lay awake in his bed. His son told him that a car from the insurance company had come to pick him up after he had left the house for work two days earlier. Mun Ho said nothing about that but said instead, ''Chunsik, bring your violin here.'' He could not enunciate clearly and Chunsik just stood there helplessly, not knowing what to do.

'' I say bring your violin here,'' he repeated, almost pleading.

Chunsik brought his instrument.

''Now I want to hear you play *Humoresque*.''

The son held a trembling bow. His father might die. Anyhow, he certainly would not regain his health even if he survived the stroke.

Now Mun Ho was dreaming of a huge orchestra and, of course, he himself was the conductor. His body heaved. It was his will to live. ''I must get well, I must get back to my art!'' He sighed deeply.

They heard the sound of a car braking to a stop at the front gate and the blast of its horn.

(end story)

Among the Marching Columns

Han Musuk

"Down with rigged elections!" abruptly shouted a friend who was marching along with him. They were part of a huge formation of students, all with their arms locked across each other's shoulders like so many rugby players. They had been shouting at the top of their voices all day, and now even the slightest attempt to utter a sound was an effort. Their veins were showing thick and vivid on their necks. They tightened their grips on their friends' shoulders. They were hot arms, hot hands. Each could feel the other's youthful heart beat through his body. This sensation of throbbing blood vessels seemed to bring about a new courage and energy—an ecstasy—as if their blood vessels had been somehow linked together, their blood intermixed.

"Down with rigged elections!" Myŏngso echoed without thinking. Being out of breath, his cry was more like the sound of something bursting. But together, all the cries formed an enormous roar, and the roar seemed to shake the world.

"Down with rigged elections!"

It was the roar of several thousand youths.

"Do something about the Masan incident!" someone took the lead again.

"Do something about the Masan incident!" echoed the roar. It was the rumbling of the sea.

Shouting, Myŏngso looked up into a clear blue sky. Trees along the street came into sight. Branches laden with young leaves were reaching out with all their might to the April sun.

Spring. Everything was reawakened and revived from the slumber and interruption of winter. It was life itself. It was life self-evident, unabashed, and unconcealed.

It was almost a revelation—it felt like the sudden opening

of a tightly shut door revealing a vast new vista beyond. Life! A shiver ran down his spine. Unconsciously, Myŏngso threw out his chest and tightened the grip on his friends' shoulders, where he could also feel the pulsing of hot blood. It was the evidence of life and youth. (We are living and we must live.)

In a kind of prostrated tension, Myŏngso could feel all individual identity and thought collapse and dissolve into this self-evident fact.

"Respect the people's rights!" someone shouted again.

"Respect the people's rights!" an infuriated roar followed.

Myŏngso joined in at the top of his voice. Now his throat felt rusty and burning. He felt an indescribable thirst, but he kept on shouting.

"Respect the people's rights!" With this the boys began to trot.

And that sent up a cloud of dust. In the dust the students galloped, shouting. They shouted and galloped as one, for they were of one will.

Myŏngso was faintly aware that he no longer had any weight of his own. He felt as though his body were turning into a transparent, weightless flag flapping in a brisk spring breeze. It was mostly a sense of relief. To release and give oneself to this huge will and fury was to him a kind of self-affirmation. He felt he could reassert himself only by becoming lost in this vast whole. It might well have been an illusion, but to him at that moment it was as true as a revelation. He was not afraid of illusions.

"Yah!"

A battle cry went up from somewhere at near the front of the column; then the column began to recede. Was it another police attack? An electric tension ran through the entire formation. The students tightened their grips on each other's shoulders.

Myŏngso looked intently forward. Although the Kwanghwa Gate intersection was not far away, he could see nothing but black-uniformed waves of people. He could not make out what was happening. One regressing foot from the row in front stepped on his foot. He felt as though something hot had dropped on his foot, and he realized for the first time that he was missing a shoe. Suddenly, a scene flashed through his head in which he had been knocked down by the police just outside the main gate of his school.

They had been a host of youths who had something legitimate to say. All they had wanted to do was to call a spade a spade and to demand in peace the redressing of wrong and injustice.

But the police had charged furiously into the formation even before the student procession was out of the school gate. Maddened clubs had danced insanely. They grappled, shoved, kicked, and shouted. Under the relentless police charge the students had been forced to retreat back into the campus.

Chased by policemen, Myŏngso had run into a tree. As he tottered and reeled, something zipped past him with a queer scream. With that Myŏngso fell down flat on the curb stone.

Instantly Myŏngso had glimpsed an enormous black figure with a chin strap charging toward him, then a thump on his shoulder. Curiously, it was painless; it was merely hot.

Then rocks had begun to fly, and red bricks too. He had wondered where the people were finding all those rocks and bricks on the cleanly swept pavement. Bricks flew incredible distances, as though they were red rubber balls.

Soon the police had dispersed. Again the student formation had marched out of the gate. It was no longer the crowd of meek young fellows of a short while ago. It was different.

Up until the clash with the police they had been merely a group of students whose youthful faces reflected contemplative scepticism and sensible equilibrium. But now they were furious young lions. Then the raging billows of life's force began to boil.

After a short while the tide was turned; the waves of students again began to move forward. Roars of shouting went up everywhere. They were now joined by citizens who crowded both sides of the pavement. Shouts of encouragement and applause persisted thunderously.

Myŏngso had forgotten long ago the pain of treading the rock-strewn pavement with his bare feet.

"We want a just government!" a harsh voice took the lead.

"We want a just government!" a roar joined in as if to relieve some pain.

They were sweating. The air was dense with the wholesome smell of young bodies. The sound of innumerable pairs of shoes thumping the pavement was enormous. Someone staggered and friends on both sides immediately tightened their grip to support him. Throats burned with thirst.

The intersection was just ahead. The column trotted again for a short while, while other waves of students from the West Gate and South Gate areas joined in. Angry roars, excitement, and confusion seemed to reign.

Now, with completely benumbed feet, Myŏngso was heaving hard.

With siren wailing, a fire engine drove up toward the government office building, steering through the waves of students. Another furious roar went up somewhere. The column again started to inch forward. Then a sudden dash like a surge of swelling waves. Then it stopped. It was the middle of the intersection.

Only a short distance away the Anti-Communist Center building was burning, puffing out black smoke. In the bright sunlight the fire seemed to have lost its color; somehow it gave the impression that it wasn't a clean and effective blaze. It was morelike a smoldering of evil will.

The fire engine did not get very far. An arch of water from the hose bridged the fire engine and the burning building like a rainbow.

But that did not last long. The rainbow of water tottered, flickered, and then disappeared. The fire engine was surrounded by a crowd of students who shouted, cursed, and shoved each other in uncontrollable confusion.

Then the water hose was taken over by students. The line of water gushed straight up in the air like a water fountain for a while, dispersing students around the fire engine.

The fire engine started to move. It inched its way among the students back toward the direction it had come. It was laden with students, triumphant and excited. They were waving their arms furiously.

"Fellow students! The time has come! The citadel of dictatorship is about to crumble!" shouted one of the students on the fire engine with his hands cupped to his mouth.

Just then, someone right behind him sent up an incredibly loud cry of delight.

"Mansei! Mansei!

He was stunned. It was so loud. It was a loud, deep, yet clear and resonant voice. It was a rich and vibrant and untired voice—it wasn't even slightly harsh, despite all the shouting and cursing.

It was instantly joined by others, and the roar of "mansei"

shook the earth. It was repeated three times, but Myŏngso thought he could distinguish the rich, resonant voice amid the roar. Myŏngso mechanically turned back to look at the owner of the voice.

It was the first time he had looked back all that day. He was stunned to find row after row of dirt-smeared faces following his. Originally each school had its own separate column, but now they seemed to have all mixed together.

He could spot the owner of the voice right away; he was two rows behind Myŏngso. He was asking something of the person on his right, and Myŏngso could see only his profile. Even his low-toned question had that rich, vibrant sound.

"What! Seoul Daily, too?"

The young man glanced back toward the Seoul Daily Press building.

Myŏngso was stunned and electrified. The young man was none other than Ch'angsu.

While he was still looking back, the column had advanced a couple of steps. He realized that he was standing in between two rows of students. He floundered a little, but instinctively recovered his balance. He looked for his spot in the formation; he couldn't find it. The rows had, as it were, all healed up without him. Now the tightly formed rows behind him were pressing hard, driving him forward. There was no place for him to join the phalanx. For fear that he should be run down and trampled, he stuck out his elbows sideways with his fists tightly griped on his chest.

He felt as though he was being refused both from within and without the formation; he was simply pushed along. Abandoned by the armlocked students, his legs now seemed to have their own will in pushing forward.

He felt he was abandoned—all alone in a vast space. With the loneliness, his old self began to creep back to him—his old self, forever tormented by scepticism, a sense of alienation, remorse, groping, and unjustifiable rebellion, and by the sense of guilt which underlay all other feelings. To him it was an old wound, still painful and still very vulnerable. Alienated, repulsed. and at times consciously withdrawn from it, he found the mysterious thing kept attracting him back the mysteriously magnetic thing known as human solidarity.

It might have been purely accidental that he went astray from the formation, but by virtue of the accident Myŏngso was forced back into his old self. Somehow, the members of the formation had, as it were, purified themselves by purging one dissonant element.

"Yah—yah!"

The stormy battle cries rising all around him now seemed to come from distant hills beyond.

The column was slowly passing the front of the burning Anti-Communist Center. Unbearably hot air mixed with black fumes surrounded the marching columns.

A stir ran through the formation. Among the dense black clouds of smoke, dancing red flames could be seen. It wasn't the only fire; there was another, though smaller in scale, across the street in the construction area by the Ministry of Communications. An overturned patrol car was sending up a thin line of black smoke.

Now the agitation was mounting to a new peak. The shouts were no longer orderly ones; everyone was making his own meaningless outcry, and put together, they were like an angry roar of ocean surf.

Myŏngso's legs were still following the formation. Blood was now seeping from his bare sole, but curiously enough he could feel no pain. The air was getting thinner around him. Inspite of his forward movement, reality for him seemed to be receding. His "self"—that perennial retreat to which he had always returned after temporary agitation—was now slowly coming back to him. It was like a clam in its shell; having once retreated into this sanctum, he was completely severed from the outer world. Yet his body was pushing forward in the formation.

He looked down. He could see a multitude of feet marching all around him. Blackshoes, brown shoes, red shoes, army boots, loafers, sneakers—and many were without shoes. The feet were moving fast, but where were they going?

"Apologize to the people!"

Someone abruptly shouted near him. It was a ringing voice, and it awoke Myŏngso from reverie into reality. Somehow, everyone around him joined in this cry without knowing who gave the lead. But Myŏngso knew. (It must be Ch'angsu, it must be Ch'angsu.) He had no evidence, but he was convinced that it was Ch'angsu.

It was the same ringing voice that had sent up the cry of "mansei" toward the captured fire engine, his face glowing with excited rapture. That's right! It was Ch'angsu's deep voice that had separated him—the only black sheep—from the rest of the formation.

He felt dizzy and swayed a little. Now the forward movement of the column was spasmodic. Waves of shoes and bare feet began to fill his dizzy eyesight. The shoes and feet began to sway slowly at first, then the pace began to quicken. Where were they going? Perhaps it's to the land of life, he thought. And he realized that it was not the first time he had watched those innumerable feet treading the road. He had seen the same tired feet seeking the land of freedom and life once before but in another situation.

Then fear began to overcome him.

Ch'angsu, life, and countless, countless feet.

What he had thought to be the distant background of his consciousness was actually a part of his consciousness, and no matter how hard he tried, he could not erase it from his mind. It kept coming back to him.

The shout of a moment ago rang back to him as if directed as a personal accusation.

"Apologize to the people! Apologize to the people!"

Myŏngso looked down again. The multitude of feet was walling him in again. His sight was filled with feet; then they began to fill the sight of his mind too.

His memory raced back about ten years to a late June day in 1950. It was raining hard. The speedometer was nearly always at zero. The car was practically crawling along, boxed in between other cars. One could see thick, slanting rain pouring down, dimming the headlights. Rain hitting the hood of the car became orange-colored spray and foam.

Frantic cries uttered by refugees on foot could be heard incessantly from both sides of the road.

Thump, thump, thump, thump.

Countless feet were treading the wet road in a confused rhythm.

The rain was pouring down mercilessly. Wet to the skin, the

128

procession went endlessly and mechanically.

Thump, thump, thump, thump.

One could hear the distant rumbling of cannon. The pace of the shabby procession seemed to quicken at every sound of artillery fire.

Myŏngso, an eleven-year-old-boy, was sitting in a corner of the car. He was too young to realize fully the gravity of the situation. Nevertheless, he was well aware of the fear, amazement, and panic of the grown-ups. He was sitting by the window, pale and small, looking at the dark outside.

"Da-d-dy!"

He could still hear the little boy's wailing, now mixed with the sound of the rain. That was the cry he had heard when the chauffeur started the motor and pulled out earlier that day. It was Ch'angsu's wailing cry. Myŏngso shuddered a little.

There were so many things that he could not comprehend. Things one had trusted,things one had always taken for granted—these crumbled down relentlessly. He could understand that somehow a war was on and that somehow his fate was being dragged into it willy-nilly. Yet the war was still some distance from him. He did not realize that the wars he had read about in history books and children's books on heroes were merely the outcome and significance of wars, not their practice and methodology. No one had told him about the dreaded practice of war. Especially,there was no way for him to know the animal nature people display when caught in the whirlpool of war.

He was afraid. It wasn't the sound of cannons that frightened him. It wasn't terror itself, but the premonition of terror that made him afraid. What was to happen terrified him more than what had happened. The scene that preceded their departure from the house was still confused in his head. It was a scene completely beyond the power of his comprehension.

The rain became worse.

Thump, thump, thump, thump.

Through the rain-washed windowpane he could still see the countless feet.

Myŏngso closed his eyes. What the headlights disclosed through the windshield was like the hell he had read about in books. Their backs to the light, people were walking hurriedly, impatiently, intently bent forward. Impatiently marching feet.

Where were they going?

No one told him. Probably no one could tell. His grand-mother, his parents, his elder sisters all of them were intently watching the road ahead with hardened faces. Around his mother's tightly colsed mouth he thought he could discern occasional spasms.

Myŏngso stole glances at the chauffeur. But now he was another man. He could not find in him the good-natured man who used to be his willing accomplice in many childish pranks and devilments. His thick eyebrows were closely knitted, and his heavy mouth was tightly closed; he blinked his eyes often. His hands gripping the wheel looked coarse and powerful as usual, but his shoulders sagged. Anger and sorrow seemed to fill his enormous body, welling out from the bottom of his heart.

Myŏngso did not know anything. He only snatched another glance at the chauffeur, thinking he looked quite different today. He watched the chauffeur's shapeless drooping neck. It was an old neck, and inside this old neck, through the throat, he thought he could hear silent wailing and sobbing. And that reminded him of Ch'angsu again.

Ch'angsu that morning had been standing by his father who was himself standing meekly by the car with his hands deferentially clasped in front of him. Ch'angsu was the chauffeur's only son.

The chauffeur faltered and stammered. He kept murmuring something inaudible. Myŏngso's own father, who was standing opposite the chauffeur, looked hard put.

"Naturally we'd like to take him along if we could, but the seats...," Myŏngso's father was both indecisive and inaudible.

"Even the trunk of the car will be alright, sir," the chauffeur said finally as though he was enunciating particularly difficult words.

"Well, but..."

His father's reply was still very indecisive. Just then his mother emerged out of the front door, followed by the maid and the tutor, who were carrying hastily packed suitcases. She looked very pale.

B-o-o-m! It was a roar of a cannon,

"What are you all doing? Can't you hear the cannon roar? Let's go, Shin. Open up the trunk and put these away—hurry, please." her voice sounded unusually hoarse.

As if spurred by what she said, the chauffeur raised the lid of the trunk and crammed the luggage inside. When the trunk lid banged shut, Myǒngso's father seemed to have made up his mind.

"Well, it won't be long in the first place. Three days at the most. We may well be back here tomorrow, so..." There was another roar of cannon. Now his father gave sharp and effective orders. "You sit in the back seat with Mother and Okhui. Put Ongnan on your lap. I will sit up front with Myongso."

The chauffeur's shoulders slumped down limply. Ch'angsu stepped closer to his father.

"Daddy." Tears began to well in Ch'angsu's eyes. "Daddy, don't go. Stay here with us."

Apparently the chauffeur had never thought about the possibility before. With a start he grabbed the boy and embraced him tightly.

"What are you doing? Listen, the cannon roar is getting closer!" screamed his mother. She was already sitting in the car. Inside, the car was full of packages, valises, suitcases, and Ongnan was crying with dismay.

"Myǒngso, get in the car! Daddy, what are you doing? We have no time to lose!" His mother was now mad at everybody. She seemed to have neatly forgotten the fact that she had been the main cause of delay so far, packing up useless things in spite of her husband's repeated warnings to pack only the valuable and the essential.

His father got in the front seat. It was full of packages too, and there was hardly a place for him to sit. When he finally wriggled himself in, he put Myǒngso on his lap.

"Shin, we've got no more time. Let's go!"

It was funny situation: no one in the car knew how to drive, but none in the car thought, not even for a moment, that the chauffeur might wish to stay behind with his own family. They attached no value to any action other than their own; they were order itself. And the chauffeur was one who had lived among this warped order for years and years.

"Shin! I am telling you to get started!" shouted his father in a loud, angry voice. It was a command.

The chauffeur picked up his son. He rubbed his cheeks against his son's. He stood like that for a moment. Then finally, as if he had made up his mind, he put Ch'angsu down.

Once in the car, the chauffeur never looked back. The chauffeur's lodging was in a corner of the large garden just inside the main gate of the mansion. His family was now standing in front of the house to see the car off. When the car started to pull out, the wailing burst into the air.

"Daddy!" Ch'angsu's voice followed the car. The chauffeur sounded the horn uselessly and needlessly, as if to muffle his son's voice.

Somehow Myŏngso felt very uncomfortable sitting on his father's lap, so he put one bag on his lap and sat down in its place.

Looking out the window, he realized that the thing he had been checking so hard up to then was a good cry.

They were now within sight of the government building. The square was now full of students, milling and jostling. It was said that some students were now talking with the government officials. No representatives had been chosen. It didn't matter who they were. Anybody who happened to be at the front might well represent them, for what they wished they wished as one, and it was so simple.

Indeed, they were not demanding too much. They certainly were not out to grab political power; they were demanding that the government recognize the basic and minimum rights of the people. Proper things should be properly handled.

They waited. Those people were now doing what they themselves would have done if they had been up front. What they wanted to shout had been shouted. Now only the administrative part of the whole business remained—proper actions on the part of the government in reply to their demands. Feeling a sudden upsurge of fatigue, they began to sit down on the pavement. All of them were wet with perspiration.

Elbowing through the dense crowd of citizens on the sidewalk, the women of the neighbourhood brought pails of water to them. Every one of them was thirsty. They quenched their thirst by taking turns at the dipper. A relaxed air began to set in. Now even an occasional low chuckle could be heard here and there.

Sidewalks were overflowing with citizens, and enthusiastic applause arose among them incessantly.

The body smell of a vast number of youths, their rough

breathing, their low-toned conversation—these were curiously mixed together and turned into a dense humming; the angry uproar of a short while ago could no longer be heard.

But Myŏngso's ears were still ringing with the angry roar: "Apologize to the people! Apologize to the people!"

It was that deep, rich, and resonant voice, Ch'angsu's voice. And what's more, Myŏngso might have been hearing the same outcry for a long, long time. Ch'angsu must have been calling it out for more than ten years, ever since that dreadful day in June of 1950 when the war broke out. But the call had not reached Myŏngso's ears.

Ch'angsu was merely crying then. But if they had thought it a mere crying, it was because they were dumb. The anger to be soothed by crying, the heart wrenched with curses—no one in Myŏngso's family was aware of the things that were going on in Ch'angsu's mind. He was too shabby an outsider to deserve their sympathy. They even showed some reluctance to have Ch'angsu's family living within the bounds of their mansion. It was September. They came back to Seoul as soon as it was retaken from the hands of the Communists. They had just arrived after three months of refugee life in Pusan. The reason they were reluctant was simple: something had happened to Ch'angsu's family while they were away.

It was late July when Ch'angsu's mother died. She was out on a forced labor gang one day, and the entire gang was bombed by UN planes. His mother was killed instantly. This was reported to the family by one of the few survivors, and they could not even retrieve her body.

"Ch'angnam? What happened to Ch'angnam?" the chauffeur looked insanely for his eldest daughter. But when he was told that she had been mobilized to work in a people's hospital and had gone north with the medical unit, he merely slumped down, with no courage to ask abut his missing second daughter. It was known only that she had joined the Young Communist Women and had made some speeches; now, after the liberation of Seoul, she was arrested and imprisoned somewhere in town.

"Oh, God, they all turned into commies! You can never trust those people," was the immediate Myongso's mother's response. But she could never stop to listen to the fact that the girls had been forced into doing what they did because their father went south with an important government official, fleeing the Communist regime. Even if she had, it probably would have made no difference to her.

Mr. Shin, the chauffeur, seemed to have become an even more faithful and loyal servant. He seemed to be grateful that his employer would not fire a man with two Communist daughters.

Mr. Shin did not even bother to find out the whereabouts of his second daughter. Alone with Ch'angsu, he lived on in the old room, which had become much larger and roomier with the departure of the three female members of the family. Then, in January of the following year, they had to leave Seoul again for Pusan. Again Mr. Shin drove Myŏngso's family car, but this time, since the luggage had been shipped by rail, Ch'angsu was allowed to come with his father.

When Mr. Shin was given a room next to the bathroom in their temporary dwelling in Pusan, he was very grateful; the congested seaport city was oveflowing with homeless people.

Living together in the same house, Myŏngso somehow began to dislike playing with Ch'angsu. He began to shun him. He acted unnecessarily rude and unkind to Mr. Shin too. People must have thought it was the self-indulgence of the only son of a high government official.

Myŏngso became a middle school student while the family was still leading a refugee life. He entered the renowned Kigyŏng Middle School with top marks in the entrance examination. He was a devil of a miniature genius.Ch'angsu also became a middle school student, entering Yangji(private) Middle School. Thus, the two boys began to lead two different lives, both at home and school. Though they were of the same age and lived together in the same house, they became more and more estranged.

It wasn't because Myongso regarded Ch'angsu as the son of an employee. Nor was it because the other was a student attending what was generally thought to be a second-rate middle school while he himself was attending the top school in the country. He merely disliked Ch'angsu. And in this case, his dislike certainly gave an impression of abuse and maltreatment. It got to be so that the housemaids often frowned secretly.

But Myŏngso thought that he was the real victim. The sense of oppression he felt whenever he saw Ch'angsu was becoming almost unbearable. It was somehow connected in his mind with fear. Whenever he saw Ch'angsu, he was reminded of the scene of that night in September. (Ch'angsu had been cryed and cryed upon his father's returned.) Now, even when he saw Ch'angsu's smiling, he could not help seeing the crying face superimposed in his mind's eye. It was like a nucleus in his consciousness which gnawed away like a disease.

Mr. Shin and his son were sincere, loyal, and perfectly trustworthy employees in every possible way. "Minister Pak has a good chauffeur" was what his father's friends used to say, but he kept on saying "No" to himself. Soon they came back again to Seoul, but this situation had not changed.

He did not know how to express his as yet immature consciousness, but vaguely he felt that to find sincerity and loyalty where hatred and grievance should have been was to face the devilish and darker side of human nature. He kept on shunning Ch'angsu, although they were living in the same house.

Thus, time flowed on. One grew up in a luxuriously decorated Western room, the other in a shabby frame house next to the garage.

Now Myŏngso was a high school senior. Throughout his middle school and high school days, he had always been the top student in his class. The funny part of it all was that he was well aware that he had never consciously tried to be the best; then he would further realize that in this very awareness was the arrogant self-confidence and conceit that disgusted him. Being the only son of a high-ranking government official with abundant material resources, he really should not have had any complaints. But something indefinable was always gnawing at him in a corner of his mind.

He was looking down at the garden one day from the window of his room, when he noticed that there was something swaying in the breeze, hung between a treetop and the eaves of the drawing room. Glistening at times in the sun, it was a spider's web.

It did not interest him. Just as he was going to look away, however, a sparrow flew smack into the web. Instantly, the sparrow fell to the ground, covered with the web.

Myŏngso leaned out of the window. The sparrow was frantically jumping up and down on the lawn, still covered with the web. The web on the sparrow now looked drab and ragged, he thought; it had had a glistening and transparent beauty of its own when it was up in the air.

The sparrow seemed uneasy. Stopping his jumping, he began to work his neck. Finally he wriggled his head out of the web. He jumped up and down again, but still looked uncomfortable. He jumped, bobbed his head, and then he jumped again.

A cynical smile spread across Myŏngso's lips. For some reason, the sparrow looked like himself, he thought.

Just then, a deep, ringing bass voice was heard singing. It sang a well-known Negro spiritual. It was rich and resonant, but doleful and plaintive at the same time. It was coming from the back yard. It carried a free and unchecked tune up in the air. Myŏngso suddenly wanted to find out who the owner of the voice was.

He ran down the stairs to go around to the back yard. He saw his father's car parked in front of the garage, and Mr. Shin smoking a cigarette, sitting on a piece of rock a little way off. A sturdily built young man with broad shouders was washing the car with a water hose in one hand. He was the man who was singing.

Myŏngso went near the car. Seeing him approach, Mr. Shin jumped to his feet. At this the singing stopped. The man looked the hose still in his hand.

It was Ch'angsu; he had grown beyond recognition. His round face was covered with a pleasant amount of pimples, and it gave out altogether a healthy look. He was completely grown up. It was the first time Myŏngso had seen him in the two years since Ch'angsu began to live with a certain wealthy family as a tutor to their children.

Myŏngso advanced a step closer; he was very glad to see Ch'angsu again. Just as he was reaching out his hand to hold Ch'angsu's, Mr. Shin rushed in to stand between them. Then he began to bow in an apologetic gesture.

"What manners, Ch'angsu! I'm sorry. He thought there wasn't anybody around in the..."

Taken aback, Myŏngso looked at Mr. Shin for a long time. Then he realized what Mr. Shin was trying to convey.

He felt as if a fire had been put out inside.

He could distinctly feel that his heart was chilled and cooling off. His two clear, girlish eyes were now giving out an icy stare. He looked coldly at them, and then turned around to walk away.

He could hear the hushed, whispering reproach of Mr. Shin behind him.

"Do I not always tell you to be more careful?" The funny thing was that he felt much relieved by that incident, as if a spell was broken that had bound him for a long time. Now he felt he could dismiss Mr. Shin and his son completely out of his consciousness. And he did.

It was early summer of last year when Myŏngso ran into Ch'angsu again. Now Myŏngso was a college junior.

He was strolling along the path in the woods of the forestry experimentation station. He was not alone; a girl, a sophomore at the same college, was beside him. She was wearing a light pink angora wool sweater and a flared white skirt. In the dominant green of the woods the color of her dress gave out a soft pastel tone. It was like the fluffy pinfeathers of an infant bird.

She was beautiful, he thought. He felt peace, love, and affection well up from the bottom of his heart. It was like the thawing out of a heart which had been frozen, frozen with dirt and filth. Or it was like his head was being cleared of an evil fog, the clear blueness of the sky seeping into its place. Suddenly she stopped.

"Look, butterflies."

Myŏngso turned to the direction she pointed. A pair of yellow butterflies were dancing and fluttering in the air.

"They are yellow butterflies. Yellow butterflies," said the girl with a gay, joyous laughter. It was a buoyant voice. She was very lovely and charming.

"Why? Do you particularly love yellow butterflies, Aehui?"

"No, not particularly. I just recalled an old story Mother told me way back, that if the first butterfly one sees in spring is a white one, one becomes bereaved of his dearest."

Silently Myŏngso gazed at her lips in fascination—soft, pinkish without any rouge. Just above her upper lip, he could see the light shadow of downy hair.

When she was serious, she talked in a very quiet tone, as quiet as the snowflakes piling up in winter. Yet her voice and intonation were buoyant and springy. He had never met a person like that. Of course, she was not seriously believing the story, he thought, but nevertheless it was striking that she should still remember a story which she had heard many, many years ago. It seemed to tell of her deep attachment and affection to her parents.

Aehui had grown up in a home filled with scholars. Her father was a renowned linguistic scientist and two of her three elder brothers were promising young scholars with degrees in the field of natural science. She was the youngest, and the only daughter of the family. When Myŏngso visited the family for the first time, he was on an errand for his father. Dr. Song, Aehui's father, used to be a classmate of Myŏngso's uncle.

Though he was generally quite averse to visiting other people's houses, he made one pretext or another to revisit Dr. Song's house after that. He could not help being drawn in more and more by the atmosphere of the family that seemed to consist of deep culture, faith, affection, and love.

He had always been welcomed by the family. But when they got around to the subject of criticizing the government, they ignored Myŏngso altogether. Never violent, they were stern and effective in their attacks upon and criticism of the government.

She had been brought up in such a family, and she was the center of love of all the members. That was why she had been christened Aehui, too, he was told; Aehui meaning the beloved maiden.

It was always beautiful to see her return the love she received, adding her own love, but he often thought that she was fortunate in having parents to whom she could devote such love and affection. He was not.

Whenever he faced his own mother, he was filled with self-disgust that he should have been born of her. All too frequently he would observe the shoe box of his house filled with women's shoes of all colors—then he would hear the muffled and unnatural laughter of women flattering his mother in her room. Then he would imagine the ugly and fat mouths of those women that would lie without shame or scruple. Why were they always there? Why did they always gather around his mother? He knew, he knew, and that disgusted him all the more.

She was not entirely without an affectionate side. She would decorate her room with the pictures of the children of her two daughters, Okhui and Ongnan, who were now in the United States, and she would watch those pictures rapturously for hours on end like a good grandmother. But, this did not happen often, and even if it did, her facial expression on such occasions simply did not connect with that of when she bade Mr. Shin hurry up on that fateful day.

She had learned to play the *kayagum*[1] some years ago, but even that did not sound artistic or refined to him. Hung on the wall, the shiny lines of the instrument seemed filthy with the fat of his mother's fingers.

His father was somewhat different; he commanded a broad knowledge of culture. But one vital point was warped and crooked in him. Myŏngso seldom contradicted his father to his face. But the father was well aware of the son's disapproval and resistance. Every morning he would find on his desk the opposition newspapers, showily spread, full of criticism of his own doings.

Once a large picture of a beggar boy sprawling on the pavement was stuck on the drawing room wall. It was on the day that the father had invited an important guest from abroad. His private secretary took it off in time, but his hasty manner seemed to have attracted the attention of the guest all the more. His son was trying to accuse him of political impotence by exposing one disastrous aspect of the society, the father thought. "You are too harsh; after all, you are my son," thought the father.

There was another incident. Once the son had driven his father's official car at an incredibly fast speed and had smashed a corner of a small store. Since the numbers on the license plate were well known, the incident was reported in a devastating manner by an opposition paper, although his name was not disclosed.

The father's exasperation was extreme. When he got back home that night after the maddening routine of government affairs, it was already past eleven-thirty.

Hearing the sound of the horn, Myŏngso, quite untypically, opened the main gate himself. When he saw the newspaper report, the father took it as an open challenge and affront on the part of his son. He became furious once more. What's more, the son started to go upstairs without a word even before the father had time to open the door of his room.

"Wait!" cried the father. He was already breathless. "I want to talk to you."

---

1. a Korean musical instrument with 12 strings.

Myŏngso could still recall the conversation of that night.

"It's an official car. Everybody knows the number," said the father. But the way he put it irritated his son's nerves.

"You mean it was bad because everybody knows the number," countered the son. At this the father's face turned pale with rage.

"Shut up!" roared out the father, but he was himself surprised at the tone of his voice. "You mean to say what you did was not bad enough?" the father said in a somewhat suppressed tone. The son had been looking at his father's face squarely.

"What I did? No, it wasn't my doing. It was the doing of something inside me that is protesting against corruption and slow collapse. It's my desperate attempt to throw out the dirty water that fills me up to here."

"It's between father and son. Let's cut out all the abstract rhetoric. Say your piece in plainer words."

"I cannot stand it any longer. I want to be a wholesome element in the society like anybody else. I want a space in which I can move about freely like other people. I want to smash all the mirrors that surround me wherever I go. I want to join others when they shout, and I want to soak myself with tears when others cry. I am always stared at with hate-ridden eyes because I am your son, the son of the powerful man who is leading the country into a slow death. I am afraid of this aloneness, this sense of alienation, this sense of guilt—," by now he was almost shouting. Then he saw his father's mournful and pathetic face watching him.

"Myŏngso," his fahter called out in a soft tone. At this the son burst into tears.

"No, Dad, no. Nobody persecutes me actually. I am the precious son of an important government official. They all treat me well. They all say at the college that I am a genius of rare quality. They all think I'm great." The son now stammered like an infant, sobbing. "But among them I feel guilty—guilty as the man who has set the fire and is now among the crowd that is trying to put it out. That guilty conscience bothers me."

The father got up to his feet and went closer to his son. He put his hands on the son's shoulder.

"You look as though you could use some sleep. Go to bed."

The son shook his head. "Do you sleep well? I cannot

sleep. I feel I could well if we all took our punishment."
He looked up at his father. He said nothing. They were silent
for a moment. It was the father who broke the silence after a while.

"Youth is a belief, but sooner or later we must part with it,"
he said as though it were a sigh. "Things change. Nothing lasts
forever. Youth hates the established values and wants to sweep
out the old, but the new force of today will be the old wall of
tomorrow and there is bound to be a still newer force which is
destined to charge against that wall."

"Then do you approve of the present regime?"

"I cannot say I approve. But still the wheel is turning, and
the wheel may well be on fire."

The son got up from the chair too. He was feeling much
better.

"Sleep tight, Father."

"You too."

Just as the son was turning the door knob, the father said
in a low tone as if to himself.

"Our forebears back in the olden days were puzzled and
troubled over the position of man in the universe, but now in
our day we must shed blood because of a mere worldly regime."

As he came through the door, the son turned his head and
said distinctly, with conviction. "Our bodies are on fire, Dad.
How do you expect us to solve the secret of the universe all at
once? We must advance step by step."

"Why are you silent all of a sudden? Was I too childish with
my yellow butterflies and all?" Aehui came a step closer to him
with her head to one side inquiringly. The pleasant odor of her
body mixed with that of the green foliage and permeated the air.
It spread and spread till she became the entire world to him.
Something hot like tears ran through his body. For the first time
in his life he felt an intense desire to kiss a person. Fearful of
the desire, he closed his eyes. But his inner vision was still bright.
Eyes closed, he could still see her sweet figure as vividly as with
open eyes.

"Why?" Aehui repeated her question quietly and worriedly.

He opened his eyes and saw Aehui's worried face.

"I love you."

He was more surprised at the abrupt statement, but he

repeated what he had said. "I love you very much." Then suddenly he started to race ahead.

Taken by surprise, she stood there for awhile before she began to follow him. There was a junction ahead, and as he took one path, he was almost sure that she would go off on the other. But her footsteps followed him.

He kept on running. He saw an elegant-looking tree laden with white flowers. He ran faster toward the tree as if it were the final goal of the race.

It was a magnolia tree, full of fragrant blossoms. Blooming in the May sun, it was sending out its perfume into the May breeze. It was as pure and fragrant as a maiden.

It struck him suddenly that he should decorate her with the flowers. Though he had never climbed a tree, he hoisted himself up speedily and deftly among the branches.

Then she arrived, running breathlessly, her cheeks flushed.

"I cannot follow you up there. It's not fair!" she pretended to nag, looking up. Surely it was her own way of confessing her love.

He felt his chest fill up. Flowers began to loom large in his vision. Every blossom just seemed to be waiting bliss fully to be picked.

"Don't move! I gotcha covered," he said jokingly and grabbed a branch.

Just then it happened.

"Who's up there!" a deep, ringing voice was heard, and a man emerged out of the woods. "Who's up in the tree? Come right down!" he roared again.

Myŏngso was stunned. He nearly dropped off the tree. It was none other than Ch'angsu himself. Myongso had heard earlier that Ch'angsu had also entered one of the private universities in town, but he had not seen him for a long time. Instantly Myŏngso became calm and cool.

"Come right down? Who are you to order me around?"

"I am giving an order as a citizen to a delinquent who harms tree in the forestry station, which is government property."

"By what right?"

"By the right of being a citizen"

"I cannot come down till I pick this flower."

"No, you won't."

"Yes, I will."

Ch'angsu jumped up suddenly and pulled down one of his feet. It was an experienced movement. He had heard that Ch'angsu had been working somewhere part-time, and this might well be his place of work, he thought, still struggling. Aehui gave out a scream.

He gritted his teeth desperately. Ch'angsu's powerful arm was ruthlessly pulling him down. He felt his hands gripping the branch getting weak. Then Ch'angsu released his foot unexpectedly.

"The branch is going to snap. Come down by yourself," Ch'angsu said in the same deep, ringing voice. In it there was a dignified quality that allowed no defiance.

Myŏngso came down limply from the tree, Ch'angsu stepped back one or two steps and waited. He stepped closer when Myŏngso was on the ground.

"They are all valuable material for research. They tempt us, but we should not touch, you know," Ch'angsu said in a quiet voice. Myŏngso glared at him wordlessly. Ch'angsu was cool as he could be. Suddenly Myŏngso felt all the blood in him gush up to his head. He slapped one of Ch'angsu's plump cheeks with all his might. He felt his palm burn. He hit him again on the other cheek.

Then he started to run for the gate. Ch'angsu did not follow him as he expected. Only Aehui's screaming, "Myŏngso, wait for me," followed him.

A flash that he had lost everything ran through his head as he was running. Aehui would never forgive his conduct. Even if she forgave him somehow, he would never be able to embrace her as he had thought he might. He himself could not forgive her just as he could never forgive himself now for what he had done.

When he got back, he found his father home. Though it was Sunday, it was rare for him to be home so early. The father at once knew from his look that something had happened.

"Anything wrong?"

"I met Ch'angsu!"

"Ch'angsu?"

"Yes, the same Ch'angsu that you had deserted and abandoned in Seoul when the Communists came down."

Not wishing to be dragged into another argument, the father looked busy and turned to the newspapers. But the son was determined to have it out.

"I hit him twice."

"Why?" the father looked up.

"Because he was so damned right!"

He had run out of his father's room, leaving the door ajar, and had gone upstairs noisily.

The sound of rifle fire was sudden and unexpected. Nobody had thought that the police would fire at their own people. It hit them like a thunderbolt.

"Yah. . ."

A battle cry rose like a whirlwind to shake the earth. The students no longer formed lines. Enraged and furious, every one of them was eager to go ahead for himself.

"It's rifle fire, rifle fire!"

"Those sons of bitches are firing at us!"

Everyone's face tightened up.

Then confusion began to reign over the students who crowded the wide square. A group of students was running back down the street leading to the presidential residence behind the government building.

Now through the sound of rifle fire a group of students was jumping over the low stone fences of the government building like a flock of black birds. The battle cries now rose from inside the building, too.

"Yah. . . Yah. . ."

And every time the cries rose, one could hear the sound of rifle fire.

Da-da-da-da-. . .

"Get down, get down!" Hearing someone shout urgently and desperately, Myŏngso was running ahead toward the presidential residence.

A sheet of paper flew into his face.

It seemed to have come from the government office building. In the front lawn inside the stone fences of the government building students were running every which way, as though they were doing some fast dance step among the hail and snow of flying papers. Someone must have thrown those papers out from the office windows. Some sheets of paper settled down, then they were blown up again, and carried by the wind, they flew far, far up into the air. Thrown up high from the top floor in bundles, they burst high in the air like paper cascades or confetti. Some shone more than others, depending on their angle to the sunlight.

Da-da-da-da-. . .

The sound of rifle fire increased.

"Take cover! Take cover! They're firing blind!" cried the same voice.

A jeep was slowly advancing toward them from the direction of the presidential residence, the sound of its horn drowned out by the students. A youth who was clinging to the side of the jeep was desperately waving his arm to make way.

It was a press car.

"Step aside! Make way! Men have been killed!" He was shouting in a hoarse voice.

There were people lying in the jeep as well as on the rooftop. There was no way of knowing if they were already dead, but blood was trickling down from the jeep onto the pavement. At last blood was shed!

An electric tension ran through the crowd. Sparklike rage and hostility took possession of the crowd instantly.

"Men have been killed! The police have killed people!" They all shouted and ran ahead. No one was afraid of death now. Was not dying for a cause the highest expression of life?

Pushed along by the waves of students, Myŏngso got as far as the corner of the government building compound. The multitude of feet was still around him. On that fateful night in June of 1950, those countless feet had been marching toward the Han River Bridge, not knowing their fate of an hour later. They had been marching as though the land of life had been promised to them if they could reach the Bridge. And now these countless feet were marching toward the presidential residence. Though they knew that death waited there, they kept marching as if they believed in a new life beyond that death.

Myŏngso's benumbed feet now seemed to have willpower of their own. Confusion reigned both inside and outside. He was well aware that he was no longer capable of orderly thinking, but even in that muddled moment he was conscious of one thing: it was that sense of alienation; that this breathtakingly historic upheaval somehow did not quite reach him. Among all these people proud to be the heroes of the historic moment, he alone felt slouched and shrunken, like the man who had set the fire and was now among the crowds of people who were trying to put it out. His goal might be his own execution ground.

Like a flash, his father's face came into his mind's eye. He had been a good and tender father to his only son. Something hot welled up in his heart. It was the bondage of blood that one could not help.

"Dad, blood is shed. At last we saw blood." It was his silent and despairing cry. It was a painful and heart-wrenching cry. "Blood is flowing, Dad! Blood is flowing!" This silent outcry kept bursting from his heart.

Blood. Why is it that people go insane as soon as they see blood? What is this sticky and dreadful fluid? They say it is the source and evidence of life. It runs through every human being warmly, liberally at times, and pantingly and gaspingly at other times, and for this very reason it may call and attract other blood. The reason people get insanely agitated over the spilled blood may also be that the blood is directly connected with their own. Yes, in this sticky, dark fluid lies the secret of the bondage of race, hatred, and love. The secret of making all these young men take part in this festival of life and willingly offer their lives as sacrifice is the doing of that same blood. And the closest linkage in this relation is the one between a father and son.

"Daddy! Daddy!"

A despairing longing and love wrenched his heart. But Myŏngso still remained in the middle of the crowd. It was not because the roads were blocked off, but because he, an individual, could not exercise his own willpower as he wished in the face of a giant order. He was still moving forward, dragging his blood-stained feet.

The sound of rifle fire went up close by. He could hear bullets zip through in the air overhead.

"Get down! Get down! Take to the side of the street!" a deep, ringing voice yelled up. Myŏngso took cover behind the stone fences.

"Let's not die for nothing! Get down!" the ringing voice roared again. Myŏngso turned over to the direction of the voice.

Ch'angsu was yelling as he rolled as protection an iron water main pipe that happened to be lying by the side of the street. Ch'angsu soon reached a barricade. On the other side of the barricade was a group of policemen with loaded rifles.

"We'll shoot if you cross the barricade," said one of them to Ch'angsu.

"We want to talk to the president. Let us pass," countered Ch'angsu.

"We'll shoot if you cross."

"We're going to cross."

"Then we'll shoot," repeated the policeman mechanically.

Ch'angsu hesitated for a moment on this side of the pipe.

The pipe seemed to roll back a few inches. Then all of a sudden Ch'angsu leapt forward and over the barricade. At the same time, da-da-da-da. . . It was a submachine gun.

Myŏngso reopened his eyes, which had closed for a moment reflexively. There was nobody standing around the barricade except the lone and giant figure of the policeman with his gun poised. By the barricade Ch'angsu was lying prostrate.

Wet with his own blood, Ch'angsu's back was still making convulsive movements.

"Ch'angsu?" Myŏngso jumped to his feet, crying out, almost unconsciously.

To Myŏngso at this instant, the name of Ch'angsu and everything attached to it seemed to spread and spread till they filled up the entire world. Nothing and no one existed except Ch'angsu and himself in the wide, wide world.

He dashed to the barricade in a jump, and put Ch'angsu's body on his shoulder.

Da-da-da-da-. . .

The policeman's gun went off again. Something hot hit the back of his neck he thought. The next moment he went down on the pavement, Ch'angsu's body and all.

Timeless time whirled around and inside him with incredible speed. White snowflakelike things dotted his vision. Soon he knew they were magnolia blossoms. They began to loom, loom, loom till they filled up his whole vision. Finally his head dropped on Ch'angsu's chest. In an awe-inspiring moment of silence, blood was flowing down on the pavement. The blood from the bodies of these two youths was mixed and flowing together as if from one body.

(end story)

The Hunchback of Seoul

Kwŏn T'aeung

For three days after she had run away, the odor of the woman
from a street in Seoul called Ahyŏndong lingered on the bed
sheets. It clung obstinately among the fibers of the fabric. Thus
I acquired a new habit of burying my head deeply in the sheets,
fervently working my nose, mourning, sucking in the odor of
the woman who had left me. The pungent smell of hair, the thick
eyeshadow along her damp eyes, the unnamable fragrance emitted
from her glass-smooth naked body—all this was enough to turn
my head. I moved the bed away from the window. I jealously
covered it with blankets each time I emerged from it—all this
was part of my futile effort to preserve that mature odor as long
as possible and to commemorate the short-lived universe of happiness that I had encountered for the first time in my life. I was
not able to look at anything that had belonged to her without
pangs of emotion, not even the flakes of dandruff on the pillow.
When she had made fun of my physical deformity by caressing
the hump on my back and saying, "Your this—your back looks
exactly like my belly when I was first pregnant," I was too
delirious, too intoxicated to be offended. I had not been able to
resist for a moment her sweet and tender skin. The harsh sound
of her rough breathing overwhelmed mine, launched me into
yet another heaven, and satiated my tragically urgent desire. Then
she had been me and I her.

"You are like a queen bee." I bit my teeth lest they should
rattle, deliriously watching her bright smile. She easily disengaged
herself from my arms locked around her waist, opened the window and said, "When is this damned war going to end?" She
coughed up phlegm and spat through the window.

"Why? Are you tired of the war?"

"Aren't you?"

I could not answer. Anyway, I had no way of knowing that those were the last words this woman from Ahyŏndong was going to leave me with. Of course it would have been useless even if I had known. I would merely have besought her in tears, clinging to her legs, to stay with me, while the war lasted at least, if she could not stay for good. I could not bear the hollowness left in me by the woman from Ahyŏndong. I exposed myself to the storm she raised and kindled inside me. The words she uttered in a moment of ecstasy kept coming back to me: "You are much more of a man than you look."

How those simple and ordinary words intoxicated me! In fact these words served me with the encouragement to interpret life in a brighter hue, but I knew I could not imitate those American soldiers by going out into the street and ogling the streetwalkers who filled the city. The picture of myself in my mind, a dwarf and a hunchback making a pass at sadly smiling prostitutes in the war-torn streets under a desolate sky, was so utterly impossible that tears rushed to my eyes. Thus the short, happy period in which she and I lived together had only left me with an empty and absurd significance. And in these moments of longing I had to idealize her, hungrily wanting her. The flood of ecstasy that drowned my heart, the rubble in the city in the wake of street fighting, and the arrogant passion that crept into the quiet of those ruins—it was an actual castle. The nostalgia of the ruins was the beat in my blood vessels, and like the highwayman who collected the proverbs of jubilation. In my inverted way, I had once been proud and compared myself to the fabulous turtle in the deep sea that never surfaced, and I had thought I would never be sorry if the world rolled along for millions of light-years without ever noticing me. But now I realized it had been a form of perverted resistance. I was now initiated into what people termed glory. And happiness. I realized there was nothing shameful about coveting that glory and happiness. "Your this—your back looks exactly like my belly when I was first pregnant." Even this did not anger me any longer. When her black hair covered my face I first learned what the world was about, and I felt a bridge strung between me and the world. It was not a dazzling ephemeral rainbow bridge that hovered over the volcanic crater of my long suppressed vengeance and anger; it was something more substantial and lasting.

On that day in June, when the rumblings neared the city, all the normal people—the people who had contemptuously called me a dwarf, a hunchback—fled the city in panic. I had watched the panic-stricken column of refugees crossing the bridge over the Han River through the window of my house, but it failed to arouse any kind of feeling in me. I was not a bit sorry that I was not among them. Perhaps it was not that I could not find a justifiable reason that I, too, should cross the bridge with them, but that rather I was simply and incorrigibly lazy. Three months had passed since then, and following the upsurge and counterattack of the Allied forces, people trickled back into the ruined city under the hot September sun. But I was neither glad nor sad to see them back.

The only thing that mattered to me now was the woman from Ahyŏndong. The thing that wrung my heart so painfully now was her fresh youth that tapped me and went off ever so casually. I could see no way out. The wall of youth was one over which I had no control.

But how fortunate it all was for me! It was another way to look at the whole affair. To explore inwardly the woman who had moistened my arid heart with springlike rain of affection. Without the war, I would never have been able to perceive the pure esthetics of womanhood. Through her I had had a taste of regality in the kingdom of my bed where she lay, and thus I had been able to forget, for awhile at least, the wrath deformed people like myself felt. The room filled with joy was my empire. The fragrance of the perfume, the harsh breathing, the upsurge of excitement, the passion.

A short while ago, climbing down from the slopes of Namsan hill, I looked at the objects of desire and greed of the people who fled the city, who used to laugh at me because I was a hunchback. Although the bright reflection of the acacia leaves patronizingly poured on me, I would certainly have gone mad and roamed around the barren and desolate streets of Seoul if it weren't for my experience with her in our kingdom.

After burying my head for a long time in the bed sheets, inhaling the amorous odor of the woman from Ahyŏndong, I rose and stood by the window. A patch of dark cloud was faintly discernible in the night sky, and a new moon, just off the edge of the cloud, hung loosely over the skeleton of a building whose side had been shot away by bombing; casting a sad shadow over the building.

The night was quiet. The hills silhouetted against the dark sky; rotten sacks and used ammo boxes littered the quiet streets. Perhaps in some dark alleys were the dead bodies of foreign soldiers covered with straw mats. Then I vividly recalled that I had not felt the least bit of fear watching the deserted streets with her. How do I explain this flood of fear and loneliness now, I wondered and sighed.

When I got back into bed and lit a cigarette, I could hear the roaring of truck engines again. It was a big American troop movement. The continual flow of troops to the north seemed to indicate a big offensive on our side, and it could be told by the faces of the soldiers and mountainous supplies loaded on the trucks.

Soon the headlights lit up the silk curtains on the windows. I closed my eyes, recalling the white naked body of the woman from Ahyŏndong wriggling against the illuminated curtain only a few days earlier.

It was only ten days ago, amid the furor of street fighting. The rumbling of guns and explosions, the fierce shots of Russian submachine guns directed against alleys and buildings, the wild shooting of mortars and automatic weapons. Amid all this the Communists searched out women from houses to have them build barricades on the key streets and traffic circles to slow down the Allied troops. Dividing them into two groups, they deployed one group to build barricades, and the other to dig up the pavement to lay mines.

The woman from Ahyŏndong was in the group building barricades. And I, ransacking houses, looting anything that was edible (everybody else did), was camping out in this very house. In the cellar of this huge western-style mansion I found a convenient haven from explosions and stray bullets. And it was there in the cellar of the ghostly mansion that I met her for the first time. She told me she had fled from the work party.

"Why aren't you out of town, Sir? I thought all the gentlemen had left the city," she said when I showed her into a luxurious western-style living room.

"Well, I sent my family south. I figured they wouldn't bother a cripple like me." I did not know why, but on the spur of the moment I said these words very casually as if I were the owner of the mansion.

"I must say it's very rewarding in this case, Sir," she said. Of course she had no reason to doubt my ownership of the house.

But I was struck by her beauty. She was around thirty and her mature beauty nearly dazed me. I now had an opportunity to sit together with a beautiful woman for the first time in my life.

"Would it be too much if I asked you to hide me somehow in your house, till the street fighting ends at least?" she begged and her beautiful voice kindled a fire in my heart.

"Please stay as long as you wish. Fortunately, I have enough food here. I should think it would be very bad if you got caught again at this time."

"Thank you, Sir! I will certainly repay you for this some day."

From that time on, I had conducted a more thorough search of the house, for I was not familiar with its details.

Willy-nilly I became the owner of the house, at least to her anyway. I had no intention of being an impostor. Honestly speaking, I did not think I had to act like the owner of the house when I first met the woman from Ahyŏndong. I was simply vague about it and she seemed to take it for granted that I was the master of the house. Once I knew that she believed so, somehow I could not tell her that she was wrong. But why had I been vague about it in the beginning? And why did I not correct her misunderstanding? How had I involved myself into an impostuous ownership? It was much later that I learned her beauty had very much to do with all this.

I learned it was a joy to work for and take care of a woman. It was a source of immeasurable happiness. I began to feel that I could understand what people meant by the word happiness. When I first held her ankle to tend to bruise, I trembled with excitement. It was an absolutely thrilling experience. I had the illusion of falling from the sky. But more staggering was the fact that even a deformed man like myself could arouse a long-suppressed sexual feeling in a coldly beautiful woman like her.

I had always existed for other people. When I was first born it was not my own consciousness that I reached for, but my mother's breasts. For thirty-odd years I lived in the humble knowledge that I was an appendage to someone else. Thus, it was quite natural for me to be surprised at the fact that I was able to produce the priceless semen that the woman desired. For two days we filled our bellies with delicious food, and when we tried to sleep, hearing the sound of shells exploding near the house next door, we dropped the "sirs" and "madams" from our speech.

"Only God knows when our house will be blown to pieces like the house next door," she said with a mixture of fear and resignation. At this I held her slim waist with one arm, searching for her bare breasts with the other hand. And, like a coward, I prayed to myself, "May the war last forever."

Meanwhile the shelling and bombing kept on, but luckily our house was spared. Then she said, "No one can tell the future, but I feel like serving you like this forever." How sweet of her to say those words, those enrapturing words! The silhouetted ruin through the window no longer looked desolate to me. In the back of my ecstatic mind, however, was a little dark spot, a spot of shame, which soon loomed large. I knew it was about the false ownership of the house. Of course, it was a trivial matter when two people loved each other like we did, but somehow I felt I should explain.

Days passed without my finding the opportunity to do so. One day when I returned from a short errand downtown, the woman was busy making herself up in front of the vanity table. I caressed her round, naked shoulders, kissing fervently her smooth fragrant skin.

"You tickle me to death. Why don't you behave like a good boy," she said, making a coquettish frown with her beautiful eyes.

"What's all this makeup for?"

"I want to look prettier for you," she said. Then after a while, she added, "Are we really going to get married?"

There was the unmistakable suggestion of a proposal. I jumped up and exclaimed, "Will you really do it for me?"

She said, "For all practical purposes we are married, you know. But I want to ask you something. The house—I suppose a rich man like you can give away a house like this. I wish you would give this house to me, to commemorate our wedding, so to speak."

I was speechless at this for awhile, but with a sigh I said, "Do you really want to have the house?"

At this her expression changed a great deal. Color rose to her cheeks and her long eyelashes trembled. "You mean you would? Of course we'll always live together, but I'll feel a lot more. . . secure that way. God, I am a fortunate woman."

"Must you really have the house?" I asked again. Then she buried her face in my chest, caressing me, shaking me.

I got out some blank sheets of paper and wrote out then and there a memorandum transferring ownership of the house to her. I handled everything with sincerity and taciturnity. I was not surprised at my own soberness; nor did I find the whole affair funny. That night, her wantonness and lasciviousness beggared all description. I emptied nearly half a bottle of whisky as she made me do, and fell into a deep sleep.

When I woke up the following day around noon, the woman from Ahyŏndong was no longer to be seen.

This unexpected situation upset me considerably. It was like being dragged back into the old, familiar world of humiliation before the war. I felt solitude, appropriate and worthy for the occasion, was in order. To fight off the hollowness in me, I wandered around the streets and alleys of the ruined city for days on end. From the top of the hill on which the church spire, the symbol of the Almighty's glory's rose, I looked down at the ruined city still shrouded in smoke.

The window was still lit up by the headlights. The sound of the truck engines now drew near. Somehow, I thought I could tell the nationality of the driver from the sound of the engine alone. The first truck out there was driven by a cowboy from Texas. I lit another cigarette and stood by the window. A convoy of trucks drove by with incredible noise. Their headlights, two parallel beams, pierced the pitch black of the night. And for the first time in days, I could watch without emotion the warriors go off to punish the Communists.

Viewing these lines of trucks moving north day and night I noticed a few changes that took place in the scenery from the window; people waved their hands at the moving soldiers, and there were a considerable number of bright electric lights in the city. When did all those people come back to town? But the fact did not arouse any particular feeling of welcome. Nevertheless I went out into the street and stood by them as if to reconfirm how shabby and pathetic I looked in comparison. I was never an equal by any means. The filthy streets reeked with the stench of things rotting. Suddenly I was acutely aware of my position—I found myself on a patch of ground at the top of the universe, rotting away among puddles and filth. Looking into myself coldly, I despised myself. Before long, the true owner of the house would return.

Suddenly I thought of my own house, a drab little shack near Sŏdaemun. Then inevitably I thought of Willy, my little dog, that I had left alone there. Had he not already starved to death? Or been torn into pieces by the bombing?

I walked back to the bed and threw myself down on it. Again I was intoxicated by the odor of the woman. But the room minus the woman was no longer my kingdom. I turned over once, thinking that it was high time I had left the house.

I left the house for good the following day after bidding farewell to my kingdom. Many groups of soldiers could be seen on the streets among sporadic civilians, walking with their helmets pushed back. I started to walk toward Sŏdaemun where my own house was. The way I walked was shabby and spiritless. I was empty handed, and I wore a pair of old army fatigues that I had bought three months earlier at the Dongdaemun Market. I knew there were a lot of expensive clothes hanging in the closet of the house I had just left, but somehow I did not want to try them on.

On the way to my home I passed by Ahyŏndong, and I stopped short in the middle of the pavement. I was thinking what I would say if I should run into the woman on one of these streets. I was well aware that I did not have the courage to ask the woman to come back to my royal suite. Under the clear blue Seoul sky, the peaceful sky with no more noise of guns, with refugees trickling back everyday, what words could I utter? That the interim had not been all darkness, not all misery? What other words could I utter with confidence?

Swiftly I turned back and hurried on. I walked by a long stretch of dreary and magnificent rubble and ruins.

Finding my own little shack intact, I drew in a deep breath. Something hot plugged my throat and I was moved to tears. Clearing my throat, I called out for Willy over and over. But Willy did not answer.

I turned around and went back to the heart of the city. The

dusk crept in, breathing quietly before the night descended. I could not tell why, but I found myself headed for the house where I had had a taste of happiness not long ago. But I was astounded when I turned around the corner from whence I could view the house. There in front of the house stood the woman from Ahyŏndong, a woman whose absence tormented me for so long and so bitterly. With a gush of delight and joy, I rushed across the street. But the next moment, I realized she was not alone. The man holding her hand so intimately and affectionately looked muscular and healthy. I felt tears streaking down my cheeks as I retreated. People who used to despise me, make fun of me, weren't they all healthy like the man whose hand the woman was holding?

A little while later I came out to a square surrounded by charry skeletons of buildings. I had no place to go. My own shack without Willy was no place for me to turn to, and I knew too well the Western-style mansion where the woman from Ahyŏndong had taken the muscular man was no place for me. I laughed and I wept. And the emptiness following the laughter and weeping was even more saddening. I knew I had to find some place to go before nightfall. Then I noticed a small boy walking in front of me. He wore an army field jacket that covered his knees. A broken helmet was on his head. He walked in a funny way, wihtout moving his shoulders. He held a stick in his hand, and he hit empty cans whenever he found one along the way.

The glowing sunset was turning the dark hair of the boy into yellow. I walked toward the sunset, tagging along with the boy.

(end story)

The Imjin River

Yu Chuhyŏn

A river, any river, tends to collect a hoard of tales and lore in its flow. Perhpas rivers alone flow tirelessly, timelessly. Soft words of lovers in low tones, tragic sorrow, passionate sighs— when these are accumulated over a long period of time along the banks of a river, they become folklore, a history of an area that is as unique as its climate.

From the beginning of time people have congregated in settlements along rivers. Then they pushed inland to the plains and mountains. The river flats with their fertile soil and wooded hills developed into cities.

However, there are places where the soil is shallow and barren even though it is near a river and surrounded by hills. There are many such places and the people who inhabit them find making a living very hard.

Why do people keep on living in such places? What makes them stay there in impoverished conditions, struggling against deprivation? Is it because of their homage to their ancestors, or is it because of their attachment to a hometown? An obsession? A force of habit? Resignation?

All these reasons may be wrong. The true conditions of human life may not be pinned down into clear-cut reasons or logic. Maybe they just go on living, walking along a given road, in the place they happened to be born.

However, I must tell you a story that has something to do with one such place.

1

Once an old woman was wandering along a river bank. She

thought she could still hear the last cry of her son, pitiably calling out, "Mah. . ." Her disheveled hair was half grey, and the deep furrows on her tanned brow told the story of her life. When people tried to console her, she talked back in an indignant tone. "What crime did my son commit to be shot to death? He's dead, you know. He's dead." She sat down on the river bank and began to wail. Her slightly protruding front teeth did not damage her looks; rather, they helped to give the impression of goodnaturedness to her.

"How do they expect us to live without heat in this cold weather? But my son would not have crossed the river to collect firewood if the river had not been frozen over." She went on wailing, blaming the frozen river. Who would swim across a river to collect firewood?

On January 2 by the lunar calendar, the old woman's son walked across the frozen river to the other side to cut reeds to heat the room, and he was returned dead.

The river is the Imjin River. The Imjin now divides North from South Korea in this area. In olden days it used to form the border between Silla, Paekche, and Koguryo,[1] and once again it divides the country into two and is the scene of heartbreaking bloodshed. "My son went across the river often to cut rushes for the fire. Is it such a crime to do so? He was shot by one of our own guns too." The old woman began to beat the exposed root of a pine tree and wailed on. "You know, this is my grand climacteric year," she said. She blamed it on her age. She was fifty nine. In Korea nine is an unlucky number.

As she had said, her son had died an unnatural, violent death. He was shot to death by an American guard while he was on his way home across the river after collecting firewood. He had crossed the river to cut reeds in an off-limits area. "To make me warm he was shot. Bad luck of the day." She kept blaming the luck of the day. She did not consider that her son had any faults. She merely blamed luck.

Now she blamed the person who had killed her son. Perhaps the person who had killed her son represented too big a power

---

1. refer to the three kingdoms that had divided the Korean peninsula until Silla unified the country. The period runs roughly from 200 to 668 A.D..

for her to rebel against. Perhaps she was accustomed to taking a beating. For a long while she gazed at Tŏngmang Mountain across the river, lost in reverie. The wind blowing across the river was quite nippy, but the old woman did not seem to care. The pine branches groaned in the wind. The winter sun was weak but bright against the twigs of the three ancient-looking pine trees under which the old woman sat. The pine trees and a loose pile of rocks near them constituted a *sŏnang-dang*, a place of worship where passersby prayed for good luck by adding more rocks to the pile.

2

It'aewŏn is a district in Seoul—an area on the southern foot of South Mountain. It is a relatively new part of the city, an oblong area between South Mountain and the Han River.

It is by no means a homogeneous part of the city; the standards of living among the population vary greatly. Slum frame houses with cardboard walls stand side by side with huge mansions. The way the slum houses are piled along the river bank would remind one of the Casbah in Algiers.

The district is noted principally for its foreign population. There is an American army post as well as a foreign residential area there. Naturally these foreigners attract a host of natives who make a living off them, adding an even more exotic look to the area.

Some suffer from indescribable poverty while others enjoy great affluence. There is decadent pleasure as well as self-inflicted idleness. There are people who make a living by robbery, swindling, and violence, while there are many women who support their children and parents by selling their own bodies. There are even more who make a living off those prostitutes.

Chicago is one of the many tea rooms in It'aewon. A man was sitting absentmindedly in this tea room. He wore brown corduroys and the collar of his black overcoat was up. He had a very short crewcut and his jaw was square. Over his heavy left eyelid was a scar about an inch long. It appeared to be a knife scar and looked very old. It glared under the dim lights of the tea room. He was not so tall, but he was husky and well built.

He nervously crushed his cigarette in the ashtray, coughed,

spat on the floor, and rubbed the spittle with his shoe. He looked frustrated but he might have been impatient or simply bored.
One thing, however, was apparent; his mind was suffering a self-
induced conflict.

Suddenly another man entered this tea room filled with
cigarette smoke, jazz, and bawdy conversation. Wearing a grey
windbreaker, a cap, and a pair of sun glasses, he looked very
slim and light. Finding the man with the scar, he came over.

"Here you are, Tŏkhwan," he said sitting down with a thump
on a chair opposite the man with the scar. "I've been looking
for you all day." Then he pulled out a cigarette from the pack
on the table, Tŏkhwan's pack, without hesitation. Putting it into his mouth, he chewed on it once, then he asked "Got matches on you?"

With a glum look Tŏkhwan fished out a box of matches from
his pocket and put it on the extended palm of the man with sun
glasses.

"Munt'ae wants to see you."

Still sullen, Tŏkhwan said with disgust, "Tell him you
couldn't find me." He pulled a cigarette out of the pack for
himself.

But that did not seem to bother Hyŏnp'il, the man with sun
glasses. He said, making smoke rings with his cigarette, "He
said he had to see you." Then after awhile he added, "I don't
think you can afford not to work." He leaned against the back
of the chair, stretching out his legs. But Tŏkhwan did not seem
to heed what Hyŏnp'il was saying. He gazed at the far end of
the room as if Hyŏnp'il did not exist. Perhaps he was busy thinking about something else, or he was merely ignoring Hyŏnp'il,
or perhaps he was simply staring absentmindedly.

Taking the sun glasses off, Hyŏnp'il said, "Let's go!"

"Where to?" said Tŏkhwan, pretending disinterest as if he
was bored to death.

"To the Ilmi Restaurant."

"No."

"The work is set for tonight."

"Go tell him you couldn't find me."

"He said we would have a drink to the success of tonight's
work."

Just then a waitress came round with a cloth to wipe the table.

"Is it *naturally* again?" she said.

"That's right. *Naturally* we don't have time to drink coffee. We got to leave right away," Hyŏnp'il said.

The waitress seemed to be accustomed to this. She said good-naturedly, "*Naturally* you can sit there all night if you like," turning back toward the counter.

It was around four in the afternoon. The wind was blowing hard outside and it was chilly. Whenever someone opened the front door, a gust of cold wind swept into the room. The sky outside was dark and low, and it threatened to snow. Then Tŏkhwan said quietly but firmly, "Listen! I won't have any more to do with you guys. My answer to tonight's job is a flat no. Remember that."

Hyŏnp'il seemed to laugh at this silently. His nostrils gave him away. "I agree with you one hundred percent. But you got to think about making a living too. Or have you already lined up a straight job or something? Of course, you don't really have to worry about your daily bread as long as that Miss Ch'oe is around, I know that. That gal is really something. She seemed to think about nothing but you while you were away at 'the big house.' I don't mean that I followed her around all the time you were away. Don't get me wrong. Anyway, let's go to the Ilmi and have a drink. You look hungry too. You may refuse tonight's work, and then you may not. It's all up to you. Let's go unless you don't even want to sit with us."

"I'm not going," said Tŏkhwan firmly, but Hyŏnp'il paid no attention to what he was saying. He repeated in a low tone, "Let's go. You can tell Munt'ae yourself that you don't want to take part in tonight's work. Let's go."

Tŏkhwan was angry now. He threw down his cigarette and rubbed it on the floor with his shoe again and again. "You go tell Munt'ae that you guys can work all you want. You guys can make as much money as you wish, understand? Alright? Then go!"

He laughed. Hyŏnp'il was laughing silently all the time. Wiping his sun glasses with his bare fingers, he said, "Munt'ae says tonight's job is a breeze. Big money, too. I think you'd do well to wash your hands of such things after tonight's job if it's so important to you. Let's go!"

Putting his glasses back on, Hyŏnp'il got up muttering to

himself, "Damm it! What a boring New Year. Nothing new, nothing to do! Ain't I right? Let's go!"

It was January 3 by the lunar calender. The stores were all closed. The people who filled the sidewalks exuded an air of festivity.

"Leaving so soon? I guess we'll close down early tonight. Not many customers with the New Year's celebration, you know," said the waitress, who came around again holding the evening paper under her arm. Tŏkhwan was getting up too, but he sat down again, taking the paper from under her arm. He glanced over some pictures on the front page. He turned the pages absentmindedly till he came to the third page. There his eyes rested on the headline. At first he could not believe his eyes. His heart began to thump. Panicked, he read the news over and over.

"She says she's going to close down. Let's get going. You can read the papers later," said Hyŏnp'il, but Tŏkhwan was not listening. His facial muscles became distorted, his face pale.

"I said let's get going!" said Hyŏnp'il, somewhat irritated.

But Tŏkhwan did not seem to notice him. He was absorbed in the paper. He was terribly upset. He folded the paper and then spread it again, rereading the article on the third page. Then he looked up at Hyŏnp'il with vacant eyes.

"What's the matter? Is there something interesting in the paper?"

But he did not answer. He put a cigarette in his mouth, more out of habit than anything else, and lit a match. Lighting the cigarette, his hand trembled slightly. He gritted his teeth to control himself—to control his confusion, rage, and sorrow. He said, "Was yesterday the second?"

"I guess so, the day before yesterday was the first," answered Hyŏnp'il. Hearing this, Tŏkhwan clenched his fists and gritted his teeth again. Then suddenly he said, "Let's go. I think I'm getting hungry too." He followed Hyŏnp'il out of the tea room. He was still holding the crushed newspaper in his hand. The waitress ran after him and said it belonged to someone else. He turned around and threw the paper at her. He walked out quickly.

3

"Mother, let's go back home. It's cold out here," a young

woman was saying to the old woman who was still sitting on the bank of the river. The younger woman was holding down her indigo skirt with one hand for it was flapping in the cold wind. "Let's go in, Mother. The living must go on living." At this the old woman turned around sharply.

"Is that so? I guess you're right. When a mother cannot follow her son in death..." What the old woman meant was that she did not expect her daughter-in-law to die of sorrow and grief, but her tone was somewhat biting. Then the old woman gave a quick glance at her daughter-in-law's lower abdomen. Muttering something, the old woman turned around to go home. The deep lines on her face were the signs of her lifelong poverty, but her tired old eyes were not without some goodness.

Tears rose to the eyes of Chŏngim, the daughter-in-law, when she saw her mother-in-law's disheartened profile. Her eyes bloodshot from crying, she followed the old woman. Her body seemed to be in no better condition than the old woman's, but nevertheless her's was filled with the sweetness of youth. Tagging along, she mused over her misery. She had nothing but fate to blame for her misfortune.

Chŏngim was a widow now six months after the wedding. Besides, she was pregnant. It would be a fatherless child. The seed of her dead husband was three months old in her. Somehow the thought of the fatherless child made her all the more sad. Clenching her teeth, she followed her mother-in-law, holding the old lady's sleeve with one hand, arranging the forelock on her brow with the other. She lost her husband only six months after the wedding. The remains of the permanent wave she got when they married were still in her hair. She secretly thought that her sorrow and grief were no less than her mother-in-law's, but she knew better than to say it outright. ("Is it really impossible for me to follow my husband in death?") She had thought this over and over since that day, but she knew she could not do as her mother-in-law suggested.

"Some American soldiers have just been to the village, Mother," Chŏngim said.

"Americans?" the old woman repeated, alarmed. "What did they want? Wasn't the shooting of my son enough?"

Another gust of cold wind swept up. Some dogs barked far away in the direction of the village.

"They say they tried to give money to Ch'angsu's mother."

"Money? Did she take it? Did she take the price of her husband's life?"

"They say she trampled on it right in front of the American officers."

"That's the stuff," the old woman seemed to be satisfied. But she quickly added, "How much did they say the money was?"

"I don't know. Should be a handsome sum though."

"A handsome sum? Did they come around to our house too?"

"No, Mother."

"Why not?"

"Would have come to our house too, if it hadn't been for what happened at Ch'angsu's house."

At this the old woman jumped up again. "What made them think we wouldn't receive the money? Why not take the money when my son is dead? Why not take the burial money?"

Chŏngim kept her silence. She seemed to be weary and exhausted by grief, and nothing seemed to interest her much any more. Her eyes were all swollen from crying.

The scenery along the river bank was desolate. The wind was strong among the old pine branches. They stepped down from the embankment. They did not say anything to each other till they approached the village. Probably they were thinking about the future. Now, without the breadwinner, prospects were black.

All of a sudden the old woman asked again, "How much did they say the amount was?"

"I don't know."

"A lot?"

"Whatever the sum was, it should be a lot for people in our condition, I should say."

Then the daughter-in-law guided the old woman to one side of the road. With a cloud of dust in its wake a jeep was speeding out of the village along the road lined with poplar trees toward them.

"Is it them, you reckon?"

"Looks like."

The jeep drove past them at full speed. The old woman groaned something while Chŏngim glared at the racing vehicle.

Villagers stood near the entrance to the village to watch the jeep, now a dark spot raising a cloud of dust.

Just then a group of young men were leaving the village. They had their A-frames[2] on their backs. One could tell that they were on their way to collect firewood.

"You don't mean you are going to cross the river again?" called the old lady incredulously.

"What can we do? We don't even have enough firewood to bury your son and the other," said Pongman, one of the men in the group.

"We mean to cross the river right by the American camp to see if they dare shoot again," another young man added.

"What if they do?" said the old woman, as if her own son, Tŏksu, was among the group. Seeing those young men, momentarily she could not believe that her son had died.

"Die, what else? It ain't such an attractive life anyway," said Pongman.

"What about those who are left behind?" said the old woman, almost to herself. Hearing this, Chŏngim cried again.

4

Leaving the Chicago tea room behind Hyŏnp'il, Tŏkhwan was almost beside himself. He kept telling himself that he should do something, but he did not know what it was.

"I must go see them," he muttered. "I must go right away." (But how can I go now? I am penniless.) It was meaningless to go back to his home village without any money.

He had just served six months in the penitentiary for theft and robbery. Let out only a few weeks ago. The hitch this time gave him a criminal record. He was an ex-convict with three previous offences.

(I had better stop at three!)

The warden had warned him that after three it could easily be thirty. He told Tŏkhwan to get a real job and stay away from "the big house."

He considered the warden right, and he had tried to get a good job ever since he had left the penitentiary. But no one gave

---

2. a back pack in the shape of the letter A, with which Korean workers carry heavy loads.

him a job. He was ready to do anything, but no one was ready
to give him anything. Miss Ch'oe was more eager than he himself.
She was worried to death that dangling like this might push him
back into his old criminal world. She did her best to find him
a job, but in vain.

Miss Ch'oe worked in a bar in Myŏngdong called Wild Roses.
She had been Tŏkhwan's common-law wife for the past three
years. Although her job was a disreputable one, a barmaid,
everyone who knew her said she was a good girl. She had never
been formally married, but she seemed to know the meaning of
love. She was older than Tŏkhwan by three years, but she looked younger and they seemed to be a well-matched couple. She
was the first one to whom Tŏkhwan ran when he was released
from the penitentiary a few weeks ago.

"I earn enough to feed us both. Take your time finding an
honest job this time. Try to do whatever you can. I don't ever
want you to gang up with those rascals again. If you do, I will
kill myself. I will kill myself and leave a letter to the police. Don't
think I won't mention your name in the letter," she had pleaded. There were tears in her eyes.

"I understand. That's exactly what I am thinking about—to
go straight. Back home folks think that I am a great success with
heaps of money. I cannot live up to their image of me, but at
least I can throw away names like hoodlum and gangster. I have
a brother back home, you know. He asked me to get him a job
in Seoul when I last visited home three years ago. I heard he
got married last year. I couldn't attend the wedding. You know
why, but I wrote them that I was terribly busy and couldn't get
away. They think I am a big executive of a large company or
something. I don't blame them because I was easy with my money
whenever I visited the village. It's a poor village. A one-hundred-
wŏn bill is still a sight for sore eyes. I must visit the village once
again soon. I have a mother, you know. She would be so glad
to see me, a successful son from Seoul. We can go there together
if you want to," he rambled on the evening of the day he left
the penitentiary. Of course she had heard this story many times
before. He had told these stories to her because he wanted her
to know him through and through.

Walking behind Hyŏnp'il, Tŏkhwan was now afraid of Miss
Ch'oe.

Just then, by sheer coincidence, he ran into her on the street. She was watching him, standing near a bus stop. He approached her, somewhat defiantly raising his head. "I thought you weren't feeling well," he said. He had told her to stay home and skip one night at the bar.

"I'll be back earlier than usual," she said.

Without makeup she was pale. It wasn't that she had any special sickness to speak of, but she was just generally weak.

"You must take care of yourself," he said somewhat glumly as he turned to go. She gave a sharp look at his back. "No one is home. You go right back to the house. You want me to go with you?" she said, noticing Hyŏnp'il, who had stopped several steps ahead.

"No, I want a drink. I am getting in on a job," he said roughly.

"Don't make me write the letter, you just remember. I don't want to die yet," she said at his back. He coughed up phlegm and spat it on the pavement, hurrying as if to run away from Miss Ch'oe.

5

"Mother, it would be better for you to go to Seoul to live. Resting for a few days first after tomorrow's burial, of course," said Chŏngim to her mother-in-law. Since she had heard that her dead husband's brother was doing well in Seoul, she thought this was the best way under the circumstances.

"Seoul? With my son buried on the mountain yonder! Do you think I can go to Seoul to my older son to live well? Nonsense!"

"The dead are dead. There is no reason why you should stay here and suffer the rest of your life," said Chŏngim. Then, as if she had already been left behind alone, she burst into tears.

"What about you?" asked the old woman sharply. Chŏngim could not answer that question. She had recommended that her mother-in-law go to Seoul for her own sake. But why would her mother-in-law trouble her with such a question; apparently her mother-in-law was implying something else.

"I said that for your own sake, Mother," she said, wiping her tears.

"You must stay till you give birth to that baby at least. I don't expect you to remain a widow all your life.'' The turn of events since the marriage had been such that the old woman thought that she could blame the whole thing on the bad luck that the daughter-in-law had brought into the family. But the old woman could not hate Chŏngim. She pitied her daughter-in-law.

"Is it three months old? You give it birth and I'll raise it," said the old woman, thinking momentarily of the fact that she had not heard from her son in Seoul. "My other son in Seoul does not seem to have any children. The family line must be perpetuated. You give birth to a son if you can. I'll send him to his rich uncle in Seoul to get the best education. The family line must go on.''

6

Tŏkhwan thumped the table with his fist. The dishes on the table rattled and clinked. Then clenching his teeth, he groaned, "What do you expect me to do? I can't sit here doing nothing!''

Tŏkhwan had followed Hyŏnp'il to the Ilmi Restaurant, but he had not mentioned what he had read in the papers. The two men and Munt'ae had drunk quite a lot when Tŏkhwan gave himself to that sudden outburst.

"What in the hell are you squawking about," Munt'ae cried out.

"Munt'ae!'' Tŏkhwan extended his glass to Munt'ae and continued, "My younger brother is dead! He got killed.'' With this, tears began to stream down his cheeks—tears repressed for so long.

"Your brother? Got killed? I didn't know you had a brother.'' Surprised, he gave a quick glance at Hyŏnp'il to see if he knew anything about it. But evidently it was new to him too.

"He got shot by an American soldier. He was out collecting firewood and got shot.''

"When?'' asked Munt'ae. "Was it your brother that was in the papers this evening?''

"During the war, we, myself and my brother, saved the lives of two American soldiers. We hid two of them who had lost their way during the retreat. Our own lives were at stake for doing that. But now those Americans have shot my own brother.''

For awhile a heavy silence prevailed. They even forgot to emp-

ty their glasses. But other customers in the place were not so quiet.
Some were shouting, some laughing, and some were making
bawdy jokes mixed with obscene laughter.

"Be quiet! Can't you guys just drink and not make such a
row?" roared Munt'ae all of a sudden. They seemed to be taken
aback. Then Hyŏnp'il added his piece, "Sorry, gentlemen, we
are the hoodlums of It'aewŏn, and we don't like a noisy place
if you please." So saying, he swept a glance around the room.
No one dared to talk back. Hyŏnp'il drank up his glass in a
breath, and said to Tŏkhwan, "Was it in that newspaper you
were reading?" Then he called out to the proprietor to get a copy
of the evening papers.

"Your home was P'aju, wasn't it? You got to go see them.
We all got to go see them," said Munt'ae nonchalantly, chew-
ing on a piece of dried fish.

"Money. You can't go there without money," joined in
Hyŏnp'il with a secret wink at Munt'ae.

"Naturally. Burying costs quite a bit of money these days,"
said Munt'ae.

"It's a good thing that we are going to pull that job tonight,"
said Hyŏnp'il.

"Is the funeral tomorrow? We can start early in the morning after the job, can't we?" said Munt'ae. Tŏkhwan was merely listening with his fist clenched on the table. Just then the papers
arrived. Hyŏnp'il took it up and read aloud.

"The guards shot'pem, eh? Two of them. Is this guy called
Tŏksu your brother?" said Hyŏnp'il, and then he began to curse
those guards. "Those sons of bitches! Why did they have to shoot
innocent wood collectors? Did they think they were hunting rab-
bits or something?"

Then Munt'ae took the papers and read for awhile. Soon he
said, "You can't really blame those guards," to the surprise of
the two.

"What?" asked Tŏkhwan, doubting his ears.

"You can't entirely blame those guards."

"Can't blame them?"

"That's right. It's too bad it had to be your brother."

"My brother or no, why are Korean lives so cheap? That's
the point. How do you mean we can't blame them?" Tŏkhwan
sounded much disconcerted and troubled.

But Munt'ae seemed set on provoking Tŏkhwan. He said, "You guys don't understand the psychology of guards."

To this Hyŏnp'il said, "Now you're siding with the Americans. How thoroughly pro-American you get..."

Munt'ae slowly emptied his glass. Extending the glass to Tŏkhwan he said, "It has nothing to do with pro-or anti-American feelings. All I meant was that it could easily happen. Litsen. It was the front line and it was getting dark. Suppose some dark figures appeared in front of you in an off-limits area."

"So?" pursued Tŏkhwan, his eyes glaring.

"The guard had probably called out 'Who goes there!' The wood collectors probably started to run away."

"It's natural."

"It's instinct," said Munt'ae. "They start to run without knowing why. Do you know why? Because it was an off-limits area. If they had not known that fact, they wouldn't have run away."

"So what? Do you mean to say that those guards were right in shooting away at innocent people? All they wanted to do was to collect some firewood so that they could keep warm," cried Tŏkhwan, enraged.

"Tŏkhwan, I was in the army myself and I know. I have been on guard duty myself. I was on a reconnaissance mission too. You don't understand how one gets keyed up on the front line, especially at night. When some stranger approaches you, your finger automatically races to the trigger. You can lose your own life in the matter of a split second. When the stranger starts to run, the bullet shoots out on its own. The guards' intention has nothing to do with it," Munt'ae was saying calmly.

"Are you saying that it's alright? Innocent people being killed?"

"I did not say that. The result is a disaster. But if the guard happens to be greenhorn, it can happen any time. And most guards are inexperienced privates. At least you cannot call it wilful murder. Especially when it is a place where the enemy line is not too far away."

Although it was unpleasant, Tŏkhwan knew Munt'ae's reasoning was right. But his own brother was dead. An innocent brother got killed. What could you do about it?

"What lies at the bottom of all this is poverty," Munt'ae went on. "You cannot blame the guard. Those wood collectors were not guilty of anything either. But they would not have gone out there if they had been rich. What we should hate is poverty," said Munt'ae emptying several glasses in a row.

Tŏkhwan did not wish to hear any more of Munt'ae's philosophizing. He buried his face in his hands, and tears streamed down through his fingers.

"Drink some more," Munt'ae was saying. Tŏkhwan wiped away the tears with his fists. He knew he pitied his brother, but he also knew he pitied himself for he knew he was giving way to temptation and his brother's sudden death was merely a pretext.

"There's got to be three million *wŏn* in cash."

It was a brick mansion surrounded by cement-block walls. They planned the holdup and proceeded under the supposition that there was three million *wŏn* in that house. Munt'ae's information had always been correct. His planning never failed either. Tŏkhwan knew that well. And he was finally in on it.

At three-thirty in the morning the three of them circled the house. It was like an army operation, soundless breathing and stealthy steps.

The house was quiet, deeply asleep. They examined the three sides of the house and agreed that their planning was sound. Munt'ae commanded, and Tŏkhwan was the first to jump over the wall. When all three of them were inside the wall, they put on black masks. Then they opened the front gate noiselessly.

Hyŏnp'il stayed in the garden to stand watch. It took nearly half an hour for Munt'ae and Tŏkhwan to steal into one bedroom of the house.

They had searched the drawing room first, but there was no money to be found. So they had to try the bedroom.

Fortunately the bedroom was lit with a low, blue-colored bulb, and they didn't even have to turn on their flashlights. There was a double bed in one corner of the room. A couple was sleeping in the bed. The man was wearing pajamas, but the woman was stark naked. When Munt'ae threatened the man with his dagger, he closed his eyes. Tŏkhwan pulled away the quilt and found the woman, naked, her back bent like a shrimp, trembling. She was young enough to be the man's daughter.

It was Tŏkhwan who found the package under the bed. It

was bulky enough to hold three million *wŏn*. They left the room with an air of perfect composure.

But the unexpected happened. Even before they got down to the front yard, lights came on everywhere. Shouts came from the houses all around, "Burglars!" Evidently they had an alarm system.

They three were stunned. Panicking, they forgot the prearranged getaway route. But somehow Munt'ae and Hyŏnp'il got away through the front gate. Tŏkhwan took to the wall in the backyard. It was very high, and there was a stretch of barbed wire entanglement on the top. He made a go at it. After several repeated failures he at last climbed up the high wall. The barbed wire pierced and slashed him. He jumped down to the other side. He began to run toward the hillside. He ran in the dark, tripping breathelessly. Then suddenly he realized something.

He turned around and started to run back to the wall that had just taken all his might to hurdle. He could hear people making a commotion inside the wall and saw several flashlight beams jumping up and down. But he paid no attention to them.

When he reached the wall, he groped for something in the dark. "One of them climbed over the wall here," a voice was saying inside. Just then Tŏkhwan located the package of money. He had thrown the package over the wall just before he climbed over it.

(How can I go without this?) He smiled triumphantly in the dark.

"Maybe he got hurt climbing over the wall," another voice said. A flashlight beam lit up the barbed wire fence on the top of the wall. Tŏkhwan smiled again and said, "No, sir!"

Dogs in the neighborhood began to bark.

"Turn the police dogs loose." another voice suggested inside. He started to run toward the hillside again. The baying of dogs became louder. His steps were lighter than before. He was excited with the satisfied feeling of success. He ran agilely in the darkness.

Then he noticed for the first time that he had many bad cuts. After a long, long run he hid himself under a small pine tree that grew between two huge rocks. He looked up at the dark sky. The dawn was yet to break.

He wiped the blood stains on his body with his handkerchief

and some toilet paper. Then for the first time the thought about his two friends.

(They got away safely, I suppose.) Then he realized he was all alone. Somehow the fact excited him greatly. I am alone! I am all alone with this package of money! No one can find me. I shouldn't even contact Miss Ch'oe. I should not try to see Munt'ae nor Hyŏnp'il. The police in the district must have been alerted by this time. I shouldn't try to go down there. Nor should I expect to see anybody from the village. To be alone is to be safe. For the time being anyway.

Then he realized that today was the day of his brother's funeral. A strange idea entered into his head and gripped him. When he thought of the poverty-stricken hometown village, this strange idea welled up inside him. (What about giving away the whole lot to those people?) The idea stirred and excited him greatly. (About three hundred thousand *wŏn* per house?) Three hundred thousand would be an alarming sum of money for those people for whom a mere three hundred would be a rare hoard. How proud Mother would be! She might even forget the sorrow of the loss of her other son. (I am going to throw bundles of money into the arms of those who are carrying the bier, saying they are no longer poor.)

He could no longer hear the sound of dogs barking. His hands and feet were numb from the cold.

7

The old woman was praying again at the *sŏnang-dang* situated under the three old pine trees. After the stretcher carrying her son's body left the village, she came out here to look at the frozen river.

The old woman no longer cried. Were her tears finally dried up? The villagers had borrowed a colorful bier from the neighboring village, but the old woman had insisted that stretchers were more suitable for the occasion. Thus her son, along with Mr. Shin's body, was carried away to the burial ground on a stretcher, the same stretcher on which he had been brought in two days earlier.

"Without its pillar the house must fall down." This was what the old woman had been thinking repeatedly since that morning. It was a premonition as well as determination.

Her premonition was right. Her daughter-in-law fell. Chŏngim had fainted and fallen down in the front yard when they carried her husband out on the stretcher. With the fall she shed a lot of blood.

There was her older son in Seoul, but he did not belong to the house. Nor did he belong to the village. He was a success. He should have no connection with this miserable village. This was a kind of resignation on her part. She had often longed to see her older son, but resignation had enabled her to control herself.

The surroundings were very quiet. She could see the quonset huts of the American troops on the other side of the river and some figures walking around near them. Now and then the sound of army vehicles could be heard.

The village was quiet too. The men were at the burial, and the womenfolk seemed to be depressed and exhausted.

She knew her daughter-in-law would die soon. She had once experienced an abortion herself, but the amount of blood her daughter-in-law had shed was far too great. She would soon die.

"One must die before one becomes senile," she thought. She stood up on the embankment. She looked round, and she noticed a dark spot on the gravel road far, far away to the northeast of the village. She thought it might be a man in a dark suit. Maybe the town clerk or somebody like that, she thought.

But now she had to hurry. She had to get it over with as soon as she could. She looked up at the pine-branch just over her head. "This will do," she thought. She could grab the branch on tiptoe.

A gust of wind blew her skirts. Since she had nothing heavy on underneath, it was chilly. She looked around again. Looking at the frozen river, she tried to draw in her mind the picture of the flooded river in summer. She looked up at Tŏngmang Mountain on the other side of the river. The hillside was dark brown now, but she tried to imagine the green of the warmer weather.

She tearfully watched for awhile the guard post of the American troops where her son had been killed.

The peak of the mountain now appeared to be very close. By now her son's body must be in the ground. "What if dirt gets into his eyes?" She could not bear the thought. "Although they told me it was a sunny spot. . ." She turned to look at the village again.

The dark figure of the man approaching the village loomed much larger than before. She wondered why Tŏkhwan, her rich son in Seoul, could not come back to the village like that.

(That bad boy, doesn't he know his brother is dead? Doesn't he ever hear anything?)

She now regretted very much that she had insisted on not informing her older son of the death of the other son when the villagers so suggested. But the truth was that she did not know where he lived. He had written to her last summer that he had moved to a larger house, but that was all she knew.

She looked up at the branch again and loosened her belt. It was of heavy cotton, an exceptionally long one. She made a noose with the belt. Tossing one end of it over the branch, she tied it. She turned her eyes to the approaching figure again. He was now quite close to the village. The old woman thought he might be a man going into the American camp, turning off to the right just before entering the village. She stood up erect, hesitated a moment, but she told herself firmly once more, "It's far better to die." Her bloodshot eyes began to swell out, her facial muscles distorted.

She looked for the noose. When she put her head through the noose while on tiptoe, her foot slipped.

The strong cotton belt became taut instantly. The branch swayed once or twice. The old woman's mud-stained skirt flapped in midair. Her legs and arms writhed a few times in vain, then drooped. Her body turned once or twice, dangling.

Fifty-nine. Did she blame her climacteric age at that instant?

8

At the entrance to the village Tŏkhwan ran into a man who was hurrying into the village also.

"Isn't it Tŏkhwan?" the man asked. "I am Pongman. Aren't you Tŏkhwan from Seoul?"

"Ah, Pongman. How have you been?" Pongman was a native of the village like Tŏkhwan.

"How did you know? Read it in the papers?"

"The funeral is today, isn't it?"

"Yes, but the party is already at the burial ground."

"Were you with the group collecting wood too?"

"Yes, everybody in the village was. It's safer that way. It used to be anyway. I'm sorry it had to be your brother." Then explaining how it all happened, he added, "They ran. Mr. Shin ran first, then your brother followed suit. Those Americans had stripped them naked, and Mr. Shin took off in the middle of their questioning. Your brother couldn't hang around there alone, so he took off too. He got it first, and Mr. Shin was shot down on the middle of the frozen river." He added he had just been to the police station for further investigation. "Here firewood is even more scarce than rice," he added with a sigh.

"Well, poverty is at the root of it all. I should have done something about it sooner, but I have been terribly busy, you know," said Tŏkhwan, sighing too.

"Well, now you should think about doing something for your old mother. Take her back to Seoul. We all talked about it and thought you would," said Pongman with another sigh.

Tŏkhwan was not a little taken aback by this, but he said calmly, "Well, I have insisted on doing so for a long time, but Mother wouldn't hear of it. She is obstinate in her own way, you know. She says country people should stay in the country. She says people who are used to misery die when their misery ends." He laughed an empty laughter. He dug out a pack of Saenara cigarettes. He lit one, giving one to Pongman.

"Are there nine households in the village altogether?"

"Ten."

"Pongman."

"Yes?"

"Do you think three hundred thousand *wŏn* for each family would help them any? With that money the whole village can move to a better place."

Pongman stopped short in the middle of the road, dazed.

"Three hundred thousand each?"

"I am mad about what happened this time. You remember how my brother and I helped two American soldiers during the war, don't you? Everybody in the county knows that!"

"Sure! That's why we said they bit the hand that had fed them!"

"Where is the grave?"

"It's on Tŏngmang Mountain."

"I don't understand why people stick to this place in lifelong poverty and misery," Tŏkhwan said breezily. With this, he looked far away at the embankment of the river. Then he gave out a cry of horror. "Isn't that a human being dangling over there from the pine tree?"

The next moment Pongman was running. Tŏkhwan followed him for a few steps, but resumed his normal gait. He became self-conscious, and laughed a little derisively. Approaching the embankment where he used to play when he was a child and the river beyond the embankment, which one could not cross any longer, the Imjin River, he laughed a derisive little laugh again.

(They would rather die like that than leave this crummy village.)

He drew a picture in his mind; he would dump the bundles of money under that strangled woman's skirt and tell the villagers to come and get it. Then he would leave the village ever so casually.

After all, he was the only one that had freed himself from the village, he thought. Another thought crept into his head. "Would Miss Ch'oe really write the letter? Would she really give me away to the police?" He laughed again derisively.

(end story)

When the Cricket Chirrs

Ch'oe Chŏnghŭi

Sungnye, their daughter, went out of the house hurriedly as soon as breakfast was over, shouting the usual "I'll be back" in the general direction of their room. Their son and his wife had already gone out. As was customary with so many Korean homes, the old couple was living with their son's family in the same house.

"Where are *you* going? These young kids must think that Sundays are for nothing but outings. I don't understand," said the mother, looking toward the gate through which her daughter had already disappeared. She had been plucking gray strands from her hair, using a small hand miror to reflect the back of her head in a large wall mirror. The old man could easily sense from her tone that it was not so much their daughter's going out as their son and daughter-in-law's departure that aggravated her. Living together with a married son in the same house has its advantages and disadvantages. The father thought that this was one of the bad instances.

Take breakfast that morning, for instance. Their daughter-in-law had been thoughtful enough to make some extra of the seaweed rolls which she had packed for their picnic lunch to put out on the breakfast table of the elder people. The mother had plainly shown her disgust while the father munched his roll savoring its taste. He knew, but he had pretended that he had noticed nothing.

That had been the basic attitude of the father throughout his long married life. He knew so well his wife's rather nagging disposition and her constant habit of finding fault with other people. He had always been very careful when he sensed she was in one of her moods. Sometimes he tried to cope with the situation by making some facetious remark. She was eleven years yonger than he.

"What's bothering you? Have you pulled out a black hair instead of a gray one?" he asked, looking up at his wife with a smile.

"Don't make a fool of yourself. You don't even resent impudence."

"I know how exasperating it is to pull out black hairs," he went on as if he didn't know what she was driving at.

"I don't know where you got this notion of pulling out black hairs, but can't you see that our family is floundering?"

"Floundering? What's wrong with our family? Since the coming of our new bride you haven't had to fight with the housemaid I notice. Don't you like it?"

"I don't like anything. Sungnye used to be a good girl. Now she goes out every Sunday with all her finery on. Bad influence, that's what I say." Apparently she was referring to their daughter-in-law.

"That's an unkindly thing to say. She's already a college sophomore, don't forget. It's about time she began to make boyfriends too, you know. It's nobody's teaching. I wish you wouldn't speak ill of our new bride."

"That's enough. Always our new bride, new bride. That's why she becomes so unruly and impudent. You don't want to ruin your own daughter, do you?" She slammed the hand mirror down on the dresser.

"Ruin what daughter? You used to wish to see the day when Sungnye would become grown up. Just when she is turning into a lovely young woman, you speak of ruin." This time the father deliberately left out any reference to their daughter-in-law.

"My God, you are the damnedest happy-go-lucky man I have ever seen, and I have grown old because of your happy-go-lucky attitude."

"I don't know if I made you grow old or not, but isn't everyone doomed to grow old sooner or later?" It was easy philosophizing, but he uttered the last phrase with a small sigh in spite of himself.

It wasn't certain whether she was moved by what the husband had said or whether she was simply pressed for time, but she picked up the hand mirror again and walked over to the wall mirror.

He looked up at her from his prone position. He could see the reflection of fleeting white clouds in the large wall mirror. While watching the white clouds he became envious of his wife pulling out white hairs. For he himself had given up long ago.

"Pulling them out won't help. Kim Chaewi used to pull out an awful lot of gray hairs, but he died," he mumbled half to himself, but he was startled by what he had said. A cold shiver ran down his spine.

This was a new symptom he had acquired since he attended Kim Chaewi's funeral not long ago. It was a fear of death. Over two weeks had already passed since the funeral, but the fear did not lessen. The old friend's image, pulling out gray hairs with his trembling hands, came back to him abruptly several times a day. He used to make some facetious remarks seeing him do it while he was alive, but now after his death the thing was altogether hideous and ghoulish.

After putting on makeup his wife went out. She said she was off to attend the wedding of a friend's daughter.

The house became suddenly quiet after the wife's departure. Even the maid, who had been busy cleaning the house all morning, seemed to have retired to take a nap or something, now that the moody mistress of the house was absent.

Then out of nowhere a cricket jumped into his room. The old man was startled at first, but soon he decided he should drive it out because of what he had heard long, long ago from his grandmother. She had said that winter rushes in exactly three months after the first cricket crawls into the house. Another winter could only mean that he would be a year older, he figured.

He went after the cricket, trying to catch it, but soon he found that it wasn't such an easy job. He was out of breath in no time, and that only made him realize that he was not as fit as he used to be. Then the cricket accidentally fell into the unemptied wash basin his wife had left in the room. "Now I've got you," he thought, putting his hand into the water. But it jumped in the water too. After poking and grabbing several times he finally got hold of the cricket, but when he examined the captive, he found that he had broken off a leg in the excitement of the chase. He put the cricket just outside of the room. It did not budge. He touched its tail end softly to send it off. He wished it would go away to a far-off place. It started to jump, but its former vigor and deftness were gone. It staggered.

It staggered like palsied Pae Ingi, another of his old friends. Of course, he had not actually seen the palsied and decrepit friend walk; he had only seen him lying in his bed.

He had visited this friend two weeks ago on his way back from Kim Chaewi's funeral. He had heard the news much earlier that this friend had had a stroke, but he simply could not gather the courage to go and face him. When he was young he was the first to go and see sick friends. But now, for some reason, he was apt to put off such visits as long as possible. There were too many sick friends nowadays for one thing.

His friend Pae Ingi was in bed alone. His wife had died a year ago. The room, facing west, was very hot, but the window didn't even have a rattan blind. Pae Ingi was crouching in a corner of the room probably to avoid the shaft of the sun setting through the window.

His face was swollen and a line of saliva down his jaw could be seen from the drooping corner of his mouth. With this mouth he asked if he was on his way home from Kim Chaewi's funeral. He could not articulate sounds clearly either. When he asked him how he could have known about the funeral lying in bed and all, Pae Ingi did not answer. He merely looked back at him blankly for awhile. Finally he said, "I wanted to go. . ." He could not finish the sentence.

He recalled the day Pae Ingi's son was married. Ingi had caught him just in front of the wedding hall. "Say, none of us are getting any younger, are we?" he had said. "They are making us into old men. Now that my son is married, I'll soon have grandchildren and they will call me grandpa in no time. When kids start to call you grandpa, you've had it. Then you *are* a grandpa whether you wish it or not, you know." Recalling this incident now, he looked at Pae Ingi. Then Ingi said something about getting well soon and sharing wine with old friends like the old days. But he could feel the false, pretended cheerfulness. Saying "Sure, sure," to his friend's suggestion, he had gotten up to leave. "You are not leaving already," said Ingi disappointedly, but he had some other errands to look after. Pae had reached out his feeble hand. Apparently he had wanted to shake hands. He grabbed the flabby hand. It wasn't the springy and vigorous hand it used to be.

He looked for the cricket again, but it had disappeared. Lame as it was, it must have hopped off. Resuming his former reclining position he looked into the large wall mirror. The white clouds had disappeared too, and he could see the reflection of the blue sky and occasional dragonflies flitting around.

Watching these things in the mirror, he soon fell asleep. In his dream he met Yu Ongnye, the girl Kim Chaewi used to run around with.

She was wearing a green dress though he couldn't recall what kind of shoes she had on. There were so many tall trees around her that she was almost hidden among them. If it hadn't been for her unusually fair complexion, he wouldn't have recognized her. In the woods she beckoned to him. The hand was as white as the face. Just as he was ready to go over to her he noticed the river flowing between them.

When he signaled to her that he could not cross the river, she spread her skirt as a bird would spread its wings and flew over the river toward him. There was a halo of rainbow-colored lights, bright and beautiful lights.

He stood in the bright and beautiful lights, spreading his arms to receive her. As soon as she was in his arms, he embraced her with all his might, rolling on the grass. He had experienced ecstasy.

When he awoke, the block of wood he was using as his pillow was on the other side of the room. He got up limply. In his confusion the first thing that came to his mind was that he should find out if Ongnye was still alive. Somehow it did not seem right to make love to a dead woman—not even in a dream. Then he thought he had heard somewhere that it was a sign of death in the near future to dream of making love to a dead person.

Sitting up on the floor, he tried to figure out when he had last met Ongnye. It was two years back. She looked altogether hideous with her hair dyed black. Her withered face was covered with brownish spots, but her hair was pitch black and one could not quite make up one's mind about her age. It was unnatural. They talked about many things, but he could not recall anything except that she said she was living in Ch'ungju at the time. He even forgot whether it was at a funeral or a wedding that he had met her. Anyway, he could vaguely remember that many others were around.

He and his friends—Kim Chaewi, Pae Ingi, and several other classmates—had met Ongnye for the first time while they were attending college. They had formed a reading circle and through someone's introduction she had joined it. Since she was the only female member of the set, she soon became the center of attention. Everybody was interested in her, but the custom of the country being what it was, nobody dared to do anything about it. Each knew how the other felt about her, and no doubt the boyish code of honor was working too.

This could not have lasted very long, however. Kim Chaewi had secretly violated the code and made the first move. Of course, not everyone in the group was aware of the affair. But he, Pae Ingi, and another fellow had found out. Now he could not even remember the name of this third fellow—there was a rumor that he had died in Manchuria. Another version had it that he had died in a prison after fighting against Japanese colonialism. Anyway, he was dead he thought.

When they found out about Chaewi's sly move, they decided not to disclose it to the other members of the group. Instead, they were content with the occasional treat to wine by Chaewi, who was forced to do so under the three roguish friends' threat to bring it out in the open. Moreover, Chaewi himself had seemed to enjoy being blackmailed.

He wondered if there was any way to find out whether or not Ongnye was still alive. He had to count out Pae Ingi, who in his present condition wouldn't be of much use. Other friends had all drifted off. "When Ingi dies, I will be the only one who knows anything about Ongnye, and when I die..." He stopped short at this point. The same recurring fear gripped him. And before he knew what he was doing he called the maid.

His voice sounded unusually hollow and loud. The startled maid ran to him with an equally loud "yes." She had probably thought it was the signal for the return of the mistress of the house or some such grave event. She looked around, dazed.

"I am going fishing. Lock up the front gate, all right?" He wasn't thinking about fishing at all. He merely said so because he couldn't think of anything else to say when the maid arrived. Now he had to get out of the house with his fishing pole.

He thought that it wasn't a bad idea after all. He decided to go to the nearby pond. Then he remembered a young man he used to run into at the pond who always talked about interpreting dreams. He attributed everything to his dream the night before. A bad dream, bad luck, a good dream, good luck. He figured he would be able to get something out of the young man about the strange dream he had had awhile ago.

He went around the pond looking for the young man. He had gotten to know quite a few people at the pond besides the young man, for he had been visiting the place at least four or five times a week since his retirement as a school principal.

Being Sunday, the pond was quite crowded with people fishing. Although he made nearly a full circle of the pond, he could not spot the young man. Instead, he was hailed by another man with a dark face.

"Good afternoon, sir. You're late."

He stopped and went down the bank to the water edge where the man was fishing. Although it wasn't the young man he was looking for, he was very glad at least to run into someone who knew him. The man was probably twenty years younger, but age rarely mattered around fishing spots.

"Hello, there! How's it going?"

"Not so good. Too many people to begin with. Why don't you settle down here? This is as good a place as any. Or I should say just as bad as any," said the man good-naturedly. The man probably thought that he was looking for a good spot.

"There are many people, true, but I don't see any of the usual crowd." Saying this he began to settle down by the man with the dark face.

"They must have gone to other places expecting this one to be crowded."the younger man said. He agreed. He wanted to ask this man about the dream he had just had.

"Listen, do you know anything about dreams? What happens if you fool around with a woman in a dream? Is it a good sign? The important thing is she may be a dead woman."

"Well, that's the best dream you can have! That's a sign of great fortune. You'll catch a big fish, wait and see." Saying so, the younger man went back to watch his line. Among these people good luck automatically meant a big fish.

"No, no. You've got me wrong. This particular woman, I used to know her, but the trouble is she might be dead now. If you fool around with a dead woman in a dream. . ." He stopped in the middle of the sentence. He didn't dare finish it and say, "Aren't you supposed to die soon too?" The fact was he was afraid to say it.

"A dead woman. A dead woman, you say?" The man repeated this a couple of times and the old man was all ears, listening to what the man with the dark face was going to say. But the man did not say anything further. Instead, he concentrated all his attention on his line. Something was jerking it. The old man watched silently.

"Man! It's a big one. I can feel it. Your good luck has already started to work for me too." The man pulled hard at his pole. Sure enough, it was a big fish. It jumped around on the grass with shiny, bright scales. Triumphant, the man with the dark face looked about him boastfully for spectators. He seemed to have forgotten completely the interpretation of the dream the old man wanted.

Knowing it was useless to wait for any further development in their conversation about the dream, the old man decided to do some fishing himself. The water in the pond reflected heavy white clouds. There were many more clouds than there had been in the wall mirror back home. He was watching the clouds, but before he knew it, his mind wandered back to the dream.

"Your bobber! It's jerking!" cried the man beside him. Then he realized his line was taut. He gave a careful tug at his pole. He could feel a heavy sensation in the palm gripping the fishing pole, and then it went through his entire body. It was not unlike the sensation he had when he embraced Ongnye in his dream. He felt a sudden strength well up within his body. He pulled hard at his pole. A big fish with white and blue scales came out of the water.

The old man turned to his companion with a smile. The man also looked back at the old man with a broad smile. Although their expressions looked quite alike, what they were thinking was quite different. The old man's was an uncertain smile denoting his fear and hope that this was all the dream really stood for and nothing more, nothing really drastic and fearful. But his companion's was triumphant, a didn't-I-tell-you confidence.

"You'll catch bigger ones yet. Just wait and see," he said to the old man and went back to his fishing.

He didn't catch any bigger ones after that, but he caught many, many smaller fish. He fished them out one after another. As soon as he threw in his hook, the line jerked. Then, all of a sudden he thought the motion of the white bobber seemed to resemble that of Ongnye's beckoning hand in the dream. He didn't have the heart to go on fishing. As he was getting ready to go home, his companion said that he had caught more fish in a shorter time than usual, taking a quick glance into the old man's creel. He seemed to imply that he should get the credit for interpreting the dream correctly. The old man left the pond with a noncommittal attitude.

When he got off at the bus stop, he went into the bar he always visited after such fishing trips.

"Oh, it's you. Come in, sir."

Just as at the fishing spot, he had gotten to know many faces in the bar too. The owner of the place, an old man with a mustache and a broad forehead, was always glad to see him. Of course, any proprietor would be glad to see him; he was a quiet drinker and always paid cash.

But tonight he didn't feel like drinking in silence as he usually did. After drinking four or five bowls of rice wine in a row, he called all the familiar faces to his table. He bought several rounds of drinks for everybody. Then some of them returned his hospitality by buying more drinks for everybody.

"Let's drink to our hearts' content. Ah, let us relish these delicious potions. Good wine and good snacks, aren't these good?" He honestly thought they were good.

"Say, young man, have another drink," he handed his empty glass to a young man in the group. The young man took the glass.

"Youth is what counts. One is a man while he is young; he is no longer a man when he gets old. He is just an old man. You follow me? Ha, ha, ha, ha, ha." The old man laughed heartily. He laughed hard, because he happened to recall an incident right after the May 16 military revolution. There had been a notice from the town office calling for the attendance of one male member from each family at the early morning calisthenics. Since his son had to go to work, he went to the announced place himself, thinking he represented his family. The town official looked him over and asked what he was doing there. He asked back if there wasn't an announcement calling for one male member from each family to come. "Sure, one *man* from each fmaily. . ." the offical did not finish the sentence, but it was plain what he had started to say. "We said one *man*, not one *old man*," he meant to say. It was a foggy morning. Walking back home in the fog, he felt very, very depressed.

When he came out of the saloon, the street was dimly lit by moonlight. The moon was hidden by thin clouds.

In the clearing many children were playing as usual. He went among them. Suddenly he realized he had spent nearly forty years of his life among such kids.

"Come on everybody! I am going to hand out fish. Some are big, some are small."

He was soon surrounded by children. Just as he was with his wine in the saloon, he was now very liberal with his fish. His creel was empty in no time.

"Thank you, Grandpa."

"Thanks, Grandpa."

Everyone referred to him as "Grandpa." None of them recognized him as the former school principal. Of course, none of them were old enough to have known him while he was still in office. But still, he was vaguely disappointed.

He left the clearing and took the road leading to his house. It was a dusty stretch of road during the day, but now in the moonlight it was not without some of the idyllic features of a country road. The moon had come out from behind the clouds. He could see the landscape looming up in silhouette.

The old man started to hum a tune. It was the school song of the last school he worked at before his retirement. He had worked there for seven years, the longest he worked for any one school at a stretch. Because of all this, it was now the school to which he was most sentimentally attached.

He kept on humming as he staggered along. He didn't even try to straighten his inebriated steps. The empty creel shook drunkenly at his waist.

He straightened himself up a little when he reached the gate. The housemaid opened the gate for him while his son and daughter-in-law came out of their room to greet him. The daughter-in-law stepped down to help him in, taking up his fishing gear and helping him off with the old coat he was wearing.

"My, you didn't catch any today?" remarked the daughter-in-law looking into his creel. He swayed a little.

"That's right. I'll do better tomorrow though."

"No. I'd think it much more poetic if you didn't catch any," said the daughter-in-law, giving out a pretty, coquettish laughter. She always acted this way in front of her husband.

His own wife was in the room but did not look out. He sensed right away that she was in one of her cross moods when he stepped into the room. She asked sharply why everybody was making a noise in the middle of the night. She had heard what their daughter-in-law had said to him awhile ago, and her coquettish laughter had hurt her feelings, but he didn't say anything.

He lay down on his bed after a light supper. He could hear music coming from his son's room. Was it the radio or the record player? The young couple liked to listen to music very much. Then he figured that his wife's ill humor had its origin in the music, partly at least.

"Why don't you lie down, too?" he said softly without looking up, or opening his eyes.

"Your daughter is still on the loose," she said sharply. Then he realized that their daughter was still out and that had been the prime cause of his wife's ill humor.

"Sitting up won't make her come home sooner, you know," he said softly with his eyes still closed. His wife said nothing.

He could hear the chirring of a cricket in the yard. It chirred on and off in a sad, lonesome way. He then thought of the lame cricket he had driven out of the room that morning. He hoped this chirring cricket was the same one. Do not die, cricket, and keep on chirring, he wished. Then he opened his eyes for the first time and looked out into the yard.

It was drenched in moonlight.

(end story)

The Sultriness of a Cold Evening

Yi Hoch'ŏl

"You asking me if I'm not bored, Sir?" said Captain Kim, the general's aide-de-camp, with a moronic grin. As a general rule, one feels somewhat flattered when one is asked such a question by one's superior.

The young general, who, with his feet on his desk, had been leaning as far back as he could against the back of his revolving chair, suddenly sat up straight. Dropping his feet to the ground, he repeated the same question. "Aren't you bored, Captain? You're bored too, aren't you?" This of course implied that the general was bored. Perhaps it is a matter of plain courtesy on the part of a subordinate to answer that he shares the feeling, no mater what his actual feeling is.

The general had gotten his first star about ten days before. The first week or so was spent in a whirlwind of receptions, parties, and visits to Seoul and other large towns where senior military brass lived, but now, back at his own camp, he had been trying without much success for the past two or three days to get settled. He had nothing very much to do, and he was getting restless. It seemed as though his whole body itched.

Take last night, for instance. The general simply grabbed a private first class who had just gotten off guard duty and took him to the nearby town in his own jeep. There the two of them did the town—all at the general's expense, of course. The poor PFC, sort of flabbergasted at first, finally grew bold enough to relish the evening. Anyway, the news must have gotten around among the men this morning, and wherever the general went in the camp, all the soldiers saluted him with a grin.

"What're you grinning for?" bawled the general at the men, but they kept grinning.

It was past five in the afternoon. The electric light just outside the general's office came on. Somehow, its dim light made one feel forlorn, but at the same time it made one aware of the fresh air of the early spring evening.

"Isn't that so? You're bored too, aren't you?"

"Yes, sir."

The general got up. Taking his jacket off the coat hanger, he put it on, and sat down again, interlacing his fingers.

"I wish the war would come back again. What would you say to that, Captain?"

"Well, sir. . ."

"Well, what? What kind of an answer is that? It has to be either yes or no."

"That is, I agree with you, sir."

"Why do you agree?"

"He must be really bored," thought the aide. Putting on the same moronic grin again, the aide said, "Because of boredom, General."

"Who is bored, you or me?"

"Both you and me, sir."

Somehow the general was exceedingly pleased by the answer. He laughed heartily and said two or three times, "Attaboy! That's the way to answer questions." Then he added, "We must have a war and that's that. Having soldiers bored is no way to keep them. What we need is a war. A military revolution is alright too, but that has been done once and for all already. No sane man would try it again. What would you say to that, Captain?"

"I feel the same way, sir."

"Why?"

"I don't know, I'm not that articulate, General."

The general laughed out loud again. His laughter had a ring of self-confidence—the self-confidence of a man who was sure that his laughter had a ring of self-confidence. It had the ring of a trained laughter, and necessarily it had a certain artificial quality to it.

"All right, let's drive around a little," said the general, standing up abruptly.

As Captain Kim got behind the wheel, the general called out to him, "Captain!"

"Yes sir?"

"I want you to step down."

Captain Kim stepped out from behind the wheel.

All of a sudden the general bawled out, "Atten-tion!"

Taken by surprise, the captain came to attention.

"At ease!"

The captain obeyed the command.

"Atten-tion!"

The captain came to attention again. Probably the general was doing this to relieve boredom, but the poor captain had to obey.

"At ease. Atten-tion! At ease!"

While they were engaged in this absurd game, groups of bewildered men around the camp stopped whatever they were doing to watch the two officers.

At last the general patted the captain's shoulder with a smile. "Very good. You still have a bit of the soldier in you, Captain," said the general. Then he added, "I want all the men gathered here immediately."

A panic followed. All the men fell in ranks with full battle gear. It was like an emergency drill. When they had all assembled by battalion, the general bellowed: "Men, you are supposed to keep up a good fighting spirit and high morale at all times. Never for a minute are you to slacken. The result of today's emergency drill has pleased me very much. Everyone of you is on the ball. Dismissed!"

You might say it was a pithy speech, brief and to the point. The men dispersed and made their way to their quarters in an orderly fashion.

"Captain!"

When the captain looked up, he saw that the general already had a pipe in his mouth. The general said with a grin, "Let's drive around a little, Captain."

"Where, Sir?"

"Just any old place. Let's go into the nearest town. Let's see how the people fare there."

The captain got behind the wheel again. He was nervous now and hoped that no more impulsive ideas would strike the general.

The general was a soldier with an impressive combat record. To captain Kim the general looked somewhat frivolous these days, and he often wondered how the same man could have achieved

such outstanding martial feats allegedly credited to him. He was
told that the general had been, while engaged in critical military
operations, very grave, docile, and far less talkative. Considering this background information, the present-day general with
his simple personality and boyish innocence always perplexed the
captain. Sometimes he even despised the general for his frivol-
ity, but he had to admit that the general had a certain charm too—
the charm of a cute little boy.

A man who becomes impatient over little things must be a
man who cannot be easily satisfied with little things. Perhaps
this kind of man is one who doesn't lose himself and who keeps
a cool head at critical moments. The general certainly had the
makings of such a man, thought the captain. As an aide-de-camp,
Captain Kim had often been given a hard time over petty things,
but after awhile he got used to this. What's more, at times he
even had an illusion that the general was a little boy whom he
had to look after and protect.

The captain's eldest son was now seven years old. When Captain Kim went back home after a day's work at the camp, his
son wanted to play soldiers with him. In their game his son was
a general and he remained a captain. He willingly obeyed the
commands of the little general with the toy sword: "Atten-tion!
At ease! Atten-tion! At ease!" The funny part of the game was
that he did not feel anything incongruous in obeying the commands of a seven-year-old boy once the game got underway.
Thus, it was always his wife who came between them to rescue
him from the boy's strict military discipline: "Hold your horses
now, Daddy must be very tired."

The captain often observed that he was an ordinary man, and
could thus serve to entertain those who could not stand the
boredom of everyday life; these people might appear to be abnormal in ordinary situations, but in a critical situation, these
are the ones that can perform heroic deeds.

The general hated to be driven slowly in his jeep. "A soldier
isn't a mule driver," he would snap at the driver. Knowing this,
the captain had to step on the accelerator. The jeep picked up
speed and was doing close to fifty miles an hour in no time.
The road to the town was even and wide.

"Captain."

"Sir?"

"Do you know what kind of person is the most courageous in combat?" asked the general, leaning against the back of his seat, the pipe in his mouth. When the captain made no reply, he went on. "I spent an evening with a soldier last night, and it's his kind that wins battles for us. Kind of slow witted persons, they are the most courageous and tenacious on the battlefield. Their vengeance and hostility are simple. And the most simple is the most fearful. And do you know what kind of person is the most courageous commander?"

"That I know, General."

"What kind?"

"Your kind, General."

The general gave him a side glance with a funny sort of half smile on his lips. "In what way am I the kind?"

"You give a hard time to those who are under you, and you don't seem to be able to stand the least bit of boredom, and so you fret all the time when things are normal. I mean that kind, General."

"Right you are! It may be that you are much more intelligent than you appear to be, Captain," said the general, slapping the shoulder of the captain. The jeep jerked for a moment.

Soon their jeep drove in and through the town. Nothing worth mentioning was happening there. They were paving a strip of street in the middle of the town, and when the jeep passed the as-yet-unpaved gravel road, it left a cloud of dust behind it. A low line of houses stretched along either side of the street, and the houses had the desolate look peculiar to a small town at dusk. The street looked deserted save for a few elderly people in front of the realtor's office, a handful of housewives in front of the grocer's, and some ill-clad urchins desultorily looking for badly timed excitement. In short, nothing was happening in the town. About the only unusual thing that happened was that a policeman at the intersection, seeing the general's insignia on the jeep, gave a beautiful salute toward the jeep. The captain almost missed it, since the jeep was running at such great speed. Not the general though. He never missed those, and he was returning an equally beautiful salute to the policeman.

"Captain."

"Yes, sir."

"Let's make another round of the town."

"Sir?"

"I say drive around again. Go on out to the riverbank and drive through the town again."

The captain could not figure out what the general was up to. But the general said nothing further and merely kept on sucking at his pipe.

The jeep swung around into the open clearing to go back to the northern tip of the town. The smell of early spring soil was refreshing, and the river water looked gray-white in the dusk on the other side of the embankment. For awhile the jeep followed the embankment, trailing a cloud of dust behind it.

"Captain."

"Yes, sir."

"Some people jump impatiently while others go on living more or less ordinarily."

"Yes."

"You know what I mean?"

"I think I do."

"Do you think those impatient people are happy?"

"I don't know if they are happy, General. But I do know they can be very efficient. They can achieve something efficiently or destroy something efficiently. Their efficiency works either way."

The jeep drove into town again. The speed dropped somewhat when it passed over the gravel road. The captain could see the sign flag up on the realtor's office fluttering in the evening breeze; it was written in red ink on a piece of white cloth. Somehow the flag made him feel what seemed to him the sultriness of living. "Sultriness," thought the captain, "the damp, heavy heat of July's rainy season when people are too tired to move, and only mosquitoes have the energy to act; this is what living is to most people. It's so for me anyway. The outcome of having to make a living among the swarm of people is sultriness." He thought of his son.

"Daddy, atten-tion!" He comes to attention.

"Daddy, at ease!" He eases up.

Attention! At ease! Attention! At ease! His wife intervenes. She says, "That's enough. Daddy must be very tired." Then she laughs pleasantly. Living is sultriness. His wife takes his coat. He has to put on an artificial expression in order to maintain

194

dignity as the head of the family. She puts water into the basin
for him to wash up. He washes his hands. Sometimes the moon
is up, and other times it isn't. It doesn't really matter whether
the moon is up or not. His wife starts to talk—only on the sultry
things of making a living. It tires him out.

Compared with that, riding along with the general in a fast-
running jeep was far more refreshing, he thought.

Soon they came by the intersection, and the policeman again
gave a beautiful salute toward the jeep. He was a middle-aged
man with a bad complexion.

"Captain."

"Yes, sir."

"Make another round."

"Sir?"

"I say make another round."

The general seemed to be a little agitated. In vain the captain stole a glance at the general to find out what he was up to.
The jeep swung around and again it made its way through the
clearing and embankment into the northern edge of the town.
Soon the jeep came by the same intersection, and again the
policeman saluted beautifully toward the speeding jeep, and again
the general returned the salute very militarily.

"Once more, Captain. Another round," cried out the
general.

At last the captain caught on. A thin, knowing smile came
on his lips. Giving a quick glance toward the captain, the general
said, "You get it, Captain?"

"I do, sir!"

"What do you say to that? I say, what do you say to that?
What do you think of it?" The general's face was flushed with
excitement.

All of a sudden the captain began to pant too. What's this?
Without any reason he too became very agitated, and somehow
he felt welling up inside himself a violent urge, a vicious impulse,
to destroy something, anything. He felt that he could no longer
stand the sultriness of everyday living. He saw that the general
was sweating profusely, and he was himself sweating.

Now the jeep was doing close to seventy miles an hour; it
must have appeared to an onlooker, as it raced down the embankment, like some monster dashing headlong towards an

abyss.

Funny, the jeep itself seemed to catch the fever. Now with headlights on, it seemed to become contaminated with life. It seemed to run not on its own mechanism or logic, but on, ridiculously enough, the logic of the two officers. Symbiosis? They wished this state would last forever. Was it because they were intrigued by the intense heat the jeep put forth? What few townspeople there were in the street followed the speeding jeep with bewildered eyes. The elderly people in the realtor's office rushed out to the street, and the urchins stopped doing whatever mischievous things they were engaged in at the time, all to stare at the racing jeep. The grocer and his customers were also watching.

The jeep dashed along the street at the same feverish speed. The policeman looked somewhat bewildered, but he saluted again quite solemnly. Was he catching on too?

"Another round," cried out the general; he was sweating profusely, his swagger stick in his hand.

It was completely dark by now. Again the jeep rushed by the intersection. There was the same policeman, and he saluted again in the same fashion.

"Stop!" bellowed the general.

The jeep screeched to a stop, and suddenly an intense quiet set in. And with it, the sultriness of everyday life rushed in toward them. The general got out of the jeep and accosted the policeman.

"How old are you?"

"Thirty-eight, sir," the policeman answered, coming to attention.

"Give the chain of command."

The policeman hesitated.

"The chain of command, man! Don't you know what a chain of command is?"

Finally the policeman managed to mumble out his own name and that of the chief of the local police precinct.

"You ought to start from the Minister of the Interior on down," snapped the general.

It was apparent that the policeman did not know the name of the minister; after some hemming and hawing he started with the name of the National Police Bureau Chief.

"Where do you live?" said the general.

Captain Kim jotted down the address. Of course it was the general's wish. The two officers got back in the jeep.

"Shall I head back to the camp, sir?"

"I want to go to that address. Let's stop at a butcher's first though."

The captain started the jeep, but it was no longer the fiery monster of a moment ago; it had already reverted back to a clumsy metal lump. The captain wiped sweat off his face with his handkerchief.

At the butcher's they bought two pounds of chuck meat, and at a nearby store they bought some cookies and candies. Then they slowly drove to the address given by the policeman.

It was a ramshackle clapboard house, and out came a shabbily dressed woman. She could not have been more than forty, but she looked much older and untidy. When the captain asked if it was the home of such-and-such policeman, she nodded and said with a worried look, "What's the matter? Did he do anything wrong?"

The captain explained who the general was and the purpose of their visit—to pay a compliment to an outstandingly exemplary policeman. The policeman's wife looked much disconcerted; she looked more disturbed than pleased.

The general stepped forward and said awkwardly, "A fine fellow. Your husband is a fine man." But he looked so out of place in this new role. Even his tone was like that of a schoolboy reciting something in class. The aide had to put his hand to his mouth in order to stop an outburst of laughter. "You are fortunate in having such a fine man as your husband," went on the general. "That's what I came here to compliment you on." But when he realized he was not getting much response from the woman, the general got impatient and snapped at the aide, "Captain, why don't you bring out the stuff?" pointing his stick at the jeep.

The captain handed the packages to the general.

"How many children do you have?" asked the general, the packages in his hands.

"Six of 'em."

"You must be very happy. I mean, you must be happy having that many children.''

The woman said nothing.

''Your husband is a very fine man.'' The general was saying the same thing over with awkward little bows. The woman seemed to be completely at a loss. She took the packages with an idiotic smile.

The general, who now got in the jeep, looked very much displeased. Sensing this, the aide followed the woman into the house and after awhile returned to the jeep. The general was sucking at his pipe glumly.

''General, you have done a good thing. The whole family is overjoyed. They are so touched that every one of them is crying with the packages of cookies and candies spread in the middle of the room. They are wondering how a general can be so kind and generous,'' said the captain.

All at once the glum look disappeared from the general's face. ''Well done! Let's go back to the camp,'' said the general out loud.

(end story)

Christmas Carol

Ch'oe Inhun

Again a burst of cheerful laughter, laughter that reminded him of the splendor of a huge magnolia bouquet thrown up in the air. The merrymaking in the next room, his sister's room, seemed to pick up and ripen. But the cheer no longer buoyed him up; it now got on his nerves. Their laughter still reminded him of bouquets, but now they were made of lifeless, tissuepaper flowers.

Sitting at his desk, he turned to the window without getting up. His face was reflected in the windowpane, framed against the darkness outside; a face so familiar but so pitifully lacking wisdom and confidence after all these years. Tonight he felt this more than ever. For a second he thought he might reread the letter lying on his desk, but on second thought he picked up the empty envelope instead. Aimlessly he scrutinized the postmark and the design of the foreign stamps as though they had a direct bearing on his present, absurdly empty state of mind. On closer scrutiny, he could make out the picture drawn on one of the stamps. It was a bird's-eye view of some European town, packed with massive, old-fashioned brick buildings. It was the town of R—. Then, for the first time, he realized that drawings on stamps are made up of fine lines just as newspaper picturers are nothing but a series of small dots. He kept looking at the fine lines that made up the town of R—. but soon the lines turned into the creases and wrinkles of an aged face. It was the face of an old woman he used to know in that town. Naturally, this took him back to the days he had lived in that town while attending school there.

He used to think that he had made a right decision in going to Europe. Furthermore, he considered it fortunate that his university was located in an old town like R — which flourished during the Middle Ages as a center of commerce and which was known as one of the cradles of protestantism. It was specially noted for its tanning. The leather produced there was still very expensive and all the society ladies and debutantes were said to wear shoes made from leather tanned in R—. Tanning was still the town's chief industry and so it was noted for its unpleasant odors. Once he visited a tannery and the odor made him sick. It was a small tannery—perhaps no larger than the ones in which the present employees' forebears had worked in the Middle Ages. There were many such small tanneries in the town. The peculiar odor was particularly bad in the early morning when the fog from the canals shrouded the town.

The apartment in which he lived during his stay in the town was an old somber brick building on the eastern edge of the town. It used to be the dormitory of the theological seminary, but it had been sold when the seminary moved to the other side of the town. Except for installing gas and electricity, no renovations had been made when the building was turned into apartments. His rooms were on the third floor (the building was three stories high) at the end of the west corridor. His window commanded a view of the whole town, and the canal stretched out to the west as far as the eye could see. His rooms became very sultry in summer, but he did not mind because the view was worth it.

Perhaps the hollow feeling that had taken hold of him when he first moved into these rooms after a long journey from Korea had nothing to do with the surroundings. He should have felt satisfied, for his long-cherished desire was at last fulfilled—to study Western history in Europe. Many of his friends had gone to the United States for advanced studies, but he had always had Europe in mind for his studies abroad. It was probably due to the influence of the snobbishness of characters he had read about in English novels that he regarded America as still being a culturally inferior colony. At any rate, the university in the town of R— had many noted scholars of Western history and he had nothing to complain about concerning the school. Nevertheless, the hollow and somber feeling persisted until the end of his stay in Europe. With the same heavy feeling, he had made the round of the lecture rooms every day. He could not help seeing the cobbler in the professors, eminent scholars of Western history. He saw in them the cobbler, grey haired, enlarged knuckles, and drooping shoulders. It was not so much their physical features as their manner of handling academic subjects that impressed him. Once he thought he had almost verified this impression; it was during a lecture on medieval industry and went into tanning techniques in detail. At that time he thought that learning was not something vague and abstract to these old scholars with huge hands but something concrete and practical, such as tanning the pelt of a mare or nailing on the sole of a shoe. To them learning was not ideological logic but something resembling manual work and this very idea weighed down on the heart of the Oriental student, who had always regarded learning as something cosmopolitan and ideological.

Even his ideas about the spirit of Protestantism had to be adjusted and corrected. Protestantism there, he had learned, was roughly equivalent to what he had regarded as Catholicism back home. He came to understand the Jacobinic blackness of Calvinism as the direct opposite of liberalism. It was like the jealously and obstinately guarded body of rules of an old family; there again he saw the enlarged knuckles of the professors. This feeling was everywhere. Even his apartment was permeated with it.

It was one summer afternoon when the sky was overcast with the thin layer of clouds perculiar to this part of the country, and the hot summer sun filtered through into the mild summer mellowness. He had been there two months already and he was getting accustomed to the view of the town from his apartment window. Directly below his room was the backyard of the building. From that height the square plot of lawn looked like the bottom of an empty well. And old woman was sitting there on the bench. In the half-light of the overcast day everything looked soft and calm. There was no one in the backyard except the old lady, and for no coherent reason he was intensely impressed at the sight of her. He could not explain it; it was one of those strange sensations we receive at a certain time, or in a certain place, or from a certain person. He started at the old woman aimlessly. She had a book open but the way she held it was strange. She was not holding it; rather she was shielding it as if protecting a cat or some other pet and was leaning slightly forward. He figured it was the Bible or a prayer book. As a foreign student, he elaborated on his impression: an old woman living alone in an apartment—a quiet summer afternoon—basking in the sun on a bench—the Bible serving the role of a cat on the lap. That's it, this is religion—this is Christianity—religion blended into living, learning and the soles of shoes—religion and an old woman—the Bible and a cat—that's right, there is a cat crouching in every fold and crease of the people's lives here—the cat weighs down on the loneliness of life—the cat is the learning that measures the weight of life—the cat is also of utility and practicality in the political system of their world as is the needle of the cobbler—the same cat can turn into a panther for a foreigner at any moment.

He heard a knock on the door and turned. A blond young man of medium height walked in. He introduced himself saying that he was a student of engineering at the university and that he came because he had heard that there was another student living in the same building. Herr H — (for that was his name) went over to the window and looked out. He pointed out the old woman, shrugged his shoulders, and said:

"She is the guardian saint of this building."

"Saint?"

"Yes. She has been living here for over twenty years now and no one knows anything about her except that she was once a nurse."

"What's that book?"

"The Bible. That's why she is called a saint, I guess. But I'll say she is a funny saint."

"How so?"

"Well, they usually do penance and good works. Not this one. She doesn't like meeting people. She always holds onto the Bible like that."

"Perhaps she accumulates her good works in the Bible."

"I don't know. She doesn't seem to read the Bible, she merely holds onto it. No one has ever seen her without it, day or night. Maybe it's a kind of penance too, to have to carry it around all the time."

His veiw was clearly different from H—'s idea, but he did not wish to go into it since it would involve a lengthy discussion. The "saint" continued her penance in the sun without moving even once.

This was how he came to know H—. As might be expected from an engineering student, H — sometimes made fun of the foreign student who seemed to be so steeped in and concerned with culture, tradition, and the like. He argued that the trouble with Orientals was their humility in trying to find universality in their own tradition. Then the humble stranger would retort by saying that it is easy for a student of natural science to dismiss everything like that, but to him it wasn't so simple as long as he saw massive medieval walls everywhere and women crouching over the Bible as over a pet cat.

"It follows that the guardian saint's (they always referred to the old woman thus after their first meeting) Bible is not for rational analysis of logical demonstration but a living thing like a pet cat. You said she never read it, didn't you? It is quite natural, for no one ever reads a cat. To her, other cats don't mean a thing. She wouldn't care for other cats even if they were finer cats than hers. She would stick to her own, however dirty and insignificant it might be. That's religion. It's not like garments that you change according to the seasons. Moral science is devoted to the recording of individuality while natural science handles illustration. There is a wall built around individuality. There is a gap between individuals and this widens when it involves individuals whose languages differ and. . ."

"What you are saying amounts to racial discrimination," broke in H—.

"No, cultural discrimination," he said.

"Well, isn't it the job of science to clarify the extent of that discrimination to establish the basis for mutual understanding?"

"Yes, but living itself is not science. Science is merely a means of living. You Occidentals have what might be termed a vested interest in this matter, and it is not likely that you would be willing to relinquish it," he said.

"A transitional period is inevitable, is it not?" said H—.

"I agree," he said. "It is diffcult for an individual to go through the transitional period, especially from our point of view."

"Is it difficult while you are staying here too?" H— asked.

"It's the same everywhere."

"Why? If I may ask."

"Back home, we have our version of *you*, you know."

"God knows I am not responsible for that!"

"Certainly not."

"Who is responsible for it?" said H—.

"Who knows? Maybe Columbus," he said rather facetiously.

"Right you are! May the filthy Italian go to hell!"

But he knew consigning Columbus to hell would not solve anything. You make fun of your greats as though they are your inferiors but in fact you are cashing in dividends and profits from their achievements, and maybe that is the very reason why you want to speak unkindly of them.

It was early the following spring and nearly six months after his arrival. He left the library earlier than usual to return to his apartment. As he started to climb the stairway to the third floor, he heard a short cry of dismay and something dropped at his feet. Standing about halfway up the stairway was the old woman. Her eyes stared at a spot near his feet, at a small book. She must have let the book inadvertently slip from her hand. It was one of those things, and no real harm was done to anything or anybody. But he was shocked to see the expression on her face; she looked, he thought, as though she were seeing the end of the world. Embarrassed, he picked up the book. It was a small Bible bound in yellowish leather. After a moment's hesitation he handed it to the old woman with an awkward smile. Then another shocking thing happened; she rushed toward him, two steps at a time as a young girl in a hurry might do, stopped in front of him, and snatched the book from his hand. Dazed, he merely looked into her eyes. Clutching the book, her arms shivered. Her face—eyes wide open and the muscles around her mouth twitching—showed terror and hatred. Then for the third time a change took place that baffled him; suddenly all the tension disappeared from her face. He heard her say dispiritedly, in a low tone, "I am sorry, stranger, I really am." She mumbled the words, almost to herself, and went on descending the stairs. He stood where she had been and watched her till she disappeared. A ray of the early spring sun about the size of a handkerchief, coming through the skylight, rested on the handrail of the stairway. The building was quiet as usual. The deserted stairway seemed to extend both ways, up and down, interminably. He sat down on one of the steps. Violent loneliness took hold of him, and he thought he would feel better if he could throw up.

Coming back to his apartment, he sat down astride a chair by the window and looked down at the canal. The canal stretched out straight and endlessly. Then he thought about home and his friends there. He pictured the face of a friend who had been killed in the war just before he left for Europe. A kind of guilty feeling began to mix with his loneliness—guilty because he was so far away in a safe place while his own people were going through the hellish tortures of the war. Then he recalled what another friend had said to him at the farewell party given in his honor just before his departure. He had said: "Go, go if you can. Do you know what books we young Koreans should pack in our combat bag when we go to war? None, absolutely none. In other words, our country doesn't even offer the romantic and sentimental flare of war. Why die in this war? Why spill blood for nothing? To die in this war is no better than to die in a traffic accident." His friend rambled on and on in this vein while he quaffed rice wine with self-abandonment. It followed that he went abroad to a foreign country to learn how to satisfy that romantic and sentimental urge. One spoke of the dead as those to be pitied, but wasn't living far worse than death? History was always there, but what good can history do for a decaying corpse? *Then, there is nothing to feel guilty about. We cannot live for others. We have ourselves to look out for. Let's not deceive ourselves. Man is always a wolf who preys on men.*

His wandering thoughts inevitably returned to the incident with the old woman. She snatched the book from his hand as though he had been trying to take it away from her by force. It was merely a hand-worn Bible, not a holy relic of Christ or of some saint. Stingy faith. To her faith was like money. It was not something to share with others. It was a savings passbook. Her facial expression on the stairway was not unlike that of an old miser caught counting and recounting the money he has taken out of his old safe. To them foreigners would never look like normal persons. "I am sorry, stranger, I really am." Was it not the usual apology of a white woman to a Negro whom she had mistaken for a thief or a rapist? Loneliness only ends with either hatred or love for someone. So does humiliation.

He lit a cigarette and blew smoke against the windowpane. Then he muttered to himself: "Man is always a wolf who preys on other people, and that's what I've got to learn.''

He often woke up in the night. He would get up, dress, and go out to see the canal, for he knew he could hardly get back to sleep again. It was quite nice to walk the quiet, deserted street to the canal. The moon would be pale on the cobbled pavement. At night the town was really scenic. The quiet town in the middle of the night looked like fertile ruins, if such things existed. Sometimes he would see other such things existed. Sometimes he would see other people taking a midnight walk, but that was quite rare. The buildings seemed to show their faces without makeup. He felt at home with them during such moments. Since they were of neither brick nor stone, it was not unlike looking at sculpture.

The canal itself was a delight to look at, too. With one or two all-night lamps burning, the moored barges seemed to be sound asleep. He would sit down on the bank. The water was about a fathom below his dangling feet. It looked heavy with darkness and floating oil. He groped for pebbles around where he sat but finding none he dug in his pockets for coins. He would drop one into the water. Drip. Nothing more. Then he spat into the water. Drip. Nothing more. He got up and started to stroll along the quay. Then it occurred to him that it might not be possible for him to enjoy such nocturnal walks back home. No, it would be out of the question. The curfew alone would be enough to make it impossible. Don't be a wet blanket, don't think about home. He would go through the park on the way back to the apartment. The acacia blossoms were in full bloom, and the scent almost suffocating. But the faint, fishy smell of leather mixed with the scent of the acacia.

One night he came back to his apartment from one such nocturnal walk. He started to climb the stairs slowly so as not to disturb the others in the house, but suddenly he stopped frozen, a cold shudder running down his spine. He saw a young woman silently descending the semidarkness of the stairway. Her steps were so stealthy that she took him by surprise. As she drew closer, however, he realized that she wasn't young at all. In fact, she was the old woman with the Bible. This shocked him again. She was clasping the book to her bosom as she passed by him silently like a ghost. When he had recovered enough to be able to move, he realized that his back was cold with sweat. When he reached his room he was nearly exhausted, and he knew it wasn't from his walk along the canal.

Toward dawn he stole out of his room, tiptoed downstairs to the second floor and, reaching the end room on the left, he opened the door without knocking. On the bed he saw the old woman, with the face of the young woman of his illusion on the stairway, making love with a young man. Her corpulent white buttocks heaved wildly like those of a mare. The young man was H—. He tried to run but his legs forze. He became desperate. . . Then he awoke. It was a dream. His bed was wet with sweat. He had masturbated and was completely exhausted. After this he fell asleep again and dreamed. He was sitting by the canal and throwing coins into the water. Drip, drip. He spat. Drip, drip. Soon he ran out of coins, and with that he fell into a deep, dreamless sleep.

He did not come into contact with the old woman during the remainder of the three years he stayed in the town of R—. He only learned that she was a recipient of the Florence Nightingale Medal and that she was a member of the Evangelical Society. Maybe her attachment to the Bible might serve certain purposes of such a society. Other tenants in the building seemed to regard her with a certain respect, for she was really harmless save for the fact that she disliked meeting people. Besides, being a recipient of the Florence Nightingale Medal and a member of the Evangelical Society, she was bound to command respect and reverence, for she was thus assoicated with both kinds of crosses, secular (Red) as well as religious. The unpleasant impression she once made on him wore off. In the course of three years she even became to him a mysterious figure with a halo around her head.

Perhaps his reaction to the incident, as foreigners are apt to do, was stronger than normal. It was probably more common among members of the society. In fact, he ran into many characters like her during his stay abroad, old people, living on a pension or on their savings like mice gnawing away at a wooden pillar but stil enjoying some secret and jealously guarded hobby or the like. Of course they were of many kinds, but in essence they did not differ from the old woman who carried her Bible around as she would a pet cat. An old man, a retired sea captain, living in a room two doors down from his, was another of them. But he never got to like the captain. The old man's hobby was the collection of hydrographic charts, and he pestered everyone with rambling accounts of how he fought German U-boats during the two world wars. But he tried to avoid the old man ever since the captain asked him once which part of China Korea was. He could not stand the old man's good nature. It was different with the old woman; she had cut off all human contacts, and to him it seemed a form of enviable stoicism. Twenty years—for twenty years she had been engaged in only one thing. No matter what that one thing was, it was something in itself to be able to concentrate oneself on doing only that one thing for twenty long years. The same work, the same appearance, the same expression, the same routine, the same obsession. He envied the magnificently huge accumulation of hand-worn time. Time is the start of everything and it must precede changes or revolutions. He felt the same thing when the old captain showed him a chart which was said to have been used by pirates in the Middle Ages. It bore the skull and crossbones, symbol of pirates. He thought, "Europeans must understand these symbols physically while outsiders understand them mentally. They live among such symbols. Such symbols are their nerves, their cells, eyeballs, the dirt under their fingernails. But to us they are learning, logic, culture, and ideas." He could see the gap between the two approaches. The old woman was simply one such symbol of Europe. He had seen in her eyes that night on the stairway how obstinate and consistent those symbols were. It was enough to "grab" the Bible; God was to be grabbed like a savings passbook. He knew how hard the task of bridging the gap would be and later, after his return to Korea, he verified it while teaching Western history at a university. With a sense of despair he felt his lectures lacked the tenacity of those old cobbler-professors and the almost hostile obsession of the old woman with the Bible. The human being is *not* the same everywhere. That is merely a shallow illusion born in the mind of the colonial intellectual. Man, as the product of history, is soaked in time, history, tradition. . . he believed all this most strongly up to a little while ago. But now this belief was completely shattered.

He picked up the letter which he had pushed aside as though it were something to dread.

Just then his sister stepped into the room without knocking, "What's holding you up?" she said jovially, "I've already asked you to join us. My friends are dying to meet you." Then she noticed the letter in his hand. "My, my. Is it a love letter? From a blonde with blue eyes?"

"No." He laughed awkwardly.

"What pathetic laughter!" and she went on teasingly, "A heart-wrenching love affair separated by a whim of fate, is that it? This *is* news!"

"Alright, stop it. I'll join you in a little while."

"Make it quick. Make hay while the sun shines, as they say."

"What are you saying? This is Christmas. Do you think Christmas is some kind of carnival of something? And you are not even a Christian."

"You are more old-fashioned than most people who have never been to the West. The new generation has its own ways. You must learn them in order to get along with them."

"Anyway, you go ahead," he said.

Winking at the letter, she said, "Show it to me later, will you?"

Then she left the room, slamming the door behind her. He watched the closed door blankly for awhile, then began to read the letter for the second time. It was from H—, his former fellow tenant in the town of R—.

. . .Recently there has been a campaign going on here to recapture the ancient spirit of Christmas. People have become fed up with the commercialized version of Christmas of recent years, it seems. What is striking about the campaign, however, is the fact that it is whole-heartedly supported by the young people while the older generation seems reluctant to join in. I think of you often in this connection, you who obstinately refused to join Christmas parties while you were here. If this campaign succeeds, I mean if our young people succeed in becoming older than our old people, then I fear that the wall of your theories concerning cultural discrimination will become higher and higher. Speaking of the old people, I have some news to share with you. You remember the guardian saint, don't you? She died not long ago. But she confessed a shocking story on her deathbed. There were quite a few people besides the minister present because she had been a member of many societies. She said it was both her confession and her apology to the people of the town of R—. She said that she had deceived people for thirty years, that she was not worthy of her membership in the Evangelical Society, that she had never been really interested in the Bible though she still clutched that same Bible at that very moment, and that she had kept the Bible for such a long time only to keep the leather cover. She disclosed the shocking fact that the leather cover of the Bible was made from the skin of her lover who had died in an accident nearly forty years before. Her lover died in the hospital where she worked, and she had removed part of his skin the night before his burial. She had been a nurse in the surgical department, and so she had no problem. Upon her retirement she had come to the apartment to live, and one day she had thought of the idea of covering the Bible with her lover's skin. Of course, she had feared the profanity, but she had thought it was the best way to preserve his skin, for she covered the most sacred thing in the world with the dearest thing in the world to her. In this way she was able to be near her lover at any time and in any place. She said she had to confess this on her deathbed, this unpardonable sin, and she begged for mercy.

Well, doesn't it shock you? You used to say something about her being a symbol of Europe, Christianity, and so forth. But her lifelong obsession had nothing to do with Christianity. It was rooted in and sustained by love, which is common everywhere. And most human. I hope this news will be of some use to you in your research into Western history. Wishing you a merry Christmas and a happy New Year, I am.

Yours Sincerely,

H—.

He again heard a cheerful burst of laughter from his sister's room.

He put the letter in his desk drawer and locked it. He put on his overcoat. Stepping out of his room, he could hear the merrymaking coming from his sister's room even louder than before. He stood in front of his room for awhile and mumbled something to himself. "H — argues that she was being merely human and that her act had nothing to do with Christianity or tradition. But did she not confess her deed as profane and sacrilegious? A race of people who must hold onto love in the form of a piece of skin. . . can you imagine a Korean woman keeping the Book of Fortune covered with the skin of her dead lover?''

He felt sick. And he knew it was a familiar to him. He passed the door to his sister's room silently. The record player was blaring Christmas carols sung by a male voice. Just then he was caught by his sister, who was coming back to her room from downstairs.

''Going out?'' she asked surprised.

''Yeah, I forgot I had to...''

''But you promised you would join...'' She did not finish the sentence. She looked very hurt. Ordinarily, if she had looked that way he would have softened immediately, but tonight was different. He felt completely indifferent to her. With a stony stare he turned away and walked down toward the front door.

'Where are you going? I know you don't have an appointment,'' said his sister reproachfully.

''Appointment?'' he thought. ''What sort of appointments do you kids need to make you get together and frolic like this? Christmas. Christmas parties. Christmas in this country is nothing but a pretext for the younger generation of both sexes to get together and romp. A female who preserved a piece of male skin using the Bible as a shield. Is there any similarity between the two? Have our kids jumped over the cultural wall? No, there is a difference. The old woman had partner to renew her contract with on her deathbed. She returned the Bible to God. The Bible, the cat, the skin of the lover, then back to the Bible, thus the cycle was complete. But what about these kids? They don't have partner to renew contract with.

''Is Pat Boone your cat?'' he asked his sister quite abruptly. Now she was giving him an icy stare. He saw the stony eyes of the old woman on the stairway in his sister's eyes. He turned the door knob slowly and stepped out into the darkness. Where to? He was aware that he did not have either of the old woman's possessions—neither the Bible nor the piece of skin. Moreover, he did not have those kids' Pat Boone records. ''Well, I don't even have an appointment to keep. What am I then? The sweet and sour puke that is brewing inside me, that's me.'' Just then he knew where he should go. To R—. To that gloomy-looking dormitory building that belonged to the theological seminary in an old town where a man can leave a piece or two of his hide when he dies. "Then I should sit on the stairway to the third floor and lean against the handrail where the ray of sun coming through the skylight rests. There I will throw up what's inside me and chew it as a cow chews her cud. I will keep on doing it till this night in Seoul where Christmas rampages like a beast is over."

(end story)

Chaos

Nam Chŏnghyŏn

I too may wind up being a run-of-the-mill carpenter even before I know what's befallen me. The thought is discouraging, if you ask me. Life becomes something terrible. Like father, like son, it is said. For me such a dreadful life cycle was probably drafted and set in motion even before I was born. No use trying to get out of the rut. You feel you are a mere puppet with a giant pulling the strings that make you click. Looking out on a horizon with no prospects, you feel so frustrated that tears come to your eyes. Such a gloomy outlook overpowers me and, more often than not, I let the hammer or whatever I happen to be holding slip from my hand in my pessimistic reverie. Why must it always be my toes? I don't know, but always they seem to be the target. Ouch! Damn it! Why the hell. . .

Not that I despise being a carpenter. No. You don't have to argue for of the loftiest democratic ideals, that all legitimate trades are equally honorable. All you have to do is just try to picture a world without carpenters. It would be so drab and ugly. Beginning with the small things such as these tables and chairs, the bulk of what's above the earth would not have existed but for the hands of carpenters. It is some achivement to bow your head down to. I have a fair amount of respect for my dead father on this account; he was a carpenter all his life. What's more, was not Joseph, the father of Jesus and one of the most influential persons in the making of history, a carpenter? No need to add more to prove my point. Just take this house for example. Nothing in it escaped the carpenter's hand, and so I have no intention of slighting his achievements.

So it naturally follows that my misgivings about being a carpenter have nothing to do with its social prestige. Rather, it is something personal. I don't know how to go about explaining this, but let's say that I once made up my mind not to follow in my father's footsteps. By this, of course, I mean his dying in prison. Dying in prison is the worst thing that can happen to a man, having to take leave of the world, forlorn, bitter, and alone. The mere thought gives you the creeps. It may be alright for a worm, but I, a normal man with a normal name like Tŏksu, cannot finish my life like that. No, sir! But the trouble is my hands; the more firmly I resolve not to be a carpenter, the more deftly my hands move about picking up the hammer here and nails there. Now, it is a serious problem if your hands start to work against your will. It's a betrayal, an insurrection. When you have to stand by and watch your hands mending broken doors and tables always against your will, you taste the absolute in frustration. Then you feel an overwhelming depression. I am not authoritarian by nature, but I cannot help being a bit touchy when my hands, which are supposed to be my best and most obedient members, work against me. Watching my hands working ever so cleverly, I sometimes whisper imploringly: "My dear hands, don't do that. Can't you listen to me just for once? Oh, my dear, lovely hands?" But that's all. Nothing changes. My hands make no indication of having heard me. They work even more deftly and swiftly than before with no sign of fatigue. It's disturbingly subversive. Considering our relationship, I don't think I deserve this really. When I observe the skillful movements of my hands, which are no longer those of an apprentice, handling the saw or the plane, a sudden horror takes hold of me.

Then suddenly I realized one day that it wasn't my father but these two hands that should have been accused of subversive plots against the government. Horror-struck, I debated whether I should file a formal accusation against my hands. I should waste no time reporting them to the authorities. I would be punished if I failed in my duty as a citizen. One can never condone subversion, however dear and intimate one's personal relationship may be with the guilty party. Following this line of thought, I felt very patriotic which, in turn, made me feel good and secure. I have been a fool not to have thought about it sooner, but it's still not too late. We must never confuse what's public and what's personal. Go ahead and make the report. Of course, it will agonize you to indict your own hands, but thorny is the way of all patriots, and so on.

Thus resolved, I started out by admonishing my hands with the sternest possible expression on my face. Then I hesitated and backed down. I had to. It was because of the look of my hands. They were too rough, with far too many scars, to be human. Looking down on these hands that had so many scars from the carpenter's adze or chisel, I lost the courage to accost them with an accusation. That's not all. What suddenly struck me was their resemblance to my father's hands. The round, coin-sized scar on the second knuckle of the right thumb was an exact copy of the one on my father's right thumb. I could do nothing but close my eyes and sigh deeply. To whom do these hands belong? This might sound very unfilial but I was unable to distinguish my hands from my father's. That was only the beginning of a series of new troubles. My inability to see my hands in the right perspective began to apply to other things. Things around me began to take on blurred outlines. Lines indefinite, colors nebulous, like abstract paintings. Watching these things happen, the illusion took hold of me so that my body itself was dissolving into a gluey mass. Sensing the crisis in such moments, I would call my own name loudly, "Tŏksu, Tŏksu," as if that would help bring form back to my body. But what came forth on such occasions, thrusting itself before my eyes, was not my identity but a fearless object. What was it? Emerging out of the opaque fog that surrounded me was a hand. My father's! That would put me on guard instantly.

Once I held my father's hand in the visiting room of the prison. Of course, I had no way of knowing then that it would be our last meeting. On that occasion, for no clear reason, he thrust out his hand toward me, his body trembling. He glared at me as though I was his dread enemy, his bloodshot eyes dilating. Fear took hold of me.

"Stop it, Father. Please."

"Look here! You understand me, don't you?"

"What do you mean?"

"What? You mean you don't understand me?"

"What about?"

"How dare you talk to me like that? Tell me you understand me even if no one else does."

I could not understand why he was suddenly upset. Then suddenly, without really meaning it, I told him he was truly my father, the husband of my mother, and therefore would have been the father-in-law of my sister's husband, if I had had a sister. This, of course, only added to my father's rage. In fact, he was so infuriated that he suddenly seemed restored to sanity. With a deep, long sigh he said, "That's all you understand about your father," almost to himself. Then his face changed to that of a sobbing child.

"I'm sorry, Father."

"That's not the point. If that's all you know about me, how can I expect the authorities to do better? I cannot blame them. You know I am unjustly accused."

"I guess you are right. Forgive me."

"Guess? You only guess? How can you say such things to me? Tŏksu, I love you so dearly."

"I'm sorry."

"Being sorry won't help at this stage. Give me your honest opinion. Was it really such a crime for me to love my own son? I loved my son so dearly that I made a dining table for a certain powerful man in the government, hoping he would look after my dear son in some way. Was it really such a crime to warrant this treatment?"

"Father, I am not saying that it was a crime. I only say that the authorities understand such matters far better than lowly and ignorant people like us. Won't they look into the matter and judge it fairly and squarely?"

"You, too, are on their side, I see. You are determined to ruin your own father, to break his heart."

"No, what I'm really determined to do is not to get involved in this affair. Would you rather have me dragged into this on your side, for me to be behind those bars?" I said this sullenly and breathed a long sigh. This quieted him down and kept him brooding for quite some time.

"I'm sorry, Tŏksu," he said, "I didn't quite look at it that way. I have been selfish, Tŏksu. But, then, I was merely eager to have the truth out. You understand that much, don't you?"

I don't know why, but my father had never seemed more untruthful than when he spoke those words, tearfully talking about truth. He seemed such a liar and so insincere that it was almost comic to look at him. In spite of myself, I burst into empty laughter, "Hi-hee-hee."

I know it was dreadful under the circumstances for a son to laugh like that but, I tell you, I had no other choice. Whenever the word truth was mentioned by anyone, I tended to see the untruth behind it and everything around me seemed like some sort of joke. Then I had to laugh. Can you blame me for that?

Such grandiose terms as patriotism, government, national assembly, the revolution, all seemed like pages torn out of a comic book, and obscene one at that. Things that happened around me just could not be real—they had to be some game, mere acting.

Anyway, the fact that my father, a dull but honest man, was at the time awaiting his final trial did not strike me as real. I thought at the time, "Somebody must be joking, but whoever he is, he is overdoing it.

I have no intention of slighting my father's personal integrity and intelligence, but after all, he couldn't even read the newspaper with full comprehension and here he was accused of subversive ideas. Ideology, my eye! Let me now give you a brief rundown of the case—State v. My Father.

It all began with the cutting down of the gingko tree that had stood in our backyard for nearly two hundred years. He did this for his only son, meaning me. Well, the tree was a kind of household treasure and he would not have cut it down for any other reason. After carefully drying the lumber he made an elegant dining table out of it for a minister of the government. For some reason he had the notion that the present would lead the minister to favor me. Anyway, it took him over a month to make the table and, finally, he was successful in effecting its delivery through the good offices of various people. That was all. What I don't see is how the fact that one leg of the table broke has anything to do with my father's ideology. The fact that the leg broke while the minister was entertaining several very important Japanese businessmen, thus resulting in his losing face, was purely a question of physics; he had loaded the table beyond its capacity. Anybody can understand that.

But that was not the case with the minister. He certainly had a strange power of reasoning. He insisted that the present was made with the explicit purpose of embarrassing him; that embarrassing a minister was not different from embarrassing the country; and that none other than the Communist sympathizers would engage in such subversive activities. So it naturally followed that my father was immediately arrested and investigated.

The situation was truly farcical, and when I heard the word truth coming from my father, blue with the fatigue of imprisonment rage and I could not help but laugh out loud.

My father heard the derisive laughter of his own son but was no longer capable of being infuriated. He looked dumb and dazed. Resting his head on his hand for what seemed to be a long while, he breathed harshly. Then suddenly he roared, "How dare you laugh at me!" Then he shivered violently. I knew I had overdone it.

"Forgive me, Father. We've gone too far with our joking," I said.

"What? Joking? You mean to say that what I have said and all I have been through is a joke?" he gasped.

"You don't think all this has been in earnest, do you?"

"There is really no end to your impudence and audacity. Then you must regard the fact that I am imprisoned as nothing but a joke."

"What else?"

His shriveled and parched limbs fell into a fit of convulsions. Why?

"Father, your legs are shaking," I advised him as if to warn him of some imminent danger. But he seemed to have no time to heed such trivialities. Instead he said, "Listen, you, you must be determined to destroy your already ruined father. Tell me, do you regard my love for you as part of the joke too?" Suddenly thrusting his hands toward me, he said, "Look at these hands."

A look of blue rage flashed across his eyes. His hands were covered with scars. The large one on his thumb especially repulsed me. It began to loom large and emit a strange, fierce light. It was a silent accusation of an unfilial son. As if to save myself from being blinded by that light, I held his hand in mine and hurried to say, "Forgive me, Father. I am unworthy of your love," as I knelt down before him.

"Forget it, son. My only wish has been to make you somebody, something better than a carpenter," he said in a surprisingly mild tone.

"I know. I'll try. But right now, don't worry about such things." I don't know why, but I spoke on in a tone of repentance and then left the prison promising to visit him again soon. But my father died a few days before the final trial, unilaterally breaking our agreement to meet again. A prison official, upon my visit, told me that my father had one day closed his eyes and would not reopen them as if determined not to do so. Somehow I was more amused by the facetious description of my father's death than I was grieved by the news. Really, I thought, his power of description was worthy of admiration by any standards, and I said, "Congratulations, congratulations." He must have thought I was a nut.

Anyway, after my father's death, I resolved to fulfill his last wish—to pursue a better life than that of a carpenter. But my confounded hands! As I mentioned earlier, my hands seemed to work on as they please. In spite of me, they picked up a hammer here and nails there and skillfully went to work. Naturally they collected scars here and there, including the large one on the thumb exactly like that on my dead father's thumb. It was my constant tormentor and reminder of my father's anguish.

My first move to get out of the rut was to change my environment. After an ardous search, I was able to rent a room in a Western-style house. I considered myself fortunate in being able to get the room, although the rent was considerably higher than that for a room in a Korean-style house, for somehow I had the notion that my pursuit of a better life had more chance of success in this new location.

I soon noticed something strange about the house, however. Although it looked new and clean, closer observation showed that everything about it was either crooked and warped or distorted. There again my carpenter's eyes were at work. But even more strange were the faces of the family that owned the house—they looked all distorted like the ones you see in a cheap mirror.

At first I doubted my eyes, but soon I learned that it was due to the constant bickering and quarreling in the family. Not a day passed in peace. No one ever smiled. Fights broke out on the slightest pretext among members of the family—the old couple, their daughter, and their son and his wife. A few harsh words and pieces of furniture or household goods would fly across the yard. Name calling, grappling, hair pulling, and scratching would ensue. When exhausted, they would lay down among the debris of broken glass and splintered wood and wail themselves to sleep. One would think that they had been born to fight among themselves. No sense of decency or respect, let alone of family love. Such barbaric chaos!

Mungil, the old man and head of the family, would often call on me between these routine fights, soliciting my sympathy and friendship. When he addressed me, he would talk in a soft, faltering tone as if he were in the confessional.

He usually began with name dropping, and by naming several high government officials, he seemed to think he had established his social respectability.

"This is one damned family. I am ashamed of my family. I don't know what will become of it. The children don't respect their father, the wife doesn't respect her husband. Of course, I don't expect today's younger generation to have the same sense of respect for the aged you used to see. But this is going too far, far too far."

Naturally I would do my best to console him, citing myself as an example, telling him how bad I was to my own father, and assuring him that his children were by far a better breed. I told him this rebellion of the young was something like influenza and that it would soon pass away.

But if you listened to Myŏnghŭi, his daughter, who had been forced by her father to give up her high school education, it was another story entirely. According to her, her father was the most inhumane tyrant who ever lived. He was an impossible old goat and was so stingy that he would not allow his daughter a decent education nor decent clothing. Naturally, she didn't pay any attention when her father told her to do something, even to bring a glass of water. That would in turn enrage him and some ghastly name calling would follow. One by one other family members would join in.

The strange thing, however, was that whenever the daughter-in-law joined in a fight, everybody except the son would gang up on her no matter whose side she happened to be on that day.

However, the most formidable fighter in the family was

Hyŏnggi, the son. He was around thirty years old and I heard
he had been fired from a bank job for embezzlement. Being a
perpetual drunkard, he was naturally seldom around the house,
but as soon as he stepped into the yard all hell would break loose.
He called his parents and sister all kinds of names. Ond day he
came round to my room, drunk and began to pester me to join
him for a friendly drink. Being a teetotaler, I tried to decline
the offer cordially. Naturally he would not listen and finally I
was dragged into a nearby booze joint. Over the next hour or
so he told his side of the story in the family conflict.

"I think you will readily agree that the most important thing
in a democratic society such as ours is the readiness to talk things
over and solve problems through mutual understanding, but the
fossils at our place (meaning his parents) fearfully lack this spirit.
Down with the fossils, I say. They think my wife is their chattel
slave or something. What should have been a happy and fruitful
companionship for me and my wife has been wrecked due to their
selfishness. I am miserable in more ways than one. Do you know
why I had to quit (he didn't say fired) the bank? The old man
kept on whining how he was short about two hundred thousand
wŏn when he built the house. So I sort of "borrowed" the money
from the bank where I was working.

"Then some son of a bitch in the accounting section found
out about it not long ago. So I had to quit. In other words I
sacrificed my career and honor for my old man. Now that I'm
broke, I ask him to return the money. You know what he says?
He flatly refuses to pay me back. I know he's got a snug little
hoard of money stashed away somewhere, but he says he doesn't
have any. So I tell him to sell the house. To this he says he would
rather die. Now this is what I get for doing a favor. Ingrate! Now
you know why I take to drinking." He guzzled down his wine
as a wronged man might do in desperation.

That night, after he had sufficiently warmed himself up with
the cheap wine, we headed for home. Rather, he headed for home
with me following and feeling miserable because something fearful might happen when he arrived there.

"This goddamn house is cursed!" he roared out as he kicked open the front gate. "This is my day for a showdown with
the old rascal. Come on out and face me. You either pay me
off right now or, or. . ." Then hell as usual broke loose.

Everybody jumped on everybody else, grabbing, pulling, screaming, whining. Sometime during the confusion, the son got hold
of an old pick handle and began to swing it blindly. The daughter
jumped into my room wearing little more than her panties. She
buried her head under my quilt, sobbing violently. Her plump
buttocks shook and heaved as she sobbed, which gave me a pleasant sensation. Ah! I wondered about the dirty mind I had to
be sexually aroused under such grotesque circumstances. But
nothing happened. After awhile things quieted down, and the
girl went back to her room.

What I still don't understand is what happened the following morning. I got up early, even before dawn broke, and set
about fixing broken window sills, nailing down loosened pieces
of wood and glueing together broken furniture. I was doing this
against my own will. My hands did all the work, automatically
and skillfully. "Am I really going to be just another carpenter?"
I stopped in the middle of my work, looked down at my hands,
and felt frustrated.

Suddenly a hand grabbed my shoulder. It was the son, drunk
as a skunk.

"Do me a favor. Give me a break," he pleaded.

"You are drunk," I said.

"Naturally. What do you expect? But I am sure you can
understand my plight. In fact, you are the only one who
understands me and can help me now. Please do me a favor and
be a witness for me."

"A witness? For what?"

"You mean you didn't know? I tell you, my old man is a
Communist spy. Why else should he act so undemocratically?
It all adds up, you know. I've given up trying to collect money
from the old man, but I can collect the reward money from the
government by informing on him. In this case the reward money
happens to be exactly the same amount as the sum he owes me.
Some coincidence, eh? Ha-ha-ha. Only thing is that someone
has to support my report to the authorities. This is where you
come in. All you have to do is to relate what you have observed
at our place. I am not asking too much, am I? Of course I won't
forget a pretty share for you when I get my money."

"You must be very drunk," I said.

"What? You think I say these things because I am drunk? My God, even you, my last hope, turn against me." So saying, he picked up a sharp-edged tool, poising it as if to thrust to it into his chest. Instantly I held on to his arms, begging to be forgiven.

"Forgive me, I don't know how I could have been so cruel," I said on the spur of the moment without realizing what it meant.

"That's better. That's more like you," he said with a triumphant smile spreading over his face. Putting down the tool, he grabbed me by the collar. "Let's get going then. What are we waiting for?"

Withoug knowing where we were headed I was led away, shambling, teetering, my heart pounding, in this impossible and absurd situation.

(end story)

At the End of the World

Son Sohŭi

"Look, our dog is giving birth to puppies. One, two. . . wait, there is another, and that one makes three," was Kŭmsun's jubilant cry. "Hey! You ain't supposed to look while they're getting born. Come back in right now," was the upset cry of my stepmother. "I didn't look on purpose, Mom. I just wanted to feed our dog because she hadn't eaten since last night, and then I found them puppies. Each one is a different color—yellow, white, and black." As her voice with its mock nagging tone disappeared toward the kitchen, the house became quiet again.

I was lying in my bed. I had the chills and felt a numbing pain in my legs and arms. A mixture of overworked fatigue and flu. "I must get up, I must get up," I kept saying to myself. Then slowly my body temperature rose, my head ached, I started running a fever. As I lay there, I thought of the new born puppies. "Let's see, a yellow puppy, a white puppy, a black puppy. It must be atavism. Its grandfather must have been yellow, the great-grandfather white, and the great-great-grandfather black. What will the color of the next one be? I hope it's spotted. Maybe the father is. I hope so. It's interesting, the way atavism works. Wait, I hear someone's footsteps. By the sound, it's Kŭmsun."

"Drink this herb medicine, Brother." Opening the lattice door, Kumsun placed a tray with a bowl of herb medicine and a bowl of water beside my pallet. "Ah, alright," I said with my eyes closed. "Do you feel really bad? If you do, Mom said she would send for a doctor." "No, don't worry about me, I'll be alright soon." "It must be really bad, your lips are all swollen." "Stop gabbing, this medicine is enough to make me well." "You better get well soon, and don't forget to get me a wild azalea for the garden before you go back to camp. You promised me that three years ago, remember, but you went into the army instead.'' ''Alright, how big a one do you want? Now with them puppies, I suppose you want a medium-sized one.'' ''Great, I'm really happy. Say, is it bad luck for someone to look at puppies while they are being born? Do puppies get sick or die if you do?'' ''I don't know, I don't think so,'' I said.

Kŭmsun was sitting on the other side of the open lattice door. The cold air blowing in was bad for my nose and made me cough a little. But I didn't tell her to close the door, nor did I ask her to come into the room. Suddenly I felt I had some urgent business to look after. I knew this was an illusion, but I was restless as if I were on the run, running away from something. It was as if I were eagerly waiting for her to leave me alone so I could tend to that unfinished business. But I didn't dare tell her to leave me alone. She was only thirteen, but somehow I could never feel at ease around her and able to say such things. I don't think it was because she was my stepsister. Perhpas I didn't want to make her feel embarrassed. Holding the tip of my nose between the thumb and forefinger, I kept answering all her wonderridden questions.

''Why, you bad girl, why are you sitting there with the door open? What if your brother catches a worse cold?'' Stepmother's upset cry was heard from afar. Coming to the door herself, she added, ''How are you feeling? The herb doctor said that his medicine would fix you up.'' She looked into the room over Kŭmsun's shoulder, and finding the bowl of medicine still on the tray, she cried again, upset, ''Why, you haven't even drunk it yet! It must be cold by now. Why, you little chatterbox, you just sat there gabbing away. You should've asked your brother to drink it.'' Then she stooped and picked up the bowl. ''I'll heat it up again.''

''Don't bother, Mom. I feel alright and I don't think I need any more medicine,'' I said.

I felt restless again. I wished they would go away and leave me alone. Why didn't they just go away and leave me be? Just then, as if to tell me what I was running away from, Father's sharp and angry roar was heard.

''You damned women, what are you bitches up to anyway? What is this? Why are you women always flirting with that young boy? You always have the best service for the boy, medicine and all. But you don't care whether the master of the house comes home or not. God, what a family! What is this family coming to? Incestuous bitches!''

That was Father all right. The words were familiar, and the squeaky voice was familiar too. At the slightest pretext he always jumped to nasty conclusions. Of course, his anger was actually directed at me, his only son. But this time he was shrewdly leaving me out of his attack. Maybe it was because I was on leave from the army for a very short time, or maybe it was because I was sick.

"It's not me who's sick, it's him. We ought to put our strength together to cure him of his sick mind," I said to myself. But on the other hand, I kept telling myself to cover up under the bed quilt because Father and his sick mind might jump at me any moment with a club or something. I kept telling myself to do something to protect myself from his assault, but actually I did nothing. I was lying flat on my back and I didn't budge. "I'm in a hurry, I'm in a hurry," I said to myself, but scenes with unpleasant memories kept coming back to me. "No, I have no time to dwell on such things, I'm in a hurry, I have no time, not even a minute, not even a second, I have no time, no time..." This idea that I was in a hurry and had no time filled my body and wriggled and squirmed within me like a huge worm. My nose went dry, my tongue was scorched.

The bright window turned gray, then dark as dusk set. That's natural enough. But why was I lying there like that? Was it because I was an orphan of the universe? I thought to myself, "Isn't that absurd? No, I am absurdity itself. That's why I am pressed for time now. I am so pressed for time that I may not be able to get back to the camp on time. A bunch of MP's might come after me. I'd better hide before they grab me. Where should I hide? Not in this house. But where? Let's see, there's Suni's in the village. And there is Poksun's house too. She's kind of cute.'' She's the one who secretly gave me five boiled eggs when I first enlisted. Yŏngsun gave me a bottle of hair tonic as a present. Ilsun gave me ten stamps and a pad of stationery. Chŭngsun two handkerchiefs. . . I used up all of Ilsun's stamps and paper to write to Poksun. It was unfair of me to do so. After all, they belonged to Ilsun. I only kissed Chǔngsun, though. Once she asked me to meet her in the woods, waving her pretty handkerchief. I went up there, and this gal, Chǔngsun, threw herself into my arms and told me to do whatever I wished to do, then she flushed. So I proposed a kiss. She said it was alright with her. So I held her ears and kissed. My heart began to beat faster and faster and she asked me what it tasted like. I said it wasn't sweet but a little bitter like a herb, and she said my mouth tasted like pine juice and I said I had just eaten a pine flavored cake and she said I was a fool. She married a guy in a neighboring village not long after that.

"Turn on the light, Brother, I've brought your supper." It was Kumsun's cheerful voice. Then I heard the sound of a tray being put down on the other side of the lattice door. "What supper?" I said in a dazed voice. "What you mean what supper. Supper is supper. Just turn on the light." Ah, ah, after stammering several times, I asked her what time it was. "It's eight. I had to wait till Daddy fell asleep. He must have drunk an awful lot. He threatened to beat Mommy and me up, and at last he fell asleep awhile ago. Have you waited long?" she said. I turned on the light and she brought the stray into the room. "Go ahead and eat your supper now," she said, then she noticed that the bowl of herb medicine was still untouched. "Why, you haven't taken the medicine yet!" Then she sort of glared at me. They were beautiful eyes, very much like stepmother's. She is a stepmother to me, but a blood mother to Kumsun, and there's nothing added Kǔmsun taking after her own mother. Her round chin looked like her mother's, and the slightly upturned nose too. Then I wondered who I took after. Kǔmsun was still making a motherly fuss over the bowl of herb medicine. She was a bit taken aback when I asked her whom did she think I took after, thrusting my face toward her. "Well, let's see, you don't look like Daddy, nor do you look like your mother as I saw her in the picture, and you don't look like my mother, so I don't know what to say." I wanted to be alone again, and I asked for a glass of water just to send her out of my room. Just then the lattice was opened from the outside. Stepmother was there with another tray.

"Here's the water. Give me that bowl of medicine and I'll heat it up again. Cold herb medicine ain't no use." I handed her the bowl in silence. She took it without a word and turned away. After awhile she was back.

"You finish it up this time. It'll make you get well quicker. Eat a lot too. That's where you get strength from." She started back a few steps, but turned around and added, "Kŭmsun, bring the tray out when your brother gets through. Meanwhile I'll build a fire for the heated floor." Stepmother closed the lattice door, completely expressionless, not looking at me, not looking at Kŭmsun. Was it total resignation on her part? But it was odd that she should not show any emotion at all in the face of Father's vulgar and nasty remarks. I watched the closed lattice door for awhile absentmindedly. She seemed to be a little donkey destined to pull too heavy a load, too heavy a burden. Is that what they call karma? Retribution? For what and for whom was she enduring such a heavy burden?

"Your herb medicine is getting cold again, and your supper too. Go ahead and finish it up." "Alright, I'll take the medicine first." I picked up the bowl of medicine. "Daddy was awfully drunk, it's the day of county fair, you know." Kŭmsun was making an excuse for Father's unreasonable behavior, sitting down across from the supper tray. She is getting more and more like her mother, I thought. She was even taking after her mother in her leniency toward Father. Nothing more was said about Father. After awhile I put down my spoon and pushed the tray away. Kŭmsun looked at me, then at the tray as if to say, "Is that all your're going to eat?" Then she picked up the tray and left the room.

Almost as soon as she left I put the light out. It was because I wanted to be left alone. But still in a corner of my mind I was wishing that Father, now sober, would drop in to see how I was doing. Of course it would never happen, but just in case, what should I do and say? It had been four days since I came home, but the only time I saw him was when I first got home. Even that time I merely bowed, I did not look up. I doubt if he looked into my face that time either. When I said I was home on leave, he gave some kind of a cynical grunt. That was all. Of course I never expected more than that from Father. But now I was wishing Father would drop in to see me. I must be sick!

I was getting chills again. There will be a fever after the chill. Just as I was pulling the quilt over my face, I heard mouselike shrieks from the direction of the kennel. "Is there a rat hole near the kennel? No, it must be the puppies, that's right, we now have puppies. I wonder why they are whining like that. Do puppies have worries like we human beings? Don't they like their mother-dog licking their bodies? There, they are still whining. Maybe there are too many puppies and they can't find the nipples."

I do not know how much time passed. Finally, the whining stopped and the kennel was all quiet again. The puppies must have fallen asleep. Hamlet's soliloquy—death is like sleep and nothing more. Maybe Hamlet was right. Sleep is a lot like death. The only difference is that death lacks dreams. I do not know where many of my childhood friends are, and maybe that's part of the process of death. The experience of my past emotion, the exotic euphoria and beautiful sorrow I once enjoyed among the azaleas are now gone forever. Poksun and Chŭngsun married, but no one knows what happened to Yŏngsun since she went off to Seoul. Ilsun is still in the village, but I don't suppose she expects to get the pad of stationery and ten postage stamps back. I was happy among their colorful and gay laughter, but the happiness was often interrupted by the angry yells of my father. Shall I call on Ilsun tomorrow? What will she say? I wonder if Poksun has changed? Will she still smell of herbs? No, it was more like the smell of spring sod, and it was like the smell of my dead mother. I liked that bittersweet smell very much. Whenever I dug in for that smell among Mother's breast, there was Father near me, glaring. Whenever he found me with my arm around Mother's waist, he roared, "Take your hands off, ain't you a big boy now!" Then Mother died and I had Stepmother. But why was Father jealously watching me all the time? I think I am sleepy. Am I falling asleep? Or am I walking away somewhere? Is this the ravine of sleep or the brink of death? Let's see, I command a company at the post, don't I? But I don't really think I am a good company commander. Take the incident the other night, for instance, when Sergeant Kim was beating up the poet-turned-private. I got shook up myself watching, and I groaned everytime the poet shrieked as the sergeant hit him. And what about the Officer's Training Course I took? Every time I had to go through the infiltration course, I sweated a lot under the barbed wire. That means I am not much of a soldier. Shall I get back to the post? But that's not an important question to brood over at this moment. What then is an important question? Whether to live or die is not important, what to do is not important, how to repay is not important, how to make people understand is not important, whether it is possible to communicate is not important, how to shock people is not important, whether I should make people penitent and contrite is not important, to prove my innocence is not important, and what should become of me is not important. What then is important? Is it just to fall asleep? Is that important?

When I awoke, it was dawn. The paper lattice had a dim blue hue. I was feeling much better. Let's say that the herb medicine worked. But what's that noise? That's Father being difficult to the womenfolk again. But why is he so noisy at this time of day? What? What's wrong with the puppies? The mother dog ate them all up except one? No, impossible! It can't be!

I sat up and looked toward the kennel through a hole on the paper lattice door. It was very quiet. Then it's true. What a terrible thing! That explains it. The whining and yelping of last night was the gasping of their last agony. Father kept on yelling. "Even dogs understand the conditions of this family, otherwise why would a dog eat its own offspring? What, Kŭmsun looked while they were being born? Why, you good-for-nothing little bitch! Why the hell did you have to look? Anyway I have never seen a dog eat its own puppies, not one but four or five. It's no ordinary omen, mind you, the curse is on the family. An amoral family gets amoral dogs, I tell you. In this goddamn family the mother treats her son as a husband, and the son makes eyes at his mother. You ain't any different from dogs. The dog eating its own puppies ain't no ordinary omen. I tell you, that's what Buddha thinks of this family." Father's rage thus kept on till it was completely light.

I got up and went outside with a towel around my neck. No sign of the tragedy was visible around the kennel, and the dog was lying down with her neck sticking out from the entrance. Recalling what Father was raging about, I went over to the kennel to look in. Pulling the dog out of the way, I looked inside. There was a puppy, sand colored like its mother, about the size of a medium-sized rat. "Idiot! You are a foolish bitch to eat up your own puppies just because someone looked in while you were giving birth. Not one but several at that.'' Just as I was giving a kick in the dog's rear end Kŭmsun came out with another bowl of herb medicine placed inside a wash basin. I told her I would go out by the well to wash up, so I would not need the basin. She said, ''Daddy is **mad and** he is out there, you know. You'd better wash your face here in the garden.'' ''I don't see any connection between Daddy's anger and my washing.'' ''I don't know, but **Daddy** doesn't seem to like having people around.'' ''That's enogh, why don't you go off to school?'' ''I haven't been to school for four days.'' ''Why haven't you?'' ''I am told to stay home to look after you.'' ''Who told you that?'' ''Mom did.'' She pursed her lips and put the medicine bowl on the wooden floor by the lattice door. Then she noticed the hole in the paper of the lattice door. ''Who made this hole here, did you, Brother?'' ''Wasn't it there yesterday?'' ''No, it wasn't. Mother pasted a new sheet of paper while you were sick in bed.'' Recalling that I had peeked out of the hole earlier in the morning in the dirction of the kennel, I asked Kŭmsun who was the first one to notice the tragedy of our puppies. Again she pursed her little lips judiciously and said it was Father who had first found that the puppies had been eaten up. She was getting more and more like her mother, beautiful. ''That dog of ours is really nasty. I meant no harm when I looked on, I was merely trying to help her, but she ate up her own puppies.'' While Kŭmsun was gabbing away like this, I watched the hole, round, about the size of a man's figer. Maybe Father wanted to peek into the room to see what I was doing. If so, the hole was his doing too. Putting his eye at the hole, he must have watched me inside very, very carefully. Is it possible that he conceived a murderous design, to kill me, to kill his own son by his first wife? To kill his offspring as the dog had done?

"Go ahead and drink the medicine. It'll get cold again." With this interruption I could gather up the shattered pieces of my mind. "Alright, I will, and I think I'll have a shave too. Will you get some hot water for me to shave?" After shaving and washing up, I changed into my officer's uniform. Finishing breakfast, I went out and picked up a shovel. I felt in my trouser pocket to see if the sharp-edged piece of iron was still there. My stepmother, feeding the pigs at the sty, mumbled something without looking up at me. "Wish you would stay in. You aren't

well enough, you know. You still have a day's supply of herb
medicine to take too." She was still looking away.

"I'm all well now. I need some fresh air, and I want to do
what I promised Kŭmsun I'd do while I'm at it." I closed in
a couple of steps toward her.

"What does she want?"

"She wants a wild azalea bush transplanted in the garden."

"Naughty girl. Shouldn't have asked for such a thing when
you are not feeling well."

"It's alright. I'll be right back. Where did Father go?"

"He was wanted at the co-op."

"Things must be very trying for you, Mom."

"It's all right, I can stand it. It's the karma from my previous
life at work."

"It'll get better."

"I doubt it, but it's alright."

"It'll get better. Where did Kŭmsun go?"

"She must be in her room. Asleep, maybe."

"I'll be back."

"I still wish you wouldn't go. But if you insist, be sure to
come right back. It's terrible when flu gets complicated."

"Alright."

"Come back before lunch. You have medicine to take."

"Alright."

I left the house with the shovel on my shoulder. Not wishing
to run into anybody, I walked hurriedly with my cap pulled down.
But soon I came face to face with my father coming back toward
the house. He didn't say anything. Instead he stopped still in
front of me with a severe and angry look in his eyes. I said I was
going to the woods. "What for?" "I'm going to get a wild azalea
bush." "What for?" "To plant in the garden." "Ain't supposed to transplant wild plants in the garden. And an incestuous
son will never be forgiven, you just remember that." He gave
me a wild glare, turned back, and went away. Falteringly I
followed him. I wanted to cry out aloud, "Father, it's a
misunderstanding on your part, it's you who won't be forgiven."
But in actuality I did not say a word. Father turned off in the
direction of the co-op market, the tail of his coat flapping in the
wind. I took the path leading into the woods. Weeds among the
dead grass were getting greener, though the wind was still nippy.

I started to climb toward the top of the ridge line. I enjoyed the cool air. Then I found a fair-sized azalea by a huge rock. It was in this same woods that Chŭngsun threw herself into my arms. It was spring then too. Under which tree was it? Was the tree still there? I smoked a cigarette. Then I began to dig around the azalea, taking care not to cut its roots. Within the circle there were a couple of violets with tiny buds. I thought it a pity to have to kill the violets when all I wanted was the azalea. So I carefully transplanted the violets first. Still, they looked pensive and doleful. "They resemble Stepmother," I thought. It's the pale color that does that. I shoveled hard. The dirt was piling up. Father had married Stepmother when he was thirty-five. I was ten then, and Stepmother was nineteen. She always wept whenever she thought nobody was around. I did the same thing; I missed my mother, who had died in childbirth. That always made Father angry. Not wishing me to cry in Stepmother's presence, he punished me severely whenever he found me crying. That made me cry all the more, and the beatings became worse and worse.

"Don't cry. You'll make your father angry again," she often comforted me, and I could see tears in her eyes too. She told me that she had also grown up without a mother. I worked harder and harder with the shovel. The pile of dirt was like a huge mound now.

"That's how I came to marry your father, old enough to be my father."

"You could have run away."

It was on the anniversary of my mother's death. We had gone up to her grave. While Father was away to gather sod, Stepmother and I sat together by the grave and had that conversation.

"I wanted to run off to a faraway place, but I had no place to go."

"But I am happy you're with us."

"How come?"

"Because I'm afraid of Father."

"Why?"

"Ain't you?" I had been so self-conscious that I could not make myself call her Mother.

"Of course, I am. But I'm different. He is your father, and why should you be afraid of him?"

"I'm afraid of him all the same," I said.

"Alright, but don't forget that I'm on your side."

"But he's not afraid of you," I said. I stopped working for awhile to see how it was coming. It was almost done. Practically all the small roots had been cut. The azalea stood in the middle of the circle like an island. I decided to dig a little deeper. The pile of dirt around the circle was getting higher and higher.

I don't exactly remember when I started to call her Mom. Anyway she blushed when I first addressed her that way. From that time on there was more laughter than tears in her eyes.

"You want to go picking chestnuts with me?"

"Not unless you give me something to eat."

"I knew you would say that. Here, here's an apple and a pear."

"Mom, I'm going to sell the chestnuts I'll pick to buy you a pair of rubber shoes."

"My, I'll be a rich woman."

"Mom, when I grow up I'll buy you all kinds of things."

"You mean that?"

She treated me as a younger brother or a friend rather than a stepson. It was around this time that Father began to cast suspicious eyes at us. Then Kŭmsun was born. Stepmother was twenty-one. Of course he had never been kind to me, but from that time on he showed definite hostility toward me. And after I moved on to a middle school, he often tormented Stepmother insinuating that there had been some affair between myself and her. He openly showed hatred toward me. It was unbearable. Fortunately, from the junior year of my college days, I did not have to go back home during the vacations, for I was taking ROTC training. But when I was not home, Father was said to have checked the mail himself every morning for fear that I might write to her secretly. Of course the seeds of such suspicion and fear were already there even when my own mother was alive. Meanwhile, the azalea was already out of the hole, but I kept on digging, deeper and deeper. I kept on doing it unconsciously, engrossed, as if to dig myself down into the depths of the past. When was it that I first began to think of Stepmother as an affectionate sister? When was it that I first began to find a source of happiness in her beautiful eyes? When was it that the look of her slightly upturned nose first began to tickle me? When was it really? Generally, they seemed to coincide with the time Father began to show me hatred and hostility. Ah, my legs and arms hurt. "Let me lie down in there to rest. I felt so busy yesterday and I felt so leisurely this morning—all for this rest. Dad, don't ever pour dirt on my face, don't ever cover up my body with dirt. I want to lie down here forever under the blue sky. To sleep and to die, aren't they the same thing?"

I was lying flat in the hole I had dug. It was very comfortable. Maybe it was because I was tired. "Don't anybody touch me. I want to be left alone like this. I just want to fall asleep." I fished the sharp-edged piece of iron out of my pocket. I aimed it at my heart. Ah, death is like sleep. When I heard the sound of my right hand hammering the piece into my heart, a dark shadow descended before my eyes and a shock passed through my body. It was a deep darkness and a terrible shock.

(end story)

Notes on the Writers

Chang Yonghak is one of a rare breed among Korean writers, an idea novelist. Born in 1921 in North Hamgyŏng Province in North Korea, Mr. Chang studied at Waseda University in Japan before he was drafted into the Japanese Army during World War II. While teaching at secondary schools in Korea after the Liberation he began to publish stories in magazines. He won critical recognition in 1955 with the story "The Poems of John the Baptist," which the author himself says is deeply influenced by Sartre's *Nausea*. An avid reader of philosophical ideas of both Oriental and Occidental origin, Mr. Chang packs his stories and novels with abstract ideas. He has written one novel and several novelle in addition to a dozen or so stories of very high quality; many of his works have aroused critical controversy. It is a mystery to many admirers of Mr. Chang's works why he had been silent since 1970.

Ch'oe Inhun is probably the most Western among the Korean writers of any consequence. His whole approach to fiction is Western, and his free use of stylistic experiments such as dream, fantasy, diary and journal, interior monologue, and above all, the parodying of older and better-known literary works, reminds us of the works of the Absurdists in recent American and European literatures. Born in Hŏeryŏng, North Hamgyŏng Province in North Korea, Mr. Ch'oe was a law student at Seoul National University when he joined the army as an interpreter. After his discharge, he did not return to school, but instead began to write stories. He has written many novels, novells, and short stories since 1959, and has won several important literary awards.

Ch'oe Chŏnghŭi was born in North Hamgyŏng Province in 1912. After receiving her education in Seoul she joined the editorial staff of *Samcho'li* magazine in which some of her early poems appeared. She also published many stories in the 30s, but that period being what it was, her writing was deeply influenced by the tendencious quality of the literature prevalent during that decade. However, many of her later works may be called mood pieces in which the drift of feeling is much more important than, say, the sequence of events. She has won several literary awards, including the Korean Academy of Arts Award for Literature in 1971 in recognition of her outstanding contribution to Korean literature.

Chŏn Kwangyong originally from Pukch'ŏng, South Hamgyŏng Province, was educated at Seoul National University, where he has been a professor of Korean literature for many years. His formal recognition as a writer came rather late in life; his first short story "Huksan Island" won the story-writing contest sponsored by the Chosŏn-Ilbo in 1955 when he was thirty-six years old. He is a writer of a traditionally realistic bent, and likes to depict the dignity of men and women in the face of flagrant social ills and absurdities. Mr. Chŏn has published several novels and collections of short stories to date. Teaching and academic works connected with his professorial position seem to take up more and more of his time lately, for his literary output seems to have slowed down somewhat.

Han Musuk, a native of Seoul, was born in 1918. Her first artistic ambition was painting, but subsequently she decided to become a writer. Dividing her time between housekeeping and writing, she nevertheless wrote an astonishing number of novels and stories, whisking away one literary prize or award after another. Mrs. Han has had quite a number of her stories translated into English in two volumes: *In the Depths* (1965), and *The Running Water Hermitage* (1966). She represented her country at International P.E.N. Meetings in 1965 and 1969.

Hwang Sunwŏn was born in South P'yŏngan Province in 1915. A graduate of Waseda University in Japan, Mr. Hwang began his literary career first as a poet, then as a writer of stories and novels. As befitting his poet-turned-novelist literary career, his works are marked by a unique understanding of a distinctively Korean lyricism. His long and distinguished career has brought him many prizes and awards. Two separate six-volume *Collected Works* have been published, in 1964 and 1968 respectively. His academic carrer is equally impressive; he has been a professor of literature at Kyung-hee University since 1957.

Kim Tongni, born in 1913 in Kyŏngju, the ancient capital of the Silla Dynasty on the southeastern coast of the Korean peninsula, began publishing stories in 1934. Mr. Kim's literary activity was blighted temporarily by the oppressive Japanese colonial rule when he refused to cooperate with that government. After the Liberation in 1945, however, he has shown a strong commitment against the leftist-oriented writer organizations which were present on the Korean literary scene up until the outbreak of the Korean War. A prolific writer by nature, Mr. Kim has many volumes of collected short stories in addition to innumerable volumes of novels and critical essays. His five-volume *Selected Works* was published in 1968. His long and distinguished literary life has been honored by many important literary awards, including the Korean Academy of Arts Award and the March First Culture Award. Though a very versatile writer, his earlier pieces, collected in *The Sorceress and Other Stories* (1946), which drew their inspiration from native Korean folk beliefs, are still considered his most original contribution to modern Korean literature.

Kwŏn T'aeung, originally from North P'yŏngan Province in North Korea, moved to Seoul while still in his teens. A graduate of Sung Kyung Kwan University in Seoul, Mr. Kwŏn is a pharmacist by profession, but has engaged himself in various editorial works besides writing stories and novels. His writing was most prolific in the 60's, and social satire criticizing social ills and absurdities is his forte. He has two volumes of collected short stories and a novel, *The Bridge of Freedom* (1964), to his credit.

Nam Chŏnghyŏn, a native of Tangjin in South Ch'ungch'ŏng Province, was born in 1933. After graduating from an agricultural high school he made his literary début in 1957. Mr. Nam has so far published 3 volumes of short stories and several novels. Freely drawing on various techniques of allegory, fantasy, as well as realism, Mr. Nam's works straddle that delicate borderland between satire and exposé.

O Sangwŏn graduated from the French Department of the College of Liberal Arts, Seoul National University. Beginning with his "A Respite," which won a story-writing contest sponsored by a daily newspaper in 1955, Mr. O wrote many short stories during the following decade. Many of his stories raised critical controversy. For awhile he was considered by critics as a spokesman for the postwar generation. His works are permeated with a keen sense of reality and with a deeper understanding of social awareness and the need for human solidarity. It is regretted by many that he has kept away from creative writing since 1965. He is currently working for the Dong-a Ilbo, a daily newspaper published in Seoul.

Pak Yŏngjun, born in South P'yŏngan Province in 1911, is a graduate of Yonsei University, where he is currently a professor of Korean literature. His recognition came, beginning in 1934, with his winning several important novel and story writing contests sponsored by leading newspapers and magazines in the country. With eight collected volumes of short stories and over a dozen novels to his credit, Mr. Pak has won several important litertary awards, including the Korean Academy of Arts Award and the Seoul City Cultural Award. Though he began his literary career as a so-called agrarian writer, his subsequent writings show that he never shied away from writing about modern cities and city dwellers. *The Bell Gabel* (1965) is considered his best novel.

Sŏ Kiwŏn, a native of Seoul, was born in 1930. Mr. So, in 1957, gave up a successful student life at prestigious Seoul National University in exchange for the career of a novelist. At the outset of his literary career, he seemed to be mainly interested in tracing changes in ethical norms among the young during and after the war. However, his later works, such as *Kim Okkyun* (1965) and *The Revolution* (1970), seem to backtrack through the whole gamut of changes involved in the course of modernization. He is the winner of several important literary awards, including the Dong-in Literary Award.

Son Ch'angsŏp, a native of P'yŏngyang, North Korea, was born in 1922 and was educated in this country and Japan. His stories began to appear in leading magazines and newspapers in 1949. His unique quality was recognized by the public as his ability to create eccentric characters which were immediately identified as *après guerre* characters of the 50's. Mr. Son has published half a dozen novels and innumerable shorter stories, some of which have been collected in his short story collection, *The Rainy Day* (1959), and in *The Collected Representative works of Son Ch'angsŏp* (1969).

Son Sohŭi, a woman writer, was born in North Hamgyŏng Province in 1917. After a brief sojourn in Tokyo, Japan, she went to work for a newspaper in Manchuria in 1939. After the Liberation in 1945 she crossed the border to South Korea. Recognition for her came when she published a few stories in such literary magazines as *Paengmin* in 1946. She is particularly adept in drawing subtle psychological changes that take place in the minds of her characters. Having several novels and a host of short stories to her credit, she has won many literary awards including the March First Culture Award. She represented her country at the Oslo P.E.N. Meeting in 1964.

Sŏnu Hwi, born in North P'ŏngan Province in North Korea in 1922, and served in the South Korea army during the Korean War as a troop information and education officer. His stories began to appear in magazines even before he was discharged from the army as a colonel in 1958. His earlier pieces were good examples of literary activism in which the writer stresses the importance of full-fledged social participation. He has produced innumerable stories as well as several novels, some of which are incomplete. His literary creativity seems to have fallen off somewhat lately as his editorial duties for newspapers increase. Mr. Sŏnu is currently Editor-in-chief of the Chosŏn Ilbo, a highly respected daily published in the city of Seoul.

Yi Hoch'ŏl was born in Wŏnsan, North Hamgyŏng Province in 1932. Mr. Yi crossed the border to join South Korea during the Korean War. His subsequent experiences in various menial jobs, such as longshoreman, found a uniquely lyrical expression in his earlier works. He has written five novels including the popular *Seoul Is Packed to Capacity* (1967), and two volumes of collected short stories. He won the Dong-in Literary Award in 1962 with his story "Wearing off of the Flesh,"which is quite reminiscent of Chekhov's play *The Cherry Orchard*.

Yu Chuhyŏn, a native of Yŏju County in Kyŏnggi Province, was born in 1921 and educated in Japan. Mr. Yu made his début in 1948 by publishing a story in *Paengmin*, a literary magazine now defunct. During the war he edited *The Blue Sky*, the literary magazine of the Korean Air Force. His works are noted for their thoroughgoing realism and his keen analysis with regard to the nature of man and history. Probably one of the most prolific writers of all time, Mr. Yu has published over one hundred shorter stories and more than twenty book-length novels, some of which are multivolume *roman-fleuves*. The literary prizes and awards he has received include the Korean National Book Award for his novel, *The Japanese Governor-General in Korea* (1968).

About the Editor-Translator

Born in Seoul, Korea in 1929, **Kim Chongun,** the editor-translator of this book, was educated at Seoul National University in Korea and Bowdoin College and New York University in the United States. Currently, Mr. Kim is professor of American literature at Seoul National University. A frequent contributor to both scholarly and popular periodicals, Professor Kim is the author of several books dealing with American literature, and in addition has translated many volumes of American literary works into Korean.

Professor Kim completed a research project at Yale University under a Fulbright-Hays Senior Program Grant in American Studies in 1973—74. He was awarded an Asian Scholar-in-Residence Grant to teach Korean literature at the University of Washington for the 1982—83 academic year.